Same-Sex Partners

Same-Sex Partners

*The Social Demography
of Sexual Orientation*

Amanda K. Baumle
D'Lane Compton
Dudley L. Poston Jr.

SUNY
PRESS

Published by State University of New York Press, Albany

For information, contact State University of New York Press, Albany, NY
www.sunypress.edu

Production by Kelli W. LeRoux
Marketing by Michael Campochiaro

Library of Congress Cataloging-in-Publication Data

Baumle, Amanda K.
    Same-sex partners : the social demography of sexual orientation / Amanda K.
Baumle, D'Lane Compton, Dudley L. Poston, Jr.
        p. cm.
    Includes bibliographical references and index.
    ISBN 978-0-7914-7609-3 (hardcover : alk. paper)
    ISBN 978-0-7914-7610-9 (pbk. : alk. paper)   1. Gaymen—United States—
Statistics.   2. Gay couples—United States—Statistics.   3. Lesbians—
United States—Statistics.   4. Lesbian couples—United States—Statistics.
I. Compton, D'Lane.   II. Poston, Dudley L., 1940–   III. Title.
    HQ76.35.U6B38 2009
    306.84'80973 — dc22

                                                                        2008005665

10 9 8 7 6 5 4 3 2 1

LIST OF TABLES

CONTENTS

PART III. SAME-SEX UNMARRIED PARTNERS IN THE LABOR MARKET

LIST OF FIGURES

FOREWORD

This book illustrates the power of demographic data. Drawing from what many see as a kind of bare-bones, inflexible, and narrowly focused data set, the 2000 U.S. Census, Baumle, Compton and Poston have been thorough and creative and have put together an enormous amount of information on the lives of partnered gay male and lesbian Americans. In the ways they address these issues and in their data analyses, they forge new ground here.

Their work is important and timely, and should receive wide attention. While issues involving gay males and lesbians are regularly front-page news and on the minds of voters and the general public alike, there is still a relative paucity of information about the shape of the lives of this group, even as it receives more attention. Of course, scholars in a variety of academic fields, from sociology to anthropology to political science, have been turning their attention to the lives of gay men and lesbians. But there are very few studies that present the kind of systematic overview and national picture that Baumle, Compton and Poston have been able to provide here.

The authors have worked to give us as much information as can be squeezed from the U.S. Census on the lives of gay men and lesbians in the U.S. As the authors make clear and explicit, some important issues just cannot be addressed with census data. One of the biggest weaknesses with these census data is that they are limited to gay male and lesbian partners living together. Thus, the authors are not able to address gay males and lesbians in the U.S. more generally. And as they are very quick to point out, this is a serious weakness.

But whatever the admitted gaps in knowledge these authors point to, it is what they do with these data that is the real strength of this book. Even in the process of addressing the weaknesses of the data set they use, they make a case for further and deeper study of the lives of gay men and lesbians. One of their goals is to lay a foundation for further analyses and they have done that well.

They recognize that they can't answer even all the questions that they themselves raise, but instead raise the questions, point to the answers they can get to, and suggest other questions that future researchers (and different data sets) might be able to address in other ways.

And certainly, they have plenty to contribute to our understanding and knowledge of the lives of gay males and lesbians in the United States today. Mining the Census data as far as they can, they use it to deal systematically with many aspects of social life. Each chapter addresses a discrete issue (occupation, residence, family, economic situation, and others), carefully and well; the overall effect is that the book lays out in a clear fashion what is happening to individuals in same-sex couples residing in the U.S. today.

It is important to get the numbers, to see the issues in the lives of gay men and lesbians in a systematic fashion. And demography's focus on numbers allows us to see patterns, gaps, trends, and more. In their conclusion they make the case for connecting demography and legal change. Indeed, these numbers and patterns point to the ways that policy makers and others might go about effecting change. As I write this, the California Supreme Court has just struck down the ban on same-sex marriage. What constitutes a family, a marriage, or a household is rapidly changing in the United States. This book thus permits us a snapshot of same-sex partnerships even as the meaning of partnerships undergoes change. Under these conditions, this book deserves wide readership. It has the potential to guide readers through some of the issues surrounding the lives of gay men and lesbians and to point us in the direction of future changes.

Nancy E. Riley
Professor of Sociology
Bowdoin College
Brunswick, Maine
May 2008

PREFACE

In 2003, the three of us were at Texas A&M University, independently conducting research using the same-sex unmarried partner data from the 2000 U.S. Census. We discussed our work with each other, and, eventually, *Same-Sex Partners* was the result. Our book grew out of a shared vision of the importance of generating additional, representative research examining the demographic characteristics of gay men and lesbians. The U.S. Census data offer us a means for exploring many issues which had heretofore been impossible to examine because of data unavailability. Further, the size and wealth of information available in the U.S. Census data allow the new exploration of topics which had been previously unexamined or examined only with limited data sets. This book represents the culmination of our efforts to use the 2000 U.S. Census data to offer new insights about the gay male and lesbian population. We hope the results presented in the following chapters might serve to inform academicians, the general public, and policymakers.

The research conducted in this book has received support and insights from a number of sources. First, we wish to extend thanks to our editor at SUNY Press, Nancy Ellegate, and also the individuals she selected to serve as reviewers of our book. The reviewers' and Nancy's comments and suggestions resulted in improved clarity and academic quality. We would like to especially thank Nancy Riley, who authored the Foreword for our book.

We thank a number of individuals who provided feedback, suggested improvements, alerted us to the work of others, and contributed to the development of research presented in this work. We list these individuals alphabetically. They are: Lee Badgett, Dan Black, David Brown, Mary Kathryn Cazorla, Rachel Cortes, John Delamater, Andy Deseran, Eric Fong, Mark Fossett, William Frey, Gary Gates, Yuan Gu, Don Hernandez, John Logan, Ruth Masterson, Martin O'Connell, Rogelio Saenz, Craig St. John, Jane Sell, Joachim Singelmann,

Lowell Taylor, Carol Walther, and Li Zhang. We also thank Warren Waren for producing the GIS maps used in Chapter 4.

Further, we want to acknowledge many individuals at Texas A&M University who provided support and funding, including the Dean of Faculties and Associate Provost Karan Watson, Associate Dean Larry Oliver, James M. Rosenheim and The Melbern G. Glasscock Center for Humanities Research and their personnel. We also thank colleagues, not already mentioned, in the Department of Sociology for their advice, suggestions, and support.

We acknowledge with thanks our use of the Integrated Public Use Microdata Series, prepared by the University of Minnesota, as our main source for our 2000 U.S. Census data sets.

Lastly, our long and time-consuming efforts in producing this book were assisted by the support and understanding of our families. In this regard, Amanda Baumle thanks Lawrence Baumle; D'Lane Compton thanks Dorth and Sonny Rigdon, and Megan Wright; and Dudley Poston thanks Patricia Poston.

Amanda K. Baumle, Houston, Texas
D'Lane R. Compton, New Orleans, Louisiana
Dudley L. Poston Jr., College Station, Texas
May 2008

An Introduction to the Demography of Sexual Orientation

Over the past 20 years, there has been a dramatic increase in the percentages of people in the United States who believe that homosexuality should be an accepted lifestyle. In 1985, approximately 35 percent of the public indicated that homosexuality is an acceptable alternative lifestyle. Over the next 15 years, this increased to 55 percent (Newport 2001). In addition, throughout the 1990s, many states adopted laws barring discrimination in public and private employment on the basis of sexual orientation.[1] And in 2000, the U.S. Supreme Court rendered a resounding verdict against state laws that prohibited same-sex sodomy (*Lawrence v. Texas* 2003). This type of social, legal, and political action suggests an increasing acceptance of homosexuality in the United States.

There are, however, recurring events that stand in stark contradiction to these examples of progress. The Department of Justice (2004) reports the continued occurrence of violent hate crimes directed against gay men and lesbians. Beginning in the mid-1990s, and gaining momentum during the 2004 national and state elections, states have enacted constitutional amendments banning same-sex marriage, citing the need to protect marriage as a heterosexual institution. The marriage debate has resulted in such a strong fervor throughout the nation that, in 2005, the Ku Klux Klan marched in Austin, Texas, in support of the passing of a constitutional amendment (Smith 2005). The federal government has also taken a strong stance against extending the rights of gay men and lesbians. Since the 1970s, the government has repeatedly declined to grant legal protection to gay men and lesbians in employment, and the government passed the Defense of Marriage Act in 1996, defining marriage as existing solely between a man and a woman.

This polarity with regard to the status of the social, legal, and political rights of gay men and lesbians is perhaps indicative of an absence of understanding regarding the characteristics and lives of homosexual individuals (Mohr 1998). This book endeavors to address this void. In a series of chapters we present mainly quantitative analyses of topics pertaining to gay men and lesbians that have previously been relatively unexamined, or assessed mainly through qualitative studies.

1

We explore where gay men and lesbians live in the United States, why they choose those residences, income inequality, occupations, their relationships, and their family structures. We suggest that expanding knowledge in these areas could affect a variety of social and political outcomes for this group, as well as for the communities in which they reside.

For instance, we suggest in Chapters 8 and 9 that one reason the federal government has not yet passed a law prohibiting discrimination in employment may be due to the belief that gay men and lesbians do not need such protection. Stereotypes, derived in part from nonrepresentative surveys, usually depict gay men and lesbians as professionals with higher than average salaries and educational attainment (Badgett 2001; Black et al. 2000). Stereotypes about gay men and lesbians concerning their work, relationships, families, and prevalence in our population not only shape social attitudes about them, but also have the potential of creating tensions between varying social and political stances on homosexuality.

The historical absence of large representative data sets examining issues of sexual orientation has likely contributed to the derivation of many stereotypes about gay male and lesbian populations (see Chapter 1). In the United States, this situation was partly alleviated in 1990 when a question was added to the U.S. decennial census permitting the identification of partnered gay men and lesbians. The U.S. Census contains data enabling the analysis of social and demographic characteristics of homosexual individuals that have heretofore been either impossible to examine, or explored only in a limited scope. Our book uses these quantitative data in analyses to provide a more detailed representation of many of the features of the lives of cohabiting gay men and lesbians compared to those of married heterosexuals and cohabiting heterosexuals.

We hope that the analyses in this book about the status of gay men and lesbians in the United States can, perhaps, play a role in reconciling some of the existing sociopolitical conflict about gay individuals. At times, our data and analyses reinforce current stereotypes; in other cases, they challenge preexisting beliefs. Regardless, the hope is that through the analyses of representative and current data, we will provide a foundation for future research, policy, law, and understanding regarding gay men and lesbians.

"Bringing Sexuality In": The Demography of Sexual Orientation

The field of demography is one that is constantly evolving and expanding, drawing in new disciplines and building on the three core demographic processes of fertility, mortality, and migration (Poston and Micklin 2005; Hauser and Duncan 1959). In Poston and Micklin's (2005) *Handbook of Population*, they included 28 chapters exploring subfields of demography, including a wide range of topics such as marriage and family, demography of gender, labor force, biodemography, and fertility planning. Absent from such works that have inventoried the field of demography, however, is the "demography of sexual orientation" or the "demography of sexuality."

Indeed, in early 2006 we conducted a search of all articles published in the last three decades in the population studies journals contained in the JSTOR database[2] and discovered only 69 published articles containing the phrase "sexual orientation," 48 articles containing the word "lesbian," 221 articles containing the word "gay," and 181 including the word "homosexual." Out of these, few dealt directly with demographic issues pertaining to gay men, lesbians, or both (e.g., Black et al. 2000; Saewyc et al. 1999). Many more included sexual orientation as a variable in studies addressing sexual behavior, particularly as it relates to sexually transmitted infections (e.g., Schiltz 1998; Ericksen and Trocki 1994; Smith 1991). Similarly, at demography conferences, sessions devoted solely to the examination of the demography of sexuality have only occurred in the past decade, and quite infrequently.

Risman and Schwartz (1988: 126), observing the lack of research on sexual orientation in major sociological journals in the 1980s, noted that the separation of the study of sexual orientation from other social science research "diminishes both the quality of the research on homosexuality and the quality of research in those areas of sociology that could profit from data on homosexual identities, relationships, and communities." Likewise, the relative absence of research on sexual orientation in demographic journals and at demography conferences is clearly seen as discouraging. We ask, then, in this section, what would it mean and, further, what would it require, to bring the study of sexuality more into the mainstream of demography?

Much like the comparable dearth of sexuality research in demography, the field of sociology has long suffered from a lack of focus on issues of sexuality. Although the social sciences, from their conception, "assumed a natural order linking sex, gender, and sexuality," classical sociologists neglected the concept of sexuality in their work (Seidman 1994: 167). Indeed, it was not until after World War II, when issues of sexuality rose to the forefront of American society, that sociologists increasingly focused on the study of sexuality and, more specifically, sexual orientation (Seidman 1994). Despite the growing focus on homosexuality during the postwar era, Risman and Schwartz (1988) observe that studies of sexuality remained on the backburner throughout much of the twentieth century. With this history, it is perhaps to be expected that the field of demography, which has been slower to embrace studies of gender[3] (Riley 2005; Riley 1999) and race[4] (Saenz and Morales 2005), would not yet have placed the demography of sexuality into its mainstream.

As evidenced by our review of articles published in journals of demography, the topic of sexual orientation is not entirely absent from the discipline of demography. The majority of articles that do mention some aspect of sexual orientation, however, are those that primarily focus on sexually transmitted infections. Sexual orientation, then, has been introduced into the field of demography primarily through its connections to sexual behavior (rather than identity or desire) and, in turn, reproduction. It is perhaps unsurprising that sexual orientation, and other aspects of sexuality, would have found their first entrance into the discipline through their interconnections with fertility, one of the core demographic processes. Indeed, it is noteworthy that so little demographic work has been done in the broad area of sexuality, given its undeniable tie to fertility outcomes.[5]

In the analyses presented in this book we show that sexuality affects demographic outcomes in numerous arenas beyond that of sexually transmitted infections. The overviews of the extant literature in the chapters of this book demonstrate little evidence of research on the manner in which sexual orientation, in particular, serves as an important personal characteristic that can shape and inform demographic processes. Consequently, the first step toward opening the demographic discipline to studies of sexual orientation should involve incorporating orientation into current demographic models. Much as we have done throughout this work, demographers must "bring sexuality in"[6] to their studies of migration, fertility, mortality, labor force, family, and the other subfields of demography. When possible, sexual orientation should be included as an important individual characteristic in demographic research, much as gender, race, and ethnicity have become. Having taken this step, we show in the following chapters that a focus on sexual orientation in the field of demography is not unfounded. Indeed, sexual orientation results in differential outcomes on a number of issues that are fundamental to population study, supporting the additional exploration of issues of sexuality in this field.

Riley (1999), in examining the incorporation of gender into the field of demography, notes that in addition to "bringing women in" to demographic analysis and theory, one should question whether current demographic models or theories are capable of explaining the experiences of women. In much the same way, the second step of incorporating sexuality into demographic study would involve assessing whether our current understandings of demographic processes can be applied to individuals of varying sexual orientations. In particular, the interaction of sexual orientation and gender creates unique dynamics demanding new assumptions, models, and theories. Studies in the areas of fertility, migration, family demography, labor demography, and other subfields, have been dominated by a heterosexual perspective. Research in all these areas, for example, has examined the manner in which gender affects demographic outcomes as a consequence of power differentials (e.g., women will be less likely to make migration decisions than men because, on average, they earn less money and have less relationship power than do men). When one considers same-sex couples, however, using gender as a proxy for power differentials becomes problematic and forces a reevaluation of current understandings of these models.

By assessing the manner in which empirical findings about sexual orientation fit in current demographic models and theories, one should be able to improve the general understanding of the role that sexual orientation plays in shaping demographic outcomes. For example, in Chapter 5 we examine the effect of being a gay male or lesbian on the migration decision; we find that sexual orientation affects the odds of migrating and we offer some explanations as to why this is so. To truly understand the role of sexual orientation on the migration decision, however, we need to take the next step, which is to ask how and why does sexual orientation affect one's migration decision? Our qualitative chapter moves toward answering this question through interviewing gay men and lesbians about their migration decisions, but further research needs to be done to understand the role of sexual orientation in these processes.

In both Chapter 1 and our concluding chapter, we examine some of the methodological limitations that have contributed to the scarcity of demographic research on sexual orientation. Few data sets which examine demographic issues incorporate questions designed to capture sexual orientation. As we discuss in Chapter 1, many of the data sets enabling analysis of these issues were not designed with the purpose of sexual orientation research in mind. The census data that form the basis of most of this work are limited because capturing data on same-sex unmarried partners is a by-product of a variable that was developed to measure heterosexual cohabitation. Rarely are issues of orientation a primary focus in quantitative data collection, and even when more direct questions are asked, the motivations tend to be more political than demographic. As we explore in Chapter 1 and in the Conclusion, then, there is a real need to move to data sets with a more focused question on orientation in order to gain a more complete picture of the gay male and lesbian population. Further, qualitative research is needed to flesh out the quantitative, as demonstrated by our discussion of migration decisions in Chapter 4.

This book has taken a considerable step toward encouraging the further development of a demography of sexual orientation. The findings contained in these chapters reflect the importance of sexual orientation in shaping demographic outcomes. Our hope is that this work will serve as a foundation for future research in this field, including both the reevaluation of current theories and models and the creation of new, targeted data sets.

Data and Terminology

In engaging in this undertaking, we have drawn almost exclusively on data about same-sex unmarried partners that were collected in the 2000 U.S. Census. For some of the questions we examine in this book, these data are the only representative source available; for others, they provide a larger and more attractive base for answering important questions compared to studies using other data. In Chapter 1, we discuss some of the data sources that have been accessible to researchers who wished to conduct demographic studies of sexual orientation. In contrast to these sources, the benefits of the census data become readily apparent, both in the almost 1.2 million individuals who identified as same-sex unmarried partners in the 2000 census, as well as in the fine detail of questions about their residential, family, and economic characteristics.

These data are imperfect, however, in one notable aspect: they only permit the examination of characteristics of persons who are in self-identified same-sex partnered relationships and who are living together. Consequently, our analyses exclude gay men and lesbians who are single, or who would not identify as being in a "marriage-like" relationship with a same-sex partner. Further, the census data do not capture those who might be in such relationships, but who choose not to identify their relationships on the census form. The demographics of individuals who are bisexual, transgendered, or transsexual are also not directly examined, although some of these persons might well have identified themselves as same-sex unmarried partners in 2000 and, thus, be subjects of our analyses.

In Chapter 1, we examine a number of questions about the ability of the unmarried partner census question to capture a representative sample of the partnered gay male and lesbian population. In so doing, we attempt to assess whether the data have face validity, and to set forth our understanding of what a positive response to this question communicates in terms of sexual orientation. To this end, we have elected throughout this work to refer to our non-heterosexual subjects using a deliberate subset of terminology. At times, we use the phrase "same-sex unmarried partners," which incorporates the Census Bureau's "unmarried partner" vocabulary. This phrasing has been selected by many researchers conducting economic and social demographic analyses using the census data (see, e.g., Black et al. 2000).

At times, we also will categorize our subjects as "gay men" and "lesbians." We select this particular terminology at a time when they are both common and accepted labels in the gay male and lesbian communities, as well as in the academic literature (Badgett 2001; Boswell 1980). Further, these terms communicate a largely shared understanding of sexual orientation. We opt to use the term "gay *men*," since at times both men and women are referred to as "gay" (see, e.g., Boswell's [1980] and Sullivan's [1996] use of the term to refer to both men and women). Gay men are commonly understood to be those who experience sexual desire for men, engage in sexual behavior with men, and/or identify as someone with such desires or behaviors (Laumann et al. 1994). We have chosen to refer to women with same-sex sexual preferences as lesbians. Although the lesbian identity is, at times, politicized (Zita 1992), we use this term only to refer to a woman with same-sex sexual desires or behaviors, and/or who identifies as a woman with these desires or behaviors.

Finally, the phrasing "gay men" and "lesbians" avoids many of the negative connotations that are sometimes associated with other phrasing (e.g., homosexual; queer; dyke; and so forth). For example, some have argued against the use of the term "homosexual" as a noun, suggesting that this phrase carries negative connotations reflecting issues and dimensions of psychological abnormality[7]

(Risman and Schwartz 1988; Boswell 1980; Foucault 1978). Consequently, we do not use "homosexual" as a noun owing to the above interpretation; instead, homosexual is used only as an adjective (Risman and Schwartz 1988; Boswell 1980). The term "queer" is also used by some scholars and laypersons to describe the gay, lesbian, bisexual, and transgender community, and in reference to queer theory.[8] This term, however, has not been universally embraced by the community. Some equate "queer" predominantly with white gay men; others argue that it alienates members of the heterosexual community; still others find the phrase derogatory and offensive (Gamson 1996). Due to the unsettled status of this term and the large realm of meaning it encompasses, we have chosen not to use the word "queer" to describe our subjects.

We also acknowledge that the terms "gay men" and "lesbian" are not uniformly embraced by all individuals with same-sex sexual preferences. For example, some racial minorities are less likely to self-identify using these labels, viewing them as terms associated with white individuals.[9] Since we deal predominantly with same-sex individuals in the aggregate (not differentiating based on characteristics, such as race), and because census respondents were unable to indicate a preferred label, we do not make such distinctions among particular groups of same-sex unmarried partners.

In contrast, we often refer to individuals in our comparison groups—married men and women and cohabiting (unmarried) heterosexual men and women—as partnered heterosexuals. Although Katz (1995) notes that the term "heterosexual" has its origins in labeling some opposite-sex sexual behavior as deviant, heterosexuality soon became the accepted label for what is considered to be both the dominant and "normal" sexual interaction. Consequently, we (like others) use heterosexual as both noun and adjective due to the relative absence of negative connotations associated with this term.

We must emphasize, however, that in all cases we are making assumptions about our respondents' sexual orientation based on their census relationship status. It is certainly possible that an individual who identifies as married is, in fact, a gay man or lesbian; he or she would be classified as heterosexual, however, if in a marriage with an individual of the opposite sex. Similarly, an individual who has identified as being in a same-sex unmarried partner relationship will be classified as a gay man or lesbian, even if he or she is perhaps heterosexual or bisexual. Thus, when we refer to gay men, lesbians, or heterosexual men or women, it is important to keep the above considerations in mind.

Finally, at all times in this book when we refer to census data, we are discussing the demographic outcomes of *partnered individuals*. As previously noted, the census only provides data on partnered gay men and lesbians. All of our analyses, therefore, involve partnered gay men and lesbians; these individuals are compared with partnered heterosexuals (both married and cohabiting). In no instance do we draw upon data on single individuals, or make comparisons to or among single-person households.

We address additional methodological considerations concerning the census data in further detail in Chapter 1. The remaining chapters of this book are divided into three substantive sections. The first examines the spatial distribution of gay men and lesbians, including the manner in which sexual orientation affects residential choices. The second explores the family patterns of gay men and lesbians, comparing their familial characteristics with those of both married and cohabiting heterosexual couples. And the third section assesses the stereotypes of gay men and lesbians as professionals, who earn above-average wages. We now review and summarize the chapters in each of the three sections of our book.

Spatial Distribution: How Does Sexual Orientation Affect Residential Decisions?

Do gay men and lesbians only reside in urban areas, or do rural areas also contain a high prevalence of homosexual individuals? Do gay men and lesbians live in the same residential areas as heterosexual families, or are they segregated into enclaves? For those who choose to live in enclaves, do they do so to be close to other homosexual individuals or simply because those areas have attractive natural and cultural amenities? And does sexual orientation affect one's odds of engaging in an interstate move, much as an individual's sex or race has been found to do?

The first substantive section of this book presents detailed analyses of these issues, drawing on census data in an attempt to explore the manner in which sexual orientation affects the spatial distribution of individuals. In Chapter 2, we develop for all metropolitan areas of the United States, and for most of the nonmetropolitan counties, two same-sex prevalence rates: one measures the prevalence of unmarried same-sex male partners in an area, and another the prevalence of unmarried same-sex female partners. We then test several hypotheses to account for variability in the partnering rates by examining social and ecological characteristics of the areas. Among the metropolitan areas, the most influential variables predicting levels of gay male and lesbian concentration are a physical temperature index, a poverty rate, and a heterosexual cohabitation rate. Variables focusing mainly on characteristics of the area dealing with gay men and lesbians, such as those dealing with sodomy and antidiscrimination laws, as well as those assessing the presence of political and religious conservatism, are either not statistically important predictors or exhibited only minimal influence. Among the nonmetropolitan counties, the variables shown to be the most influential are whether the counties were retirement counties and whether they were rural; also significant is whether they were farming-dependent.

In Chapter 3 we ask how cities might be expected to vary in levels of residential segregation between homosexual and heterosexual partners. For the

40 cities in the U.S. in 2000 with the largest numbers of partnered gay men and lesbians, we develop a residential segregation exposure index that measures the extent to which gay men or lesbians are likely to interact with (i.e., to be exposed to) heterosexual persons in their neighborhoods. We also examine the extent to which various characteristics of the cities are associated with their levels of homosexual-heterosexual residential segregation. Among the cities, by far the most influential predictor of variation in residential segregation is the relative size of the gay male population in the city. This supports the racial and ethnic segregation literature that suggests that size of the minority population matters in determining the degree of residential segregation. Ecological characteristics of the cities that are not related to population size do not seem to account much for the variation in segregation levels across cities. These characteristics, however, have been shown by others to be important in accounting for racial and ethnic segregation. This is very interesting in that it suggests that homosexual-heterosexual residential segregation may be a different phenomenon from racial and ethnic residential segregation. This indicates that sociologists and demographers need to develop a better theoretical framework for understanding residential segregation based on sexual orientation, rather than relying on racial and ethnic models.

In Chapter 4, we take a slightly different approach, intermixing census data and qualitative field research and interview data to explore the characteristics of gay male and lesbian "enclaves" in the San Francisco Bay Area. Moving beyond the well-studied Castro District in San Francisco, we employ census data to identify the location and characteristics of four areas with high concentrations of same-sex unmarried partners: Oakland, Sonoma County, and the Mission and the Castro Districts of San Francisco. As we illustrate by both the census data and our qualitative findings, these four areas vary in terms of the gender, race, and class of their occupants; this variation provides an interesting setting within which to examine the motivations of gay men and lesbians for choosing residences with high concentrations of homosexual residents.

We opt in this chapter to also introduce qualitative data based on participant observations and in-depth interviews in order to be better able to explore both the characteristics of these enclaves and the reasons gay men and lesbians cite for selecting these areas as their residence. We find that all respondents, regardless of residence, report the presence of other gay residents and a liberal political climate as primary factors in choosing to live in an enclave. Further, cultural and natural amenities are largely disregarded or, at times, listed as negative aspects. Factors specific to sexual orientation, therefore, seem to play an important role in drawing gay men and lesbians to these high-concentration areas, as demonstrated by both census data and our qualitative results.

Chapters 2, 3, and 4 mainly examine the ways in which contextual characteristics—those of the city or the state—influence the spatial distribution of gay men and lesbians. In Chapter 5, we focus more directly on the question of whether sexual orientation affects one's likelihood to move. Specifically, we explore whether partnered gay men and lesbians are more likely to engage in interstate migration compared to cohabiting or married heterosexuals. Although some studies have examined the manner in which sexual orientation affects the prevalence of gay men and lesbians in particular cities or states, no quantitative research of which we are aware has been conducted to examine the effect of sexual orientation on the decision to migrate. Past research has found, however, that personal characteristics such as sex, race, ethnicity, age, and education can affect one's likelihood to engage in migration.

Controlling for personal characteristics, we find that individuals who are in unmarried partner relationships are more likely to engage in interstate migration than those who are married; and they are more likely to engage in interstate migration than heterosexual unmarried partners. These findings suggest that sexual orientation, like sex or race, plays a significant role in affecting the decision to engage in interstate migration. In addition, we find that men who are both gay and black, or gay and Hispanic, have lower odds of engaging in interstate migration. Racial and ethnic minorities tend to have lower odds of engaging in interstate migration; these odds decline still further when the man is also gay. Among women, the interaction of education with sexual orientation results in increased odds of migration for lesbians. Female same-sex partners who have a higher level of education are more likely to engage in interstate migration. Individual characteristics, such as race, ethnicity, and education, thus appear to interplay with sexual orientation in ways that further affect the migration decision for gay men and lesbians.

The Family: Comparing Same-Sex Couples to Married and Cohabiting Heterosexual Couples

In recent debates concerning same-sex marriage and antigay parenting laws and regulations, comparisons are usually made between gay male and lesbian couples and heterosexual couples. Are these couples less attached to one another and, as a result, less "deserving" of the right to marriage? Do large numbers of same-sex couples live in nuclear family–like arrangements, with the presence of children in the household? How many children are present in same-sex households? Are the children from previous heterosexual relationships, or are same-sex partners adopting or using other means to have children biologically? The second section of our book uses demographic data to address some of these issues and explores what is known about same-sex families and relationships. More specifically, Chapter 6 focuses on the characteristics of same-sex families and their households, while Chapter 7 examines the ways in which same-sex couples are demographically different from and/or similar to their heterosexual counterparts.

In Chapter 6, we analyze the characteristics of same-sex parents and their households, as well as the effects of restrictive state family laws on the probability of being a homosexual parent. We examine the numbers of children in same-sex households and their relationship to the head of household. In addition, we examine both individual and contextual characteristics which affect the odds of same-sex partners having children in their household.

We find that 18 percent of male same-sex partners and 22 percent of female same-sex partners have children present in their households. Our sample includes over 20,000 children in same-sex households, most of whom are categorized as being the "child," "adopted child," or "step-child" of the head of household. With regard to the probability of children being present in the household, we find that same-sex unmarried partners who indicated that they had been "separated," "divorced," or "widowed" on the marital status question are almost three times as likely to have children in their household compared to those who were categorized as "never-married" or responded "not applicable" to the marital status question. This lends support to the notion that children in same-sex households may have mainly come from previous heterosexual relationships. Further, we find no significant effect of restrictive adoption laws and regulations on the presence of children in same-sex households.

Chapter 7 explores how same-sex couples negotiate their relationships and are affected by society. It has been argued that providing legally sanctioned marriages to gay men and lesbians is unnecessary because they provide no real benefit that cannot be gleaned through contractual agreements. In addition, the stability of same-sex relationships has been questioned; these relationships are generally considered by the current literature on families to be more unstable than relationships where individuals are married. In Chapter 7 we examine both issues. In addition to providing descriptive characteristics for four types of couples, namely, gay male unmarried partners, lesbian unmarried partners, heterosexual unmarried partners, and heterosexual married partners, we also compare variables of attachment and stability across the couple types in order to ascertain demographically whether same-sex relationships are more like those of cohabitating partners or married individuals. We further examine the effect of state level legislation (antidiscrimination laws based on sexual orientation, Defense of Marriage Acts, and the political voting patterns in the area) on the family dynamics of same-sex partners in order to determine whether being in a state that has said legislation enhances or detracts from one's standard of life.

Our findings suggest that same-sex households may be more similar to married households than suggested by prior family research and by the media. Same-sex couples consistently fall between unmarried heterosexual couples and married heterosexual couples with regard to standard of life and attachment variables, making them not entirely like heterosexual unmarried partners, as was previously thought. For example, it appears that same-sex couples have greater financial commitments and dependence on one another than do heterosexual unmarried partners, although these do appear to be slightly less than those of married couples. In addition, we find that, overall, there is little statistical effect at the state level of politics and legislation on the commitment level of same-sex unmarried partners.

While the findings regarding the effects of state-level legislation in both chapters 6 and 7 appear to be mainly insignificant, this could be attributable in part to the relative newness of most of the legislation, the lack of strong enforcement, or both. We urge that caution be used when drawing conclusions about the effects of politics and legislation concerning same-sex couples and their families. Nevertheless, the analyses in these chapters shed light on same-sex families, their children, and the manner in which their relationships are comparable with those of heterosexuals.

The Labor Market: Exploring the Stereotype of Gays and Lesbians as High-Earning Professionals

The third, and final, section of our book presents analyses of same-sex unmarried partners in the labor market. As previously noted, federal laws prohibiting discrimination in employment have repeatedly failed. Many argue that gay men and lesbians are high-earning professionals and, consequently, are not in need of federal protection in the workplace. In chapters 8 and 9, we examine this stereotype of the "wealthy," "professional" gay man or lesbian, drawing on representative data from the census to assess its validity.

We explore in Chapter 8 the degree to which income differentials among partnered men can be attributed to sexual orientation. Earlier research using data from the General Social Survey (GSS) (Badgett 1995; Berg and Lien 2002; Black et al. 2003) and from the 1990 Census (Klawitter and Flatt 1998; Klawitter 1998; Allegretto and Arthur 2001) has produced varying results with respect to the existence and the extent of wage differences between gay male and lesbian workers and heterosexual workers. Although all find a wage penalty for gay men, the extent of this penalty varies, particularly depending on whether the comparison is made with partnered heterosexual men as a whole, married men, or heterosexual cohabiting men. For lesbians, the picture is more confusing, with some findings indicating no statistically significant difference in earnings between lesbians and heterosexual women when controls are included for the presence of children and part-time work. The differences in outcomes among studies using both GSS data and 1990 Census data may be attributed in large part to conflicting perspectives on the best manner in which to construct and estimate a model of income differences.

Using 2000 Census data, we find that partnered gay men earn significantly less than married heterosexual men, but slightly more than cohabiting heterosexual men. In contrast, we find that partnered lesbians earn more than *both* married and cohabiting heterosexual women. These findings seem to contradict earlier studies that have used a similar methodology in two important respects. First, our findings indicate that a *wage advantage* is present when gay men are compared to cohabiting heterosexual men, the first time that a wage advantage has been shown for gay men over any heterosexual group. Second, these analyses reveal a large and statistically significant wage advantage for lesbians even when controls were added for part-time work and the presence of children in the household. This stands in contrast with earlier findings using 1990 Census data that indicated lesbians' wage advantages disappeared when controls were added for working full-time and the presence of children (Klawitter 1998; Klawitter and Flatt 1998).

In Chapter 9, we explore the effect of sexual orientation on occupational segregation. There have not been any representative quantitative studies, to our knowledge, which have examined at a fine level whether there are occupational differences between heterosexual and homosexual individuals. Past studies have used occupational categories, such as "managerial" or "service," as control variables when examining income differences based on sexual orientation (see, e.g., Badgett 1995; Klawitter 1998). In Chapter 9, we focus on professional occupations, and explore whether gay men and lesbians are more likely to work in these professions than are heterosexuals. We show that same-sex partners are, in fact, overrepresented in the largest professions. When compared with partnered heterosexuals, gay men are overrepresented and lesbians are slightly underrepresented. Further, findings indicate that same-sex partners as a whole are concentrated in fields that are focused on creativity, psychology/counseling, and law/social work, and are underrepresented primarily in engineering and the teaching professions.

When we examine the distribution by sex of partnered gay men and lesbians in the professions, we find that gay men are significantly more likely to work in female professions than are heterosexual males, although they are underrepresented in female professions as a whole. Similarly, lesbians are more likely to work in both elite and nonelite male professions than are heterosexual females. These findings suggest that gay men and lesbians cross gender boundaries in the professions more often than do heterosexual men and women.

The analyses in the three substantive sections of our book are detailed demographic investigations of the partnered gay male and lesbian population of the United States. With few exceptions, most of the prior studies on this population have been largely qualitative. Our hope is that the analyses contained in this book will shed additional light on the partnered gay male and lesbian population, a population for which there has been much supposition but little grounded fact.

CHAPTER 1

ᚳᚩᚷ

Same-Sex Partnering Data in the 2000 U.S. Census

An Overview

In the 1990 decennial census, the U.S. Census Bureau added the "unmarried partner" category to the list of responses a respondent could choose to represent his or her relationship to the householder. The addition of this response, which was used also in the 2000 decennial census, permitted individuals to identify as same-sex unmarried partners, creating both a large and representative data-set with which to study issues of sexual orientation. As we noted in the Introduction, we use these data to undertake the demographic analyses presented in this book. In this chapter, we provide an introduction to the "unmarried partner" response category used in the census. We discuss some of the background leading to its first use in the 1990 decennial census, and cover some of the issues related to the empirical conceptualization of homosexuality and sexuality. Further, we demonstrate the manner in which the unmarried partner household data were categorized in the 2000 Census.

The unmarried partner data from the 2000 Census have certain limitations that should be taken into account when used in analyses of homosexual and heterosexual individuals. In this chapter, we both acknowledge and evaluate the impact of these limitations for research on the demography of sexual orientation. Although there are limitations, the census data nonetheless constitute the best and largest-ever data-set on same-sex and opposite-sex partners, permitting researchers to examine heretofore underexplored issues regarding sexual orientation. In the concluding section of this chapter, we employ these new data to describe some of the characteristics of partnered gay males and lesbians and compare them with married and cohabiting heterosexuals.

A Short History of the Collection of
Census Data on Cohabitation

In the early 1970s social scientists and the general public became increasingly aware of, and interested in, the phenomenon of heterosexual cohabitation, that is, persons of the opposite sex living together. The U.S. Census Bureau was the principal federal agency tasked to provide national data on the increasing numbers of cohabiters. Data from the decennial censuses and the Current Population Surveys (CPS) were used to develop estimates of the numbers of cohabiting adults in the United States.

Until the conduct of the 1990 decennial census and the 1995 CPS, however, there were no census questions that specifically asked respondents if they were nonmarital cohabiters. Consequently, the Census Bureau had to use an indirect approach to obtain cohabitation data. The Bureau defined cohabiting households as nonmarital if they contained "two and only two adults (age 15+) who are unrelated and of the opposite sex" (Casper and Cohen 2000: 237). The Census Bureau used such data to develop nationally representative estimates of cohabiters and their characteristics (Glick and Norton 1977; Glick and Spanier 1980; Glick 1984).

This operational definition of cohabiter, along with the published data, led to the concept of POSSLQ (Partners of the Opposite Sex Sharing Living Quarters), which became a cultural fixture in the 1980s and 1990s. Indeed, Casper and Cohen (2000) note that at least two books were published in the 1980s with POSSLQ in the titles (*There's Nothing That I Wouldn't Do If You Would Be My POSSLQ* [Osgood 1981]; and *Will You Be My POSSLQ?* [Bunting 1987]), and countless newspaper stories and scholarly articles used the POSSLQ data and estimates (Bumpass and Sweet 1989; Bianchi and Spain 1996; Vobejda 1998). The POSSLQ data and the resulting publications demonstrated concretely the increasing prevalence of nonmarital cohabitation in the 1970s and 1980s and helped identify and establish the phenomenon of living together as an emerging national trend. The POSSLQ estimates showed the numbers of cohabiting couples in the United States increasing from 968,000 in 1977 to nearly 2.9 million in 1990 (Casper and Cohen 2000: 239).

But the POSSLQ data were imperfect counts of the numbers of nonmarital opposite sex cohabiters living in marriage-like relationships (Casper and Cohen 2000). For one thing, since the definition was restricted to households with only two adults, it missed cohabiters sharing households with more than two adults. It also incorrectly included households containing adults who, though living together, were not cohabiting in romantic marriage-type relationships, such as roommates, boarders, or those living in other kinds of non-cohabiting relationships. To illustrate, in the 1980 census, one of the ways in which individuals could identify their "relationship to the head of household" was "roommate." Persons giving this response had no blood relationship to the householder, but may or may not have had a marriage-like (i.e., an emotional or romantic) relationship with the householder. The POSSLQ approach categorized as cohabiters persons of the opposite sex who were living together as roommates. Consequently, prior to 1990, "couples living outside marriage in marriage-like relationships were not identified separately from (unrelated) individuals living together as roommates" (Black et al. 2000: 140).

Due to both the growing numbers and interest in cohabiters, the Census Bureau recognized the need to provide direct and more precise data on nonmarital cohabitation. Therefore, in the mid-1980s, Donald J. Hernandez, then the Chief of the Marriage and Statistics Branch of the Population Division of the Census Bureau, in consultation with Arthur J. Norton, his supervisor, made the decision to add the response category of "unmarried partner" to the basic question dealing with one's "relationship to the householder" (Hernandez 2006). This change took effect in the 1990 decennial census and in the 1995 Current Population Survey. This response was also included in the 2000 census and in subsequent Current Population Surveys and American Community Surveys.

The "unmarried partner" response was added to the list of other possible responses (husband, wife, son, grandfather, suitemate, boarder, etc.) to the census question pertaining to one's "relationship to the householder," that is, the person in the household designated as "person #1." Person #1 is typically "the member of the household in whose name the home is owned, being bought or rented" (Barrett 1994: 16). Every person in the household, except for person #1, responds to a question about his or her relationship to person #1. The "unmarried partner" response enables the identification of persons in the household who are unrelated to person #1, but who have a "marriage-like" relationship with person #1. The official definition of an "unmarried partner" is "a person age 15 years and over, who is not related to the householder, who shares living quarters, and who has a close personal relationship with the householder" (U.S. Bureau of the Census 2004). The "relationship to the householder" question used in the 2000 Census has been reproduced in Figure 1.1.

With respect to data on gay males and lesbians, the federal government made no attempt to provide data of any type on this subpopulation prior to 1990. Indeed before the conduct of the 1990 U.S. Census, a large, national-level data-set for the lesbian and gay populations did not exist. The data sets then in existence were limited in scope and were based on smaller samples of the population, for example, the General Social Surveys. In the early 1980s, for instance, Castells and Murphy (1982: 238) wrote that "there is no statistical source that provides information on sexual preferences of residents of specific urban areas. . . . Such an obstacle appears overwhelming to the researcher trying to understand the spatial dynamics of the emerging gay culture."

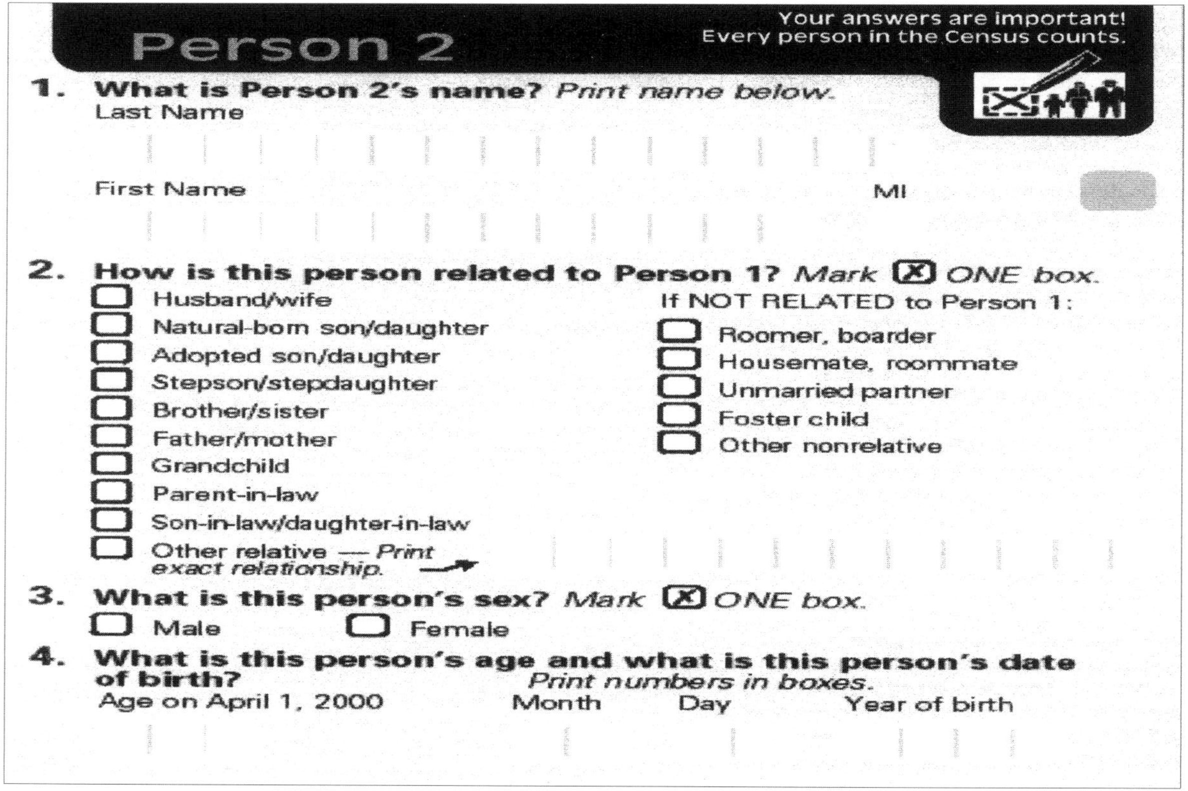

Person 2

Your answers are important!
Every person in the Census counts.

1. **What is Person 2's name?** *Print name below.*

Last Name

First Name   MI

2. **How is this person related to Person 1?** *Mark* ☒ *ONE box.*

If NOT RELATED to Person 1:

☐ Husband/wife
☐ Natural-born son/daughter
☐ Adopted son/daughter
☐ Stepson/stepdaughter
☐ Brother/sister
☐ Father/mother
☐ Grandchild
☐ Parent-in-law
☐ Son-in-law/daughter-in-law
☐ Other relative — *Print exact relationship.* →

☐ Roomer, boarder
☐ Housemate, roommate
☐ Unmarried partner
☐ Foster child
☐ Other nonrelative

3. **What is this person's sex?** *Mark* ☒ *ONE box.*

☐ Male   ☐ Female

4. **What is this person's age and what is this person's date of birth?**

Age on April 1, 2000

Print numbers in boxes.

Month   Day   Year of birth

FIGURE 1.1. Reproduction of the Question on Relationship to Householder from Census 2000

As just noted, this all changed in 1990 when the federal government decided that direct data were needed on heterosexual cohabitation and added the "unmarried partner" response to the "relationship" question. Prior to 1990, there was no direct way to use census, CPS data, or both to measure cohabitation; there was no direct way to identify persons in the household who were unrelated to the head of household but who had a marriage-like relationship with the householder. Fortunately, census procedures permitted respondents to check the "unmarried partner" response irrespective of whether their sex was the same as that of the householder. Thus, beginning in 1990, researchers have been able to use the unmarried partner data to obtain information on gay male and lesbian partnering. But what do these data truly convey regarding the identification and enumeration of partnered gay men and lesbians? To address this question we need to discuss issues involved in the conceptualization of sexual orientation.

The Conceptualization of Sexual Orientation

Most of the social science literature on sexual orientation conceptualizes the phenomenon using two basic perspectives or approaches, or a combination thereof. These two views may be referred to as "essentialism" and "social constructionism" (Laumann et al. 1994: 284). Founded in biology, the essentialist view states that there is an essential characteristic common to all homosexual individuals that is distinct and separate from heterosexual individuals. This common characteristic, or essence, is thought to be based in biology or psychology, and is a fundamental drive or trait that establishes a person's inclusion into either a homosexual or heterosexual category (Laumann et al. 1994: 285). The essentialist view of homosexuality presumes that a person may be categorized as being or not being homosexual and makes a distinction, often binary, between one who is a homosexual individual and one who is not. Thus, sexual orientation is determined by the definition of two distinct categories.

The social constructionist view of homosexuality counters and critiques the essentialist perspective. Social constructionism argues against the notion of binary categories, that is, that one either is or is not a homosexual individual (Foucault 1978; Butler 1990; Seidman 1996). Instead, this approach argues for a continuum with varying degrees of homosexuality and heterosexuality. Social constructionists point out that homosexual prevalence rates and visibility tend to vary across time and settings, and that the concepts, definitions, and practices of homosexuality are often not the same across context and cultures (Laumann et al. 1994: 285). What in one culture may be defined as "homosexual" may not be defined as such in another culture. For example, an individual may engage in same-sex sexual behavior but not identify him- or herself as a gay male or lesbian. Likewise, one might identify as a homosexual individual but never have experienced same-sex sex. Also, the sexuality definitions and labels attached to individuals by other persons and by the larger society may be incongruent with how individuals per se self-identify.

When demographers use the census unmarried partner data, they are not necessarily taking an essentialist view. They might have a social constructionist view, or understanding, of sexuality. Nonetheless, the census data only permit sexuality to be measured on one dimension, and without variation. The use of these data involves, by definition, the employment of a clear-cut and straightforward definition of what is a partnered homosexual individual (Black et al. 2000; Smith and Gates 2001; Gates and Ost 2004; Walther and Poston 2004). Consequently, in most of the chapters of this book an essentialist approach, by definition, is applied; the data do not permit any alternative. The census data are essentialist in terms of the way the question has been formulated and the way it can be applied.

However, in other demographic and social science research on homosexuality, the manner in which homosexuality and sexual orientation are measured tends to vary. This is largely due to the different ways sexual orientation has been defined in surveys and conceptualized by researchers (Saewyc et al. 2004). Homosexuality may be defined in terms of sexual behavior, sexual desire (including fantasy), and self-identification (Laumann et al. 1994; Saewyc et al. 2004). In analyses based on data from national surveys, social scientists have used one or more of the above concepts of homosexuality, but particularly those based on self-identification and behavior.

Analyses of homosexuality using data from the General Social Survey (GSS), for instance, usually employ a behavioral definition of homosexuality, such as whether a person's sex partners within a particular timeframe (such as over the past 12 months, or the past five years, or in one's lifetime) have or have not been entirely or predominantly of the same sex as the respondent (Badgett 1995; Berg and Lien 2002; Black et al. 2003). The GSS does not include a question on the self-identification of the respondent's sexual orientation.

Researchers using data from other surveys are able to use a series of different definitions of homosexuality. To date, there are two national surveys conducted in the United States that include questions dealing with sexual behavior, sexual orientation, and sexual desire. One is the National Health and Social Life Survey (NHSLS) conducted by Laumann and his associates in 1992 (see *The Social Organization of Sexuality: Sexual Practices in the United States* [1994]). The other is Cycle 6 of the National Survey of Family Growth conducted in 2002 by the National Center for Health Statistics (National Center for Health Statistics, 2004). Because these surveys allow researchers to define homosexuality in various ways, it is possible for their analyses to be more closely attuned to a social constructionist view rather than an essentialist one.

Overall, there are a few fundamental methodological limitations apparent from a review of the literature concerning the conceptualization and measurement of sexual orientation: the lack of common and consistent definitions in surveys, problems with obtaining sufficiently representative sample sizes, and the lack of sexuality-related questions in large-scale data collections. These limitations may be somewhat related to the purported social stigma attached to homosexuality. This stigma is believed to affect not only the way questionnaires are designed to address or measure sexual orientation, but also the ways in which individuals will respond to survey questions about self-identification, behavior, and desire. For example, some may be reluctant to identify as homosexual or to report homosexual behavior (Laumann et al. 1994: 284).

No doubt there are problems with data on homosexual individuals no matter how the phenomenon is conceptualized and quantified. There are likely methodological limitations and problems inherent in gathering and analyzing data about the gay male and lesbian population, as with any stigmatized minority. Nonetheless, we find that the federal census data on same-sex unmarried partners can be useful if researchers are clear about to whom the data refer. In the next section of this chapter we consider specifically the unmarried partner data from the 2000 U.S. Census and present and discuss a classification of households within which census data on same-sex partnered households are generated. This will enable us to better visualize the makeup and general definition of the populations that are captured by the same-sex unmarried partner data in the 2000 census.

Same-Sex Partner Data from the 2000 Census

In 2000, almost 5.5 million unmarried partner households were enumerated in the U.S. Census. These were households in which the couples were living together but were not married. Of these 5.5 million unmarried partner households, almost 600 thousand were same-sex partner households; 301 thousand were male-male households, and 293 thousand were female-female households (see Table 1.1). The same-sex unmarried partner households were located throughout the United States in over 99 percent of all U.S. counties. The largest number (over 85 percent) resided in metropolitan areas (Simmons and O'Connell 2003: 2).

A sorting process exists whereby a household identified in the 2000 Census came to be designated as a same-sex unmarried partner household. By detailing this sorting process, we wish to highlight exactly which households are included and which are not included in the same-sex unmarried partner census data. First, it is important to note that the "relationship to householder" question that produces the same-sex census data is one of seven so-called 100 percent census questions that are asked of all persons who respond to the census. The 100 percent unmarried partner data are available in Table PCT 22 of Summary File 2 of the 2000 Census. This table provides for various levels of geography (e.g., states, counties, census tracts, block groups, etc.) the number

TABLE 1.1. Number of Unmarried Partner and Married Couple Households, by Metropolitan Status and Geographic Region,* United States, 2000

Household Type	Number	% Metro	% Northeast	% Midwest	% South	% West
Total Households	105,480,101	79.9	19.2	23.4	36.0	21.3
Total Coupled Households	59,969,000	78.7	18.7	23.7	35.9	21.7
Unmarried Partner Households	5,475,768	81.4	19.7	23.0	33.0	24.3
Same-Sex Partners	594,391	85.3	20.1	17.8	35.3	26.9
Male–male	301,026	86.3	19.7	17.3	35.8	27.2
Female–female	293,365	84.2	20.4	18.3	34.8	26.5
Opposite–Sex Partners	4,881,377	80.9	19.6	23.6	32.3	24.0
Married Couple Households	54,493,232	78.5	18.6	23.8	36.2	21.4

*Includes Puerto Rico Not Shown.

Source: Simmons and O'Connell, 2003, tables 1 and 2.

of households in which person #1 is a male and another male in the household identifies himself as the unmarried partner of person #1; these are known as male-male households. A similar tabulation is provided for the number of female-female households in each geographic area. As mentioned earlier, because the "unmarried partner" response is meant to reflect a "marriage-like" relationship between the two same-sex persons, researchers make the assumption that these data on same-sex households (male-male or female-female) represent households inhabited by partnered gay males, or by partnered lesbians (Black et al. 2000, 2002b; Simmons and O'Connell 2003; Walther and Poston 2004; Gates and Ost 2004). The research we report in Chapter 4 of this book adds further support to this conclusion.

To show how a household ends up being classified as a same-sex household, however, we do not use the 100 percent data from Table PCT 22 of Summary File 2. These are aggregated data and do not permit the statistical manipulation of individual cases. Instead we use data from the five percent Public Use Microdata Sample (PUMS) from the 2000 Census. Following the approach used by Black and colleagues (2000) with 1990 census data, we present in Figure 1.2 a classification of households from the 2000 Census. Although the data shown in Figure 1.2 are drawn from the 5 percent PUMS, we have used sample weights to inflate the numbers to their estimated national levels.

Figure 1.2 shows two boxes with bolded outlines that represent two types of household relationships: those without a "marriage-like" relationship (A), and those with a marriage-like relationship (B). Each of the household relationship boxes is divided into subgroups. The subgroups with bolded outlines, strictly speaking, represent subgroups directly observable in the census data. Subgroups with dotted outlines are not observable in the census data.

The 5 percent PUMS data consist of 4,710,069 households containing single adults or two adults. Inflating these to national levels using their sample weights produces an estimated total number of 94,485,532 households. Excluded in this estimate are all households where the household relationship was imputed; also excluded are households with "multiple-marriage-like relationships." We begin our classification with these more than 94 million households.

In Figure 1.2 we show that of the more than 94 million households, almost 36 million are households with no marriage-like relationship (A). (Excluded here are households with three or more adults.) The majority of these 36 million households, over 27 million, are single adult households (A.1). These single adult households contain either single gay males and lesbians (A.1.1) or single heterosexuals (A.1.2). But since the census does not contain a question asking about the respondent's sexual orientation, the numbers of households in boxes A.1.1 and A.1.2 cannot be identified in the census data. This is a shortcoming of the data. Census data do not capture gay men and lesbians who live alone.

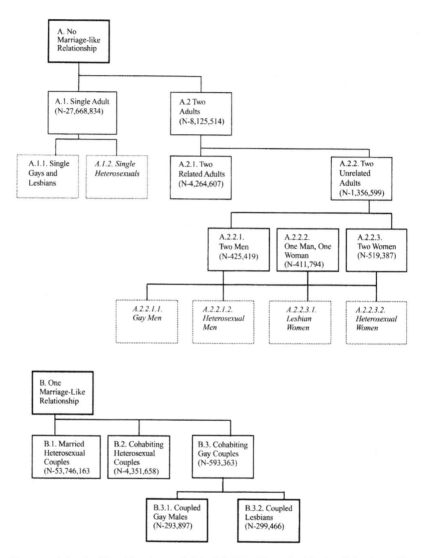

FIGURE 1.2. A Classification of 94,485,532 Households by Marriage-like Relationships for Homosexual and Hetersexual Males and Females: U.S., 2000

The remaining 8 million households are two adult households (A.2). These consist of over 4 million households containing two related adults (A.2.1) and almost 1.4 million households containing two unrelated adults (A.2.2). The box representing households with two related adults (A.2.1) are households with, for instance, two siblings, or with an uncle and a nephew, or with some other combination of two related adults. We do not use this group of households in our analyses.

We are particularly interested in the nearly 1.4 million households containing two unrelated adults (A.2.2). These households may be further subdivided into households with two men (A.2.2.1), one man and one woman (A.2.2.2), and two women (A.2.2.3). These three subgroups contain individuals who are either gay men (A.2.2.1.1), heterosexual men (A.2.2.1.2), lesbians (A.2.2.3.1), or heterosexual women (A.2.2.3.2). But there is no way to make these distinctions with census data because, as already mentioned, the census does not ask about sexual orientation. Thus, gay men or lesbians who are living with other men or women, but not in marriage-like relationships, are also not enumerated in the census.

Of the over 94 million households represented in the classification, almost 59 million are households with one marriage-like relationship (B). These may be subdivided into three subgroups: households with married heterosexual couples (B.1), households with cohabiting heterosexual couples (B.2), and households with cohabiting homosexual couples (B.3). The over 593 thousand cohabiting homosexual couples may be further subdivided into households with cohabiting gay men (B.3.1) and households with cohabiting lesbians (B.3.2). Data on these two groups of same-sex cohabiters shown in boxes B.3.1 and B.3.2 are used in this book's analyses of the social demographic patterns and dynamics of same-sex partners.

Quality of the Gay Male and Lesbian Partner Data

Although the Census Bureau instructs that the "unmarried partner" category is indicative of a marriage-like relationship, many have questioned whether the respondents understand the implications of this response and, as a result, whether the data truly reflect a homosexual relationship. In the absence of a direct question asking about sexual orientation, a number of concerns have arisen regarding the use of the same-sex unmarried partner data for the purposes of studying issues of homosexuality. Before presenting analyses using these data, therefore, we believe it is important to address these methodological issues in an attempt to appraise the quality of the same-sex partnering census data. First, we ask about the accuracy of the 2000 Census data in portraying the true numbers of partnered gay men and lesbians. Specifically, how well have the 2000 Census data on same-sex partners enumerated the actual numbers of partnered gay men and lesbians living in the United States in 2000? A second issue concerns the variation across the geographical areas of the United States in the prevalence of same-sex unmarried partners. How valid is this variation? Is there a relationship between this variation and the variation across geographical areas in the true numbers of partnered gay men and lesbians? A third issue concerns the extent to which there could be error in the same-sex partnering census data due to sex miscoding errors. We then conclude this discussion by introducing two reasons that give us further cause to have confidence in the validity of the same-sex partner data.

We first address the validity of the census data on same-sex partners. To do this, we need to know the true numbers of gay men and lesbians living in the U.S. in 2000. There are no such numbers available. However, the numbers may be estimated with data from a national survey that contains sexuality questions dealing with both self-identification and behavior; specifically, Cycle 6 of the National Survey of Family Growth (NSFG) conducted by the U.S. Department of Health and Human Services in 2002 (National Center for Health Statistics 2004). This is a survey of 12,571 persons aged 15–44 in the noninstitutional population. The male and female respondents were asked questions about same-sex behavior and sexual identification. We selected persons self-identifying as gay men or lesbians and those who reported having exclusively same-sex sex partners in the past 12 months. We reasoned that these two characteristics best typify persons who would likely be captured as same-sex unmarried partners in the census data. We combined the two groups and developed an estimate of the percentages of gay men and lesbians in the United States in 2002 self-identifying as homosexual individuals, or engaging in exclusively homosexual behavior in the past year, or both.

Using weighted NSFG data, we determined that 2.55 percent of males may be classified as gay, and that 1.81 percent of females may be classified as lesbian. The upper and lower 95 percent confidence bounds for the males are 3.2 percent and 2.1 percent, and for the females, 2.2 percent and 1.5 percent. These percentage estimates and 95 percent confidence intervals obtained from the 2002 NSFG are remarkably close to male and female homosexuality estimates and confidence intervals obtained from the only other nationally representative survey of the U.S. population that asked the same two sexuality questions, namely, the National Health and Social Life Survey (NHSLS) conducted in 1992 by Laumann and colleagues (Laumann et al. 1994).

As noted, the NSFG gay male and lesbian estimates pertain to persons aged 15 to 44. The U.S. population of males and females aged 15 to 44 counted in the 2000 Census consists of 62,647,145 males and 62,026,997 females. When we multiply these numbers by the NSFG percentages of gay men and lesbians, we obtain estimates of the total numbers of gay men and lesbians in the United States between the ages of 15 and 44, namely, 1,597,502 and

1,122,689, respectively. But how many of these gay men and lesbians are living in committed relationships in the same households?

Gates and Ost (2004: 13) have reviewed several studies to arrive at estimates "that 23.5 percent of gay men and 42.7 percent of lesbians are coupled." Using their percentage coupling figures, we estimate that in the U.S. in 2000, there were 375,413 gay men in committed relationships living in the same households (that is, 1,597,502 × 23.5%), and 479,388 committed lesbians living in the same households in the United States (or 1,122,689 × 42.7%), all between the ages of 15 and 44.

Using data from the 2000 PUMS and the corresponding person weights, we next determined that Census 2000 enumerated 334,220 same-sex male partners and 345,571 same-sex female partners between the ages of 15 and 44. Comparing these figures with the NSFG-based estimates of the numbers of partnered gay men and lesbians suggests that Census 2000 undercounted 41,193 committed gay men living in the United States, for an undercount of 11.0 percent, and undercounted 133,817 committed lesbian partners, for an undercount of 27.9 percent.

There are many problems with these estimates. For one thing, although the census questionnaire asks about identification, the identity pertains to whether or not one is in an unmarried partnership. We have already noted that the census questionnaire does not include a question asking specifically about the sexual orientation, or the sexual behavior, of the respondents. As have other researchers (Black et al. 2000, 2003; Simmons and O'Connell 2003; Walther and Poston 2004; Gates and Ost 2004), we assume that the census numbers of same-sex male and female partners reflect the numbers of committed gay men and lesbians in the population. Since there are no national-level data available on gay male and lesbian commitment rates and different studies report different estimates, we employed the male and female averages of the various studies developed by Gates and Ost (2004). We acknowledge that these estimates of partnership are, of course, less than ideal.

Despite the problems associated with our population estimates, however, these results are fairly consistent with conclusions reached by other scholars who have also found that committed gay men and lesbians were undercounted in the Census 2000 (Smith and Gates 2001; Badgett and Rogers 2003; Gates and Ost 2004). Indeed, even when widely varied methodologies have been employed to ascertain the validity of the census data, undercount estimates have been surprisingly consistent. In one instance, rather than comparing census results with past nationally representative surveys, researchers at the Institute for Gay and Lesbian Strategic Studies conducted two surveys to determine the use of the unmarried partner response by same-sex couples (Badgett and Rogers 2003). These were nonrepresentative surveys of the gay male and lesbian population; one was conducted of participants attending the gay rights Millennium

March in Washington, DC in April 2000, and the other involved an online survey that included 90 individuals who were in same-sex partnerships at the time of the 2000 census. Both of these samples were likely biased to include an oversampling of individuals identifying as unmarried partners on the census form, since such participants are more likely to be politically active and/or comfortable in disclosing their sexual orientation. Approximately 81 to 84 percent of same-sex partners participating in these surveys either chose the unmarried partner category in the 2000 census, or identified as married and would have been placed in the unmarried partner category by the Census Bureau (Badgett and Rogers 2003). Consequently, the estimated undercount from these surveys for all same-sex partners fell between 16 and 19 percent. This undercount estimate is similar to those presented in our analyses.

We now turn to the second question, that dealing with the validity of the gay and lesbian prevalence indexes across the geographic areas of the United States. How valid is this variation? There are no reliable data available to answer this question because there are no data other than census data "for calculating even the most rudimentary statistics on the [geographic] locations of the gay and lesbian populations" (Black et al. 2000: 149). However, it is possible to examine the face validity of the census-developed geographical distribution data of the partnered gay population by relating its variation with that of the spatial distribution of AIDS deaths. Unfortunately, data on AIDS deaths are only available for large metropolitan areas. Thus, we are only able to compare the variation in AIDS deaths with census-based prevalence rates of the partnered gay population for large metropolitan areas.

We are well aware, and wish to emphasize the point, that AIDS deaths are not restricted to homosexual individuals. Indeed since the 1990s in the United States there have been increasing numbers of heterosexual deaths due to AIDS. But AIDS as a cause of death continues in the United States to be the most prominent for men who have sex with men (as do most gay men) than for the heterosexual population (CDC 2004; Kaiser Family Foundation 2004). One would thus expect that among geographical areas there should be a positive association between the prevalence of gay men and the prevalence of AIDS deaths.

We obtained data on the reported number of AIDS cases for the 12-month period between July 1998 and June 1999 for the 99 metropolitan areas of the United States with populations over 500,000. Similar data are not available for smaller metropolitan areas, or for nonmetropolitan areas. We first examine this relationship in a relative way by correlating the rates of partnered gays (per 1,000 unmarried males) with the rate of AIDS cases per 100,000 persons in the area. The correlation between the two rates across the 99 metropolitan areas is .52. The relationship is positive and strong.

The actual number of reported AIDS cases and the actual number of male-male households among the 99 metropolitan areas are highly skewed so we used their natural logs in a second examination of the relationship. The correlation between the logged values of number of AIDS deaths and number of male-male households is 0.86, indicating a strong positive correlation. Similar comparisons conducted with census and AIDS data for 1990 produced comparable high positive correlations (Black et al. 2000; Walther and Poston 2004).

These tests increase our confidence in the quality of the same-sex partner data obtained in the 2000 decennial census, particularly the validity of the geographical distribution of these data in large metropolitan areas. As already noted, there are no similar data on AIDS deaths for the smaller metropolitan areas or for nonmetropolitan areas. However, the fact that the two variances are so closely related in the larger metropolitan areas gives us reason to believe that it is likely that the variances for other geographical areas would also be closely related.

In addition, there are no similar data available for examining the face validity of the partnered lesbian data from the 2000 Census. We do show in Chapter 2 of this book, however, that the partnered gay male rates and partnered lesbian rates are themselves highly and positively related (also see, Black et al. 2000; and Walther and Poston 2004). This provides some indication of the face validity of the lesbian data. Specifically, if the AIDS death rates support the face validity of the partnered gay male data, and the partnered gay male rates are highly related to the lesbian rates, then logic suggests that the partnered lesbian data also have face validity.

The third issue to be addressed is the degree to which there could be error in the same-sex partner data, perhaps due to individuals miscoding their sex. In the 1990 census, if a same-sex couple indicated that their relationship was that of married, postcollection census editing treated this as an inconsistency, and "usually changed the sex as a consistency edit. This means that in data [for 1990] released by the Bureau the couple was coded as a heterosexual married couple." (Gates and Ost 2004: 12). The Bureau changed this postcollection editing decision in the 2000 Census to treat it "as an inconsistency in the relationship to householder rather than in the spouse's sex. That is, the 'husband-wife' relationship designation was changed as a consistency edit to an 'unmarried partner' relationship. Since the sex variables were not changed [as they were in 1990], the couple was counted as a same-sex unmarried partner couple" (Gates and Ost 2004: 12).

In the 2000 U.S. Census, there was a notable increase in the total number of individuals classified as same-sex unmarried partners, with almost 600,000 couples reported as same-sex unmarried partner couples in 2000 compared to 145,130 in 1990. The quadrupling of couples identifying as same-sex unmarried partners led researchers to speculate about the cause of the "increase." Indeed, Black and colleagues (2002a) have cautioned that some of these couples might actually be heterosexual couples, misclassified by the Census Bureau as same-sex partners in an attempt to rectify contradictions between individuals' selected sex and marital status. If this is the case, they note that researchers should try to adjust for misclassified heterosexuals when using the Census data to study the homosexual population.

Because the federal government does not recognize marriage between two individuals of the same sex, the Census Bureau does not accept responses where the householder (person #1) identifies another individual of the same sex as a spouse (Fields and Clark 1999). Rather, in 2000 the Bureau accepted the sex indicated by the respondents, but reclassified the couple as unmarried partners (U.S. Census Bureau 2001). Further, same-sex unmarried partners who selected "married" on the marital status question were also reallocated by the Bureau into a category other than married. Assuming that these individuals are same-sex couples who wish to indicate a marital relationship, this strategy maintains the integrity of the responses since the unmarried partner category is designed to capture marriage-like relationships. Black and his colleagues (2002a), however, observe that a side effect of this allocation process is that married heterosexual couples who misreport the sex of one spouse will be reclassified as same-sex unmarried partners.

In the several geographical-based analyses of gay male and lesbian partnering that we present in this book, the miscoding problem is not an issue. Because the sex miscoding measurement error is very small, it does not appear to have "any significant effect on geographical distribution patterns" (Gates and Ost 2004: 14). In analyses employing the Public Use Microdata Samples, however, any sizable sex miscoding could prove to be problematic.

Black and his associates created models to test the extent of this measurement error; they also presented a method for recalculating reliable estimates using the census data. Briefly stated, to obtain the portion of same-sex unmarried partners who are actually misclassified heterosexuals, they used a figure from a 1975 Census Bureau study that indicated that the error rate for sex miscoding was less than .002 for each observation; they estimated that the error rate for miscoding one's own sex and one's partner's sex would be between .003 and .004. They then engaged in two exercises to estimate the numbers of misclassified heterosexuals: one assumes that the average number of children for homosexual households is the same for those with both allocated and nonallocated marital status, and the second assumes that the rate of sex miscoding is the same for both married and unmarried heterosexual partners.

Based on these analyses, Black and associates (2002a) concluded that between 30 and 35 percent of all same-sex unmarried partner couples are actually misallocated married heterosexual couples. Their assumption in the first exercise, however, may be problematic. Fields and Clark (1999) found in Census test studies that same-sex unmarried partners who self-identify as married couples have different characteristics than those who do not so identify. In fact, they found that the presence of children in the household (the characteristic employed by Black and associates in their analysis) was an area in which these households were particularly likely to differ, with same-sex households with children being seven times more likely to have identified as "married." Thus, the assumption by Black and colleagues that allocated and nonallocated households are similar may be problematic. They attempt to adjust for this weakness in their second exercise by allowing the average characteristics to vary among allocated and nonallocated households, and assuming that the rate of sex miscoding is the same for married and unmarried heterosexual partners. They note, however, that doing so results in increased sensitivity to the assumptions that they make regarding the rate of sex miscoding because in the first exercise they assume the value of sex miscoding only for the smaller, unmarried group.

Consequently, the analyses of Black and his associates may well contain problematic assumptions, which could result in a biased estimate of the number of misclassified heterosexuals in the 2000 Census. Nonetheless, their cautions concerning the possible existence of sizable misclassification errors need to be taken into account when conducting analyses with these data.

However, research undertaken at the U.S. Bureau of the Census indicates that the number of persons mistakenly included in the same-sex unmarried partner data because of sex miscoding is offset in part by persons mistakenly excluded because of sex miscoding. O'Connell and Gooding (2006, 2007) examined the first names of opposite-sex couples (married or unmarried) in the 2004 test census of New York and compared their names with their reported sex. They found, for instance that "98 percent of the people with the name of 'Elizabeth' . . . reported that they were female, compared with 79 percent of people with the name of 'Morgan' and 75 percent of people with the name of 'Leslie.' Some respondents with these names may have mis-marked their response in the sex item as male while others may, in reality, be male and not female" (O'Connell and Gooding 2006: 5). They then presented various approaches using "name" responses instead of "sex" responses for editing sex responses. Using the most conservative "name" approach, namely, that in which "99 percent of people with that name were of the opposite sex" (O'Connell and Gooding 2006: 5) in the census data, they found that there is as much of a gain in the number of same-sex persons based on their names as there is a loss based on their sex miscoding.

They showed that "using first names in an impartial and systematic way to invalidate reported sex responses will yield more same-sex couples than originally reported" in the census data (O'Connell and Gooding 2006: 5); indeed the number gained is near the number lost; and the characteristics of the two groups are similar. O'Connell and Gooding concluded that the inclusion of persons in the same-sex counts due to sex misclassification errors is not as serious an issue as believed by Black and his associates.

Finally, two other points may be made that further increase our confidence in the validity of the same-sex partner data from the 2000 Census. One pertains to the national "Make Your Family Count" publicity campaign that was initiated, sponsored, and conducted by gay male and lesbian communities prior to the conduct of Census 2000. Spearheaded by the Institute for Gay and Lesbian

Strategic Studies and the Policy Institute of the National Gay and Lesbian Task Force, the campaign encouraged gay male and lesbian couples to mark the "unmarried partner" category in order to be counted in the census (Bradford et al. 2002; McManus 2003; Badgett and Rogers 2003). In the months of January through March of 2000, gay and lesbian organizations and communities publicized the 2000 Census via the Internet, newspapers, and mailing lists to make their constituents aware that Census 2000 was about to be conducted. Furthermore, they encouraged gay men and lesbians in partnered relationships to fill out the census questionnaire and to be sure to use the "unmarried partner" response when answering the question on "relationship to the householder." Although we do not know the complete effects of the campaign, it has been credited by some as helping to increase the numbers of same-sex unmarried partner respondents fourfold in 2000 from the 1990 Census (Bradford et al. 2002).

A second point concerns the fact that the actual numbers and rates based on the same-sex partner census data for the census tract neighborhoods of many cities and metropolitan areas of the United States have been shown in many contexts to be large and high in exactly those neighborhood areas "known" to be gay and lesbian enclaves; and the opposite has been shown to be true for neighborhoods known as heterosexual areas. Chapters 2 and 4 in this book present data along these lines. To illustrate, the Castro District in San Francisco is well known and cited in the literature as being a prominent, if not the preeminent, gay male enclave in the United States (Abrahamson 1996; Murray 1992). According to the census data on same-sex unmarried partners, it does indeed have a very high concentration of male unmarried partners, as well as female unmarried partners (Gates and Ost 2004).

Similarly, a district in Oakland, California, known by many to be a lesbian enclave (see chapter 4) reveals a high concentration of female unmarried partners in the census data (Zamora 2004; Gates and Ost 2004). Another well-known gay enclave in the Southwestern United States, the Montrose District of Houston, also shows a very high concentration of male unmarried partners according to the 2000 Census data. Conversely, other areas of Houston, such as Kingwood and Sugarland, other areas of San Francisco, such as the Sunset and the Parkside, and many other areas in other cities also known to be heterosexual neighborhoods, report very low numbers of same-sex unmarried partners in the 2000 Census. This correspondence between the spatial distribution of same-sex unmarried partners and areas known to be gay enclaves, or known to be predominantly heterosexual, provides additional evidence about the validity of these data.

In this chapter, we have evaluated the general quality of the same-sex partner data from the 2000 census in several different ways. Despite the shortcomings of these data, we agree with Black and his associates (2000) who conducted similar analyses of the 1990 data that the census data on same-sex partners are not the product of measurement error and that, indeed, the bulk of the same-sex couples enumerated in the census data are same-sex partners.

Having examined the validity of the census data, we now turn to a general description of unmarried same-sex partners and their households, as revealed by these data. We compare them on several characteristics with married heterosexuals and with cohabiting heterosexuals to obtain a better understanding of this population.

Characteristics of Same-Sex
Unmarried Partners and Their Households

In later chapters of this book we undertake analyses examining several demographic questions pertaining to sexual orientation. Before doing so, we provide here an introduction to some of the basic characteristics of individuals who identified as same-sex unmarried partners on the 2000 Census. What percentage of racial minorities selected this category? What is the average income of individuals in this group? What is the average age of an unmarried partner? And how do these characteristics, and others, compare with those of individuals in other couple-types, specifically married and heterosexual unmarried partners? Some of the characteristics of same-sex partners and their households are presented in this section. They will provide insights into certain information on homosexuality that can be gleaned from the 2000 Census, as well as offer a foundation for the analyses to follow in later chapters of this book.

We noted previously that Census 2000 enumerated over 105 million households. Almost 60 million were households inhabited by couples, of which over 54 million were married couples. This leaves almost 5.5 million unmarried partner households. Of these, over 595 thousand were same-sex unmarried partner households (see Table 1.1). Thus, 1 in 10 of the unmarried partner households captured in Census 2000 were same-sex unmarried partner households; of these, 301 thousand were male-male and 293 thousand were female-female households.

Almost 80 percent of all households, 79 percent of coupled households, and 81 percent of unmarried partner households, were located in metropolitan areas (Table 1.1). Same-sex partner households, in comparison, had a larger metropolitan presence, with over 85 percent in metropolitan areas. This is the largest metropolitan presence of the several categories of coupled households. Also shown in Table 1.1 is the slightly different distribution by geographic region of same-sex partner households compared to other households, particularly married-couple households, with slightly more in the Northeast and West and less in the Midwest and South.

The state of California had more unmarried partner households (12 percent of the total) than any state in the nation. The percentage of same-sex unmarried partner households in California was 16 percent, also the highest in the country (Simmons and O'Connell 2003: Table 1.2). The highest percentages of same-sex unmarried households were in cities on the West and East

Coasts. San Francisco had the highest percentage of same-sex unmarried households compared to all households (2.7%), followed by Fort Lauderdale (2.1%), Seattle (1.9%), Oakland (1.8%), and Berkeley (1.8%). Only one of the top ten cities in this group was in the Midwest, namely, Minneapolis (1.6%) (Simmons and O'Connell 2003: Table 1.3). The metropolitan and regional differences examined in the preceding paragraphs receive more attention in Chapter 2 of this book.

We now examine characteristics of same-sex unmarried partners and compare them with heterosexuals who are cohabiting and with heterosexuals who are married. Here we use data from the 5 percent Public Use Microdata Samples (PUMS) from the 2000 Census. We undertake these analyses first for males, then for females. In the first analysis we compare characteristics of males who are same-sex partners with males who are cohabiting with females and with males who are married to females. The second analysis is undertaken in a similar way for females.

Since most of the analyses involve socioeconomic comparisons of the groups, we introduce several constraints. To be included in the analyses reported here, we required that the males and females were in the labor force with a job and earning at least $1,000 in 1999. We also use statistical sample adjustment methods (Stata Corp 2005) that introduce survey adjustment estimators to adjust our analyses according to the population weights assigned in the 5 percent PUMS.

Table 1.2 compares the characteristics of male same-sex unmarried partners, with cohabiting male heterosexuals and married male heterosexuals. The top panel of the table examines mean values for the three groups. On average, same-sex male partners reported annual earnings in 1999 of over $40,000, compared to almost $32,000 for male cohabiters and over $48,000 for males who were married. These earnings differences among labor force participants in the three groups require more attention. Chapter 8 in this book analyzes earnings differences between homosexual and heterosexual males and females.

We next examine mean occupational status scores for males in the three groups. The occupational status score is a score assigned to persons in each detailed census occupation based on the median earnings for that occupation. The occupational status score is meant to represent the material rewards accruing to persons in different occupations where the higher the value of the score, the higher the status (Nam and Boyd 2004). Married males have slightly more occupational status than same-sex partnered males, and both have more status than male cohabiters. Occupational differences between same-sex partners and heterosexual partners are examined in further detail in chapter 9 of this book.

Although married men have higher occupational status than same-sex partnered males, almost two-thirds of the same-sex male partners have a college degree or higher compared to less than 60 percent of married males and 47 percent of male cohabiters (Table 1.2).

TABLE 1.2. Characteristics of Male Labor Force Participants by Same-Sex Unmarried Partners, Married Heterosexuals, and Cohabiting Heterosexuals, United States, 2000

Males	Same-Sex Partners	Cohabiting Heterosexuals	Married
Means			
Annual Income (1999)	$40,813	$31,884	$48,474
Occupational Status Score	30.2	28.5	31.5
Percent with College Degree	65.4	47.1	59.5
Percent White	79.1	73.2	81.2
Percent Hispanic	13.4	13.7	10.6
Percent with Children in Household	15.9	21.7	61.2
Age Groups (%)			
Under 30	18.2	38.7	13.3
30–49	62.6	50.7	56.9
50–69	18.1	10.2	27.6
70+	1.1	0.3	2.2
Weeks Worked in 1999 (%)			
20 or less	4.9	5.2	3.8
21–30	4.6	5.4	3.4
31–40	6.6	7.8	5.1
41–50	14.6	15.9	13.3
51+	69.4	65.6	74.4

The three groups of males are mainly white, and between 11 and 14 percent are Hispanic. The race and Hispanic differences are not major, but they are significant. Same-sex male partners and male cohabiters are less likely than married males to be white and more likely to be Hispanic.

We also compare the groups of males with respect to whether there are any children under age 18 in their households. As expected, there are more children in the married households than in other households; specifically, there are children in the households of over 61 percent of the married males, compared to 22 percent of the male cohabiters and 16 percent of the same-sex male partners. Such a relatively high presence of children in the households of male same-sex partners is not necessarily a surprise, but raises additional questions regarding the characteristics of gay male and lesbian families. Chapter 6 in this book focuses in more detail on this subject.

We next analyze the age patterns of the three groups of males. Male cohabiters are significantly younger than men in the other two groups. Almost

39 percent of the heterosexual cohabiters are under age 30, compared to 18 percent of the same-sex partners and 13 percent of the married. Last, we look at the pattern of weeks worked in 1999. Almost three-quarters of the married men report working, on average, 51 or more weeks in 1999, compared to 69 percent for same-sex males and 66 percent for male cohabiters.

Same-sex partnered males are different in several ways from cohabiting male heterosexuals and married males, but in other ways they are similar. They have less socioeconomic status than married males, but more than male heterosexual cohabiters. Part of this difference could be due to age differences, given that the cohabiters are much younger on average than the men in the other two groups. With regard to race and ethnicity, their rates are closer to those of cohabiting men than to married men. And nearly 70 percent of the same-sex male partners report working 51 or more weeks in 1999, a percentage that is less than married men and more than that of cohabiting men.

We report in Table 1.3 a similar set of comparisons for females. Female same-sex partners report average earnings in 1999 of almost $35,000, compared to almost $27,000 for married women and over $23,000 for cohabiting heterosexual women. Unlike the case for partnered gays compared to married men (shown in Table 1.2), partnered lesbians report higher earnings than married women; Chapter 8 analyzes these earnings differences in more detail.

Same-sex female partners also have more occupational status than females in the two heterosexual groups. Moreover, a higher percentage of the partnered lesbians hold college degrees or higher compared to cohabiting females and married females. As was the case with the male comparisons, married women are more likely to be white and less likely to be Hispanic than either same-sex or opposite-sex cohabiting females.

With regard to the presence of children in the household, the females show the same trend as the males. That is, there is a considerably higher percentage of married women with children under age 18 in their households (62.4%), followed by female cohabiters (25.3%), and then by same-sex female partners (23%). Comparing male and female same-sex partners (Tables 1.2 and 1.3), almost one-quarter of the female same-sex households have children compared to just under 16 percent of the male same-sex households. These results have been shown in other studies (Bellafante 2004), namely, the higher representation of children in lesbian households and the substantial representation of children in gay male households.

Regarding the age composition of the three female groups, as was the case with males, female heterosexual cohabiters are younger than both same-sex female cohabiters and married females. Almost 45 percent of cohabiting women are under age 30 compared to just under 20 percent of same-sex female partners and just over 14 percent of married females.

Finally, with regard to the number of weeks worked in 1999, female same-sex partners report an average of 66 percent working 51 or more weeks in the year prior to the census, compared to 62 percent for married women and 60 percent for cohabiting heterosexual women. Among the male groups, the married have the highest percentage working 51 or weeks in 1999; among the female groups, the same-sex partners have the highest percentage.

Thus, female same-sex partners differ from heterosexual partners on a number of factors. They have more socioeconomic status than heterosexual female cohabiters and married women, and more of them worked 51 or more weeks in 1999. They are less likely to be white and more likely to be Hispanic. And they are nowhere as young as cohabiting women and roughly the same age as married women.

In this section we have compared and contrasted some characteristics of partnered gay men and lesbians with those of heterosexual cohabiters and married persons. We examined the overall prevalence of partnered same-sex persons in the U.S. population and their differential distributions compared to other couples in the metropolitan areas of the United States and in the major geographic

TABLE 1.3. Characteristics of Female Labor Force Participants by Same-Sex Unmarried Partners, Married Heterosexuals, and Cohabiting Heterosexuals, United States, 2000

Females	Same-Sex Partners	Cohabiting Heterosexuals	Married
Means			
Annual Income (1999)	$34,848	$23,351	$26,835
Occupational Status Score	29.1	26.0	27.0
Percent with College Degree	68.0	56.0	63.0
Percent White	78.9	76.0	81.8
Percent Hispanic	10.9	11.2	8.9
Percent with Children in Household	23.0	25.3	62.4
Age Groups (%)			
Under 30	19.5	44.6	14.3
30–49	63.2	46.7	59.5
50–69	16.6	8.6	25.0
70+	0.7	0.1	1.3
Weeks Worked in 1999 (%)			
20 or less	5.3	7.9	7.7
21–30	4.8	7.1	5.7
31–40	7.9	9.2	10.3
41–50	15.4	15.8	14.4
51+	66.6	60.1	62.0

areas. In Tables 1.2 and 1.3 we compared male and females according to whether they were same-sex partners, heterosexual cohabiters, or married. As a whole, the same-sex partners appear to be more different from married persons than from heterosexual cohabiters. Moreover, the patterns of differences among the males are not always the same as those among the females. The comparisons shown present a broad picture of the characteristics of the same-sex partnered population. Later chapters in this book examine many of these issues in greater detail and offer some explanations for their outcomes.

Conclusion

This chapter provided an introduction to the same-sex partnering data from the 2000 U.S. Census that will be used in most of the chapters of this book. We considered some of the background leading to the collection of unmarried partner data for the first time in the 1990 decennial census, and addressed important issues concerning the conceptualization of homosexuality and sexuality. A classification scheme of household data from the 2000 Census was next presented, which demonstrated the manner in which the unmarried same-sex partner household data were collected and categorized in the 2000 censuses.

In addition, we assessed the validity of these same-sex partner data and concluded that they are generally quite good in terms of overall quality. Although not perfect, they are not the result of measurement error. The bulk of the same-sex couples picked up in the census data are indeed same-sex unmarried partners. The last section of this chapter described some of the characteristics of partnered gay men and lesbians and compared them with married and cohabiting heterosexuals. We conclude that, on most characteristics, same-sex partners differ more from married heterosexuals than from heterosexual unmarried partners.

In the following chapters, we draw on the data just examined to examine the manner in which sexual orientation affects a variety of demographic outcomes, including spatial distribution, residential segregation, migration, family structure, and labor market outcomes.

Part I

Spatial Distribution, Residential Segregation, and Migration

CHAPTER 2

✿

Patterns of Same-Sex Partnering
in Metropolitan and Nonmetropolitan America

The 2000 U.S. Census counted almost 1.2 million same-sex unmarried partners in the country. Although these same-sex partners are located throughout the United States, the largest numbers (over 85 percent) reside in metropolitan areas. They are not, however, distributed equally among the metropolitan and nonmetropolitan areas (Simmons and O'Connell 2003). Rather, there is considerable variation in their rates of prevalence across these areas.

Quantitative assessments of the patterns of gay male and lesbian prevalence in U.S. metropolitan and nonmetropolitan areas are particularly relevant today given the active discussions in political, religious, and social arenas regarding homosexual marriage, the adoption of children by gay men and lesbians, and other issues involving sexual orientation. As Gates and Ost (2004: 3) have noted, these topics often lead to intense discussions, arguments, and debates, most of which are "marked by an astonishing lack of empirical data." It has been difficult if not impossible for policy makers, community activists, and gay male and lesbian leaders to appraise the effects that homosexual marriage laws, domestic partnership benefits, adoption rights, and other related issues would potentially have on the homosexual and heterosexual communities in the country because of the paucity of information about the locations of gay men and lesbians. Aside from everyone seeming to know that there are a lot of gay men in San Francisco, the amount of knowledge about the prevalence of gay men and lesbians elsewhere in the United States is miniscule.

The quantitative presentations in this chapter are intended to address this void. We develop for all of the metropolitan areas of the United States, and for most of the nonmetropolitan counties, two rates of homosexual partnering: one rate measures the prevalence of male same-sex partners in an area, and another measures the prevalence of female same-sex partners. We also propose and test several hypotheses to account for variability in the partnering rates.

41

Rates of the Gay and Lesbian
Partnering in Metropolitan Areas

To date, there has been one published analysis of prevalence rates of gay men and lesbians using data from the 2000 U.S. Census (Gates and Ost 2004), and three using data from the 1990 U.S. Census (Black et al. 2000, 2002; Walther and Poston 2004). The one analysis using 2000 census data (Gates and Ost 2004) constructed gay male and lesbian concentration indexes for the states, metropolitan areas, and counties of the U.S. The index is a "ratio of the proportion of same-sex couples living in an [area] to the proportion of households that are located in an [area]. . . . This ratio . . . measures the over- or underrepresentation of same-sex couples in a geographic area relative to the population" (Gates and Ost 2004: 24). This index is closely related mathematically to the one we develop in this chapter.

The partnered gay male and lesbian rates we construct are incidence rates; they specify the number of gay male or lesbian partners in an area per persons who comprise the demographic and statistical population from which gay men and lesbians are drawn. A rate is defined as the number of persons experiencing an event at a given time (the numerator) divided by the population at the risk of the event (the denominator). When calculating incidence/prevalence rates, the units comprising the numerator need to correspond with those in the denominator; that is, the denominator should include the units in the numerator. This is known as the principle of correspondence (Hinde 1998: 4).

The numerators for our rates use 100 percent data from Summary File 2, table PCT22 ("Unmarried Partner Households and Sex of Partners") of the 2000 U.S. Census (U.S. Bureau of the Census 2003). For the gay male rate we used household data in each area on "male householder and male partner," and for the lesbian rate we used household data on "female householder and female partner." We multiplied the number of male/male households by two to produce the number of gay male partners for the area, and we did the same for female/female households.

The denominators are the numbers of never married males (or females) in the population of age 18 or higher. The denominator is so restricted because according to the statistical and demographic definitions used here, as well as Census Bureau coding procedures, married persons are by definition heterosexual, and thus are not "at risk" (in a statistical sense) of being a gay male or lesbian partner. In other research we conducted in writing this book, we developed several same-sex partnering rates using both never married and married persons in the denominator, and found all of them highly correlated with those presented in this chapter. Indeed our research shows that it does not seem to matter whether same-sex partners or same-sex households are used as the numerator, or whether persons ever married, persons never married, all persons of age 18 and over, same-sex households, or all households are used as the denominator; the variances in the different rates are remarkably similar.

Our partnered gay male (lesbian) rate for an area is the following:

$$GAYMALE\ (LESBIAN)\ RATE =$$

$$\left(\frac{\#\ of\ GayMale\ (Lesbian)\ Partners}{\#\ of\ Never\ Married\ Males\ (Females)\ of\ age\ 18+} \right) \times 1,000$$

For partnered gay men residing in the 331 metropolitan areas of the United States, the rate has a mean value of 20.0 (Table 2.1), meaning that across the metropolitan areas of the U.S. in 2000, there is on average almost 20 gay male cohabiters for every 1,000 never married males of age 18 and older. San Francisco has the highest value with a score of almost 61. San Francisco contains the Castro Valley neighborhood, a well-known gay male enclave, rendering the high prevalence of gay males in this area unsurprising. Dubuque, Iowa has the lowest score, of about six gay male cohabiters per 1,000 never married males. Dubuque has strong links with the Catholic Church, including the presence of a number of monasteries and motherhouses and two Catholic universities (Wikipedia 2006a). This strong historical tie with Catholicism may be linked, in part, to the low presence of same-sex partners in the city owing to the Catholic Church's stance against homosexual conduct and gay marriage.

For partnered lesbians living in metropolitan areas, their prevalence rate has an average value of almost 27. Santa Rosa has the highest value, a score of over 72; for every 1,000 never married women of age 18 and over in Santa Rosa, there were almost 72 lesbian cohabiters. The Santa Rosa Metropolitan Statistical Area (MSA) is comprised of a single county, Sonoma County, bordering the Pacific Ocean and immediately north of Marin County, and the City and County of San Francisco. Its proximity to San Francisco, along with a somewhat more rural locale, perhaps contributes to its high prevalence score. The Provo-Orem, Utah MSA has the lowest score, at 9 per 1,000. Nearly 90 percent of Provo's population is Mormon (Hamby 2005). Further, Provo is home to Brigham Young University, a large private university that is operated by the Mormon Church. Mormons oppose marriages of gay males as well as of lesbians, and they proscribe homosexual behavior in general. Perhaps as a result, gay men and lesbians in Utah have been the subject of a great deal of litigation and restrictive legislation (Hamby 2005).

Across the metropolitan areas, the correlation between the gay male and lesbian rates is high and positive, r = .67. Thus, for the most part, the gay male rates tend to vary in the same way as the lesbian rates. Metropolitan areas with high rates of gay male partnering have high rates of lesbian partnering, and

TABLE 2.1. Means, Standard Deviations, and Minimum and Maximum Values: Gay Male and Lesbian Partnering Rates for Metropolitan Areas and Nonmetropolitan Counties of the United States, 2000

Rate	Mean	Standard Deviation	Minimum Value Area/County	Maximum Value Area/County
		Metropolitan Areas		
Gay Male Rate	20.0	6.9	6.3 Dubuque, IA	60.7 San Francisco, CA
Lesbian Rate	26.8	8.6	9.0 Provo–Orem, UT	72.2 Santa Rosa, CA
		Nonmetropolitan Counties		
Gay Male Rate	22.9	10.1	3.5 Riley County, KS	90.9 Lyon County, KY
Lesbian Rate	35.4	16.8	5.9 Brookings County, SD	173.3 Pushmataha County, OK

Gay Male (Lesbian) Rate is number of partnered gay males (lesbians) per 1,000 never married males (females) age 18+.

areas with low gay male rates have low lesbian rates. Figure 2.1 is a scatterplot comparing the values for the gay male and lesbian rates in the 331 metropolitan areas. Metropolitan areas above the line have higher gay male rates than lesbian rates, and those below the line have higher lesbian than gay male rates. San Francisco (the most extreme outlier above the line) is represented by the mark with the highest gay male index value (of 61) and Santa Rosa (the most extreme outlier below the line) is represented by the mark with the highest lesbian index value (of 72).

Over 92 percent of the metropolitan areas, 305 of the 331 areas, have higher lesbian rates than gay male rates. Four areas have gay male and lesbian scores that are the same. Only 29 of the metropolitan areas have higher gay male prevalence rates than lesbian rates. It would appear that partnered gay men have a few favorite destinations, including San Francisco; Atlanta; Los Angeles–Long Beach; Miami; Jersey City; Washington, DC; New York; and Fort Lauderdale, where their prevalence rates surpass those of lesbians. Partnered lesbians, on the other hand, are concentrated more so than gay males in metropolitan areas in general, tending not to prefer certain areas to the degree that they are preferred by gay men.

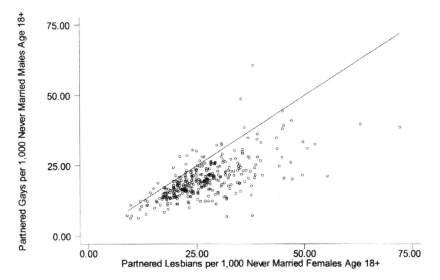

FIGURE 2.1. Scatterplot of Partnered Gay and Partnered Lesbian Rates: 331 U.S. Metropolitan Areas, 2000

We consider now the distributions of the partnered gay male and lesbian rates among the nonmetropolitan counties of the United States. We have data on 2,267 nonmetropolitan counties, comprising almost all of the nonmetropolitan counties in 2000. A few were dropped because of missing data, including many of the Alaska boroughs, Loving County, Texas, and Menominee County, Wisconsin. Of the remaining 2,267 counties, however, almost half have a small number of partnered gay male and lesbian inhabitants. We thus calculated gay male and lesbian rates for those nonmetropolitan counties with at least 20 partnered gay males (or 20 partnered lesbians). This constraint reduces the sample of nonmetropolitan counties to 1,226 for partnered gay males, and to 1,320 for partnered lesbians.

The gay male prevalence rate has a mean value among the nonmetropolitan counties of 22.9 (Table 2.1). Among the 1,226 nonmetropolitan counties of the United States with at least 20 partnered gay men in 2000, there were on average nearly 23 gay male cohabiters for every 1,000 never married males of age 18 and older. Lyon County, Kentucky, a small rural county, has the highest value on the gay index, a score of 90.9. The county with the next highest gay male prevalence rate is Monroe County, Florida, with a score of 77.4. This county is located on the southernmost tip of Florida, immediately west of Miami and includes the Florida Keys. Its county seat is Key West, long known as one of the most liberal and gay-friendly small nonmetropolitan cities in the United States (Wikipedia 2006b).

The lesbian prevalence index has a mean value among the 1,320 nonmetropolitan counties of 35.4. Pushmataha County, Oklahoma has the highest value, 173; for every 1,000 never married women of age 18 and over in this county, there are 173 lesbian cohabiters, which is almost one in five. Notably, however, there are only 48 lesbian partners residing in this county. Another of the 20 nonmetropolitan counties with the highest lesbian prevalence rates is Franklin County, Massachusetts, with an index value of 89. This is a large urban nonmetropolitan county in northwestern Massachusetts, north of Springfield, west of Worcester, and east of Pittsfield. It is located within 25 miles north and northeast, respectively, of two of the "Seven Sisters" women's colleges, namely, Smith in Northampton, and Mount Holyoke in South Hadley.

Figure 2.2 is a scatterplot of the partnered gay male and lesbian index values for those 1,105 nonmetropolitan counties with a minimum of both 20 partnered gay males and 20 partnered lesbians. Nonmetropolitan counties above the line have higher gay male rates than lesbian rates, and counties below the line have higher lesbian than gay male rates. Of the 1,105 counties shown in the scatterplot, the majority, almost 90 percent, have larger lesbian prevalence rates than gay rates. Also, the distribution in Figure 2.2 indicates that nonmetropolitan counties with high rates of gay male partnering have high rates of lesbian partnering, and vice versa. The correlation coefficient between the two indexes is .65.

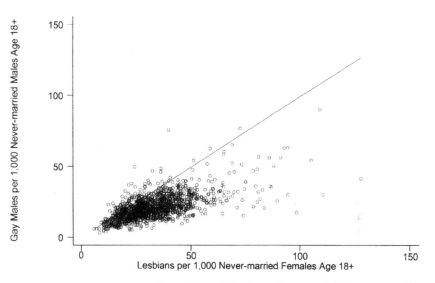

FIGURE 2.2. Scatterplot of Gay Male and Lesbian Rates: 1,105 Nonmetropolitan Counties of the U.S., 2000

Ecological Correlates of Homosexual Partnering

We turn now to the issue of accounting for variation in the rates of gay male and lesbian partnering. Among the metropolitan areas, why does San Francisco have the highest gay male rate and Santa Rosa the highest lesbian rate? Why do Dubuque, Iowa and Provo-Orem, Utah have the lowest gay male and lesbian rates? Among the nonmetropolitan counties, why does a county such as Monroe County, Florida have such a high gay male prevalence rate, and why does Franklin County, Massachusetts have such a high lesbian prevalence rate? What kinds of social, ecological, and political considerations might be influencing the variation in prevalence rates across these areas? In this section we propose and test several hypotheses in an attempt to address these questions. We use an ecological orientation for the theoretical justification of the hypotheses.

Our investigation of the reasons for the variability in rates of gay male and lesbian partnering assumes that the prevalence of gay men and lesbians in the metropolitan areas and the nonmetropolitan counties is to a significant degree the result of migration (see Black et al. 2002, for a similar kind of interpretation, one based on economics and the amenities of the area). San Francisco's and Santa Rosa's high prevalence of gay male and lesbian partnering among the metropolitan areas, and Monroe County's and Franklin County's high gay male and lesbian rates among the nonmetropolitan counties, are not due to large numbers of gay men and lesbians being born in San Francisco and in Santa Rosa, and in Monroe County and in Franklin County, but to large numbers moving to these destinations. To assist in hypothesis development, we consider sociological human ecology and its specific focus on migration.

From the perspective of human ecology, migration is the major mechanism of social change and adaptability for human populations. Knowledge of migration patterns tells us about how "populations . . . maintain themselves in particular areas" (Hawley 1950: 149). The ecological approach asserts that human populations redistribute themselves via net migration in order to attain equilibrium between their overall size and the life chances available to them (Poston and Frisbie 1998, 2005).

The theoretical foundation of human ecology is based on the interdependence of the four conceptual rubrics of population, organization, environment, and technology. The interrelationships among and between these dimensions inform our understanding of migration patterns. All populations adapt to their environments, and these adaptations vary among populations according to their social and sustenance organization, their technology, and the size, composition, and distribution of their population. The environment is comprised of both social and physical factors, and sets constraints on the population and the form and characteristics of its organization. The technology at the population's disposal sets the boundaries for the form and type of environmental adaptation the population assumes. Human ecology posits that, of the three demographic processes, migration is the most efficient agent for returning the human ecosystem to a state of equilibrium or balance between its size and organization (Poston and Frisbie 1998).

Hypotheses typically investigated in ecological studies of migration (e.g., Sly 1972; Frisbie and Poston 1978; London 1986; Saenz and Colberg 1988; Poston and Frisbie 1998; among many others) state that the variability among human groups in their patterns of migration is a function of differences in their patterns of sustenance organization, technology, environment and population. Metropolitan areas such as San Francisco and Santa Rosa are hypothesized to have high rates of gay male and lesbian partnering because of ecological factors that attract gay male and lesbian migrants, as well as ecological considerations that attract migrants in general, not only homosexual migrants. The same applies to nonmetropolitan counties such as Monroe County, Florida and Franklin County, Massachusetts.

With regard to hypothesis development, we first propose and test several ecological hypotheses to account for variability in rates of gay male and lesbian partnering among the metropolitan areas, and then do the same for the nonmetropolitan counties. Ecological structure and the dynamics of migration are decidedly different in the metropolitan areas compared to the nonmetropolitan counties.

Metropolitan Areas

One ecological factor that should tend to pull migrants in general to a metropolitan area is its level of sustenance-producing activities. Areas with low levels of unemployment should have higher net migration rates than areas with high unemployment. It makes sense to hypothesize that gay men and lesbians, as well as heterosexuals, will be attracted to areas with an abundance of jobs, and thus, low levels of unemployment (Poston and Mao 1996). We have data on rates of civilian unemployment in 1996 for each metropolitan area (U.S. Bureau of the Census 1998). We hypothesize that the greater the levels of unemployment, the lower the concentration of gay male and lesbian partners.

Two other ecological factors that should be related to the metropolitan area's net migration of both heterosexuals and homosexuals are its poverty rate and its infant mortality rate. Both reflect the general quality of life of the area. For each metropolitan area we have data on the infant mortality rate in 1994 and the percentage of persons below the poverty level in 1993 (U.S. Bureau of the Census 1998). We hypothesize that the greater the levels of infant mortality and poverty of the area, the lower the concentration of partnered gay men and lesbians.

In sociological human ecology, the environment is defined as "whatever is external to and potentially or actually influential on the phenomenon under investigation" (Hawley 1968: 330). According to this definition, the environment includes not only the biotic or physical characteristics of an area, such as climate, but also the nonphysical "influences that emanate from other organized populations in the same and in other areas" (Hawley 1981: 9).

A characteristic of the physical environment, namely, climate, is a factor that is hypothesized to draw or repel migrants, irrespective of their sexual orientation. Empirical research in the social sciences using climate as an independent variable often includes temperature as a key consideration of climate (Karp and Kelly 1971; Graves 1980; Poston and Mao 1996, 1998). We obtained January and July temperature data for each metropolitan area based on average daily temperature data for these two months from 1951 to 1970, and calculated a temperature index by dividing the average July temperature into the average January temperature. Under the assumption that persons prefer to avoid exposure to bitter and cold winters and to excessively hot and humid summers, the higher the value of this index, the more favorable the climate. This is because the index value is lowered if it is cold in the winter or hot in summer (Karp and Kelly 1971: 25).

There are also environmental factors of metropolitan areas that may be hypothesized to specifically draw gay men and lesbians, and not necessarily heterosexuals. For instance, Black and colleagues (2003) note the importance of the metropolitan area's social attitudes, and political and religious orientation as factors that should be related to the prevalence of gay men and lesbians. O'Reilly and Webster (1998) observe that the social and political characteristics of communities should be associated with levels of gay male and lesbian concentration.

Accordingly, we hypothesize that the more Republican the voting patterns in the area, and the more conservative the religious attitudes, as measured by the prevalence of Southern Baptists, the lower the concentrations of partnered gay men and lesbians.

Why should the prevalence of Republicans and Southern Baptists be negatively associated with the prevalence of gay men and lesbians? The Republican Party has long been identified, rightly or wrongly, as having an anti-gay orientation. Although there is a vocal homosexual group in the Republican Party, namely, the Log Cabin Republicans, its influence on the party is thought to be minimal (O'Reilly and Webster 1998: 501; Green et al. 1995; Guth 1995). Also, the Southern Baptist conference continually passes resolutions that consider homosexuality as an "abomination in the eyes of God" (Steinfels 1988: 6). Consequently, we have gathered data for each metropolitan area on the percentage of votes cast in the 1996 presidential election for the Republican candidate, Robert Dole. We have also obtained data for each area on the number of Southern Baptist members per 1,000 persons in the population.

There is very little literature about the relationship between the presence of sodomy laws and antigay/lesbian discrimination laws and the concentrations of gay men and lesbians. Gates and Ost (2004: 3) note that states with a large relative presence of gay men and lesbians tend to have more favorable laws pertaining to homosexuals. Such laws may be considered as another example of an ecological feature of the nonphysical environment that is hypothesized to be associated with the migration of gay men and lesbians. As of 2000, numerous states had sodomy laws that applied only to homosexual individuals, and other states had sodomy laws that applied to both homosexual and heterosexual individuals. Of the 331 metropolitan areas in 2000, 21 percent were in states with sodomy laws against both homosexual and heterosexual individuals, and 13 percent in states with sodomy laws only against gay men and lesbians. Alternately, in 2000, 23 percent of the metropolitan areas were in states that prohibited discrimination based on sexual orientation in both the public and private sectors, and 40 percent were in states prohibiting such discrimination only in the public sector.

We have constructed two dummy variables to measure the presence of sodomy laws: Sodomy-1 is scored 1 if the metropolitan area is in a state that has a sodomy law directed against both homosexual and heterosexual individuals, and 0 if not. Sodomy-2 is scored 1 if the metropolitan area is in a state that has a sodomy law directed only against gay men and lesbians, and 0 if not. We expect that both of the sodomy variables should be negatively related to the levels of concentration of gay male and lesbian partners, that is, the levels of gay male and lesbian concentration should be lower in metropolitan areas in states with sodomy laws. But owing to the pervasiveness of the first sodomy measure, we expect that the effect of Sodomy-1 will be stronger than the effect of Sodomy-2.

We have also constructed two dummy variables measuring the presence in the state of laws prohibiting discrimination in employment based on sexual orientation. Anti-disc-1 is scored 1 if the metropolitan area is in a state with laws prohibiting discrimination in the private and public sectors, and 0 if not. Anti-disc-2 is scored 1 if the metropolitan area is in a state with laws prohibiting discrimination only in the public sector, and 0 if not.

The size of the metropolitan area's total population should also be associated in a positive way with the levels of gay male and lesbian concentration. There is good reason to expect higher levels of gay male and lesbian concentration in metropolitan areas with larger populations (Abrahamson 2002). These expectations are based in part on the notion that the larger the size of the general population, the greater the likelihood for some of these people to be gay men and lesbians. Because a few metropolitan areas are outliers owing to their extremely large populations, we have taken the natural log of the metropolitan area's population size in 2000.

Finally, there is reason to expect that levels of gay male and lesbian concentration should be associated with levels of heterosexual cohabitation. If the social and political climate of an area is conducive to heterosexual cohabitation, the same should be the case for homosexual cohabitation (Black et al. 2002). Thus, areas with high rates of unmarried heterosexuals who are cohabiting should have high rates of homosexual cohabitation, and vice versa. We have taken unmarried partner data and have calculated for each metropolitan area the number of unmarried heterosexual cohabiting households per 1,000 total households.

Table 2.2 presents the results of two ordinary least squares multiple regression equations modeling the prevalence of gay men and lesbians among the 331 metropolitan areas. The dependent variable is the number of partnered gay males (lesbians) per 1,000 never married males (females) of age 18 and over; the above mentioned 12 ecological variables are the independent variables.[1] We have placed positive or negative signs to the right of the variable name indicating the direction of the variable's hypothesized relationship with the gay male/lesbian rate.

Of the 12 regression coefficients in the OLS equation predicting levels of gay male concentration, six are signed in the hypothesized direction. But of the correctly signed coefficients, only five are statistically significant. First, we find that the more agreeable the physical temperature of the area, the higher the concentration of gay male partners. As the poverty rate or the percentage voting Republican increases in the metropolitan area, the concentration of male same-sex partners decreases. And the larger the area's population, and the higher the level of heterosexual cohabitation, we find a corresponding increase in the concentration of gay males in the area. None of the four independent variables dealing with sodomy laws and antidiscrimination laws pertaining to sexual orientation are significantly associated in the hypothesized positive or negative directions with the level of gay male concentration.

TABLE 2.2. Metric and Standardized Regression Coefficients from Multiple Regression Equations of Gay Male and Lesbian Partnering Rates on 12 Ecological Independent Variables, 331 Metropolitan Areas of the United States, 2000

Independent Variable	Gay Rate		Lesbian Rate	
	Metric	Standardized	Metric	Standardized
Unemployment Rate (−)	.386*	.153	.901*	.288
Poverty Rate (−)	−.415*	−.296	−.771*	−.444
Infant Mortality Rate (−)	−.180	−.060	−.651*	−.176
Temperature Index (+)	22.136*	.449	28.906*	.474
Percent Voting for Dole, 1996 (−)	−.108*	−.142	−.089*	−.093
Southern Baptists per 1,000 Population (−)	.012*	.187	.027*	.341
Sodomy (Homo and Hetero) (−)	1.475	.087	.879	.042
Sodomy (Homo) (−)	1.123	.054	2.926*	.114
Antidiscrimination (public & private) (+)	−.379	−.023	−2.081*	−.102
Antidiscrimination (public) (+)	−.423	−.030	.698	.040
Log of Population Size of Met Area (+)	1.905*	.287	.165	.020
Heterosexual Cohabitation Rate (+)	.109*	.146	.340*	.367
Constant	−6.953		13.285	
R² (adj.)	.417		.395	

*Coefficient statistically significant at P < .05 (one tailed).

The most influential of the independent variables is the temperature index. For every one standard deviation increase in the temperature index, there is almost a one-half standard deviation increase in the gay concentration rate, holding constant the effects of the other independent variables. In order, the next most influential independent variables are the poverty rate, the log of population size, the heterosexual cohabitation rate, and the percent voting Republican. The ecological variables account for over 41 percent of the variation in the gay male partnering rate.

The results of the OLS regression equation modeling the prevalence of lesbians among the metropolitan areas are similar to those modeling the prevalence of gay men. There are three main differences. First, the infant mortality rate is significant in the lesbian equation, whereas it was not so in the equation for gay men. Second, the presence of laws prohibiting discrimination in the public and private sectors on the basis of sexual orientation is significant in the lesbian equation, although not in the expected direction. Last, the log of population size in the lesbian equation is not significant in the lesbian equation, but is significant in the equation for partnered gay men.

The most influential independent variable in the lesbian equation, as in the gay equation, is the temperature index, indicating the importance of this climate variable. The poverty rate and the heterosexual cohabitation rate are the next most influential variables in predicting high concentrations of partnered lesbians. The ecological variables account for almost 40 percent of the variation among the metropolitan areas in the lesbian prevalence rate, an adjusted R^2 value only slightly less than that in the gay male equation.

In both the partnered gay male and partnered lesbian equations, it appears that of the significant independent variables, the most important ones are amenity-based effects that apply to the population in general, and not only to gay men and lesbians. This is similar to the conclusion reached by Black and his associates (2002) in their study of San Francisco and other areas with large relative numbers of gay men. The next most influential independent variables, however, are effects that operate primarily for gay males and lesbians, such as the percent voting Republican and the heterosexual cohabitation rate. We now turn attention to the nonmetropolitan counties and examine the degree to which ecological characteristics are associated with levels of gay male and lesbian prevalence.

Nonmetropolitan Counties

For the nonmetropolitan counties we first consider three ecological factors of sustenance organization and hypothesize their effects on migration: whether the county is dependent on farming, whether the county is dependent on mining, and whether the county is a retirement county. We assume that migrants to nonmetropolitan counties, including homosexual migrants, will be more likely to seek out farming- and mining-based counties, as well as retirement counties. It is thought that nonmetropolitan migrants are likely seeking quiet and isolated spaces. We expect positive associations between whether the nonmetropolitan counties are farming-dependent, mining-dependent, and retirement-based, and their levels of partnered homosexual prevalence.

With these hypotheses in mind, we used data from the 1989 ERS County Typology Codes (ERS/USDA 1995) to create three dummy variables for each county. The farming-dependent dummy variable is scored 1 if farming in the county "contributed a weighted annual average of 20 percent or more labor and proprietor income over the three years from 1987 to 1989" (ERS/USDA 1995: 4). The mining-dependent dummy variable is scored 1 if mining in the county "contributed a weighted annual average of 15 percent or more labor and proprietor income over the three years from 1987 to 1989." The retirement dummy variable is scored 1 if the county's "population aged 60 years and over in 1990 increased by 15 percent or more from 1980–90 through in-migration" (ERS/USDA1995: 4–5).

In addition to these categories of sustenance organization, we also include a measure of whether the counties are rural or urban. Nonmetropolitan, as well as metropolitan, counties have both urban and rural components. If one nonmetropolitan county has relatively fewer persons living in urban places than another, it will be less urban. Because we expect individuals living in nonmetropolitan areas to be seeking more isolated living environments, we would anticipate that among the nonmetropolitan counties, rural counties, rather than urban counties, should be more attractive locations for migrants, including homosexual migrants. The rural dummy variable is coded 1 if the county is rural. We hypothesize that there should be a positive relationship between whether the nonmetropolitan counties are rural and their levels of homosexual prevalence.

Moving next to a specifically socioeconomic aspect of the county's sustenance organization, we hypothesize that the levels of educational attainment of the nonmetropolitan counties should be positively associated with levels of gay male/lesbian prevalence. Migrants to nonmetropolitan counties, particularly homosexual migrants, will tend to be attracted to areas with relatively educated populations. This owes in part to the generally higher levels of education of gay men and lesbians compared to the general population (Blumstein and Schwartz 1983; Laumann et al. 1994; Klawitter and Flatt 1997). Therefore, the percentage of the population in the county of age 25 and over with college education in 1990 should be positively associated with the county's level of gay male/lesbian prevalence.

We noted earlier the distinction in sociological human ecology between physical and nonphysical features of the environment. An environmental factor of nonmetropolitan areas hypothesized to specifically draw or repel gay men and lesbians, but not necessarily heterosexuals, is political orientation. We have gathered data for each nonmetropolitan county on the percentage of votes cast in the 1996 presidential election for the Republican candidate. We hypothesize that the more Republican the voting pattern of the county, the lower the concentration of gay men and lesbians.

Another characteristic of the nonmetropolitan county expected to be associated with the prevalence of gay men and lesbians is whether the county is adjacent to a metropolitan area. Although previous hypotheses expect gay men and lesbians in nonmetropolitan counties to be particularly drawn to rural and farming/mining- and retirement-based counties, we expect that if the county is adjacent to a metropolitan area, the adjacency will be another draw for homosexual migrants owing to the metropolitan area's associated social and cultural amenities. The adjacency dummy variable is coded 1 if the county is adjacent to a metropolitan area, and zero if not. We anticipate a positive association between whether the county is adjacent to a metropolitan county and its prevalence of gay/lesbian partners.

We turn now to multiple regression analyses of the gay male and lesbian partnering indexes. We use the above seven ecological characteristics of the nonmetropolitan counties as independent variables.[2] And we restrict the sample of nonmetropolitan counties to those with at least 20 partnered gay males for the gay male equation, and at least 20 partnered lesbians for the lesbian equation.

Table 2.3 reports the results of two ordinary least squares regressions, one with the gay male rates and another with the lesbian rates. For the gay male equation, five are signed as hypothesized, and four of them are statistically significant. These are the farm-dependent, retirement, rural, and Republican coefficients. If a nonmetropolitan county is a retirement county, on average it will have 7.6 more partnered gay men per 1,000 unmarried males than counties that are not retirement counties, controlling for the other independent variables. If it is a farm-dependent county, it will have on average 3.2 more partnered gays than counties that are not farming dependent. If it is a rural county, it will have 7.8 more partnered gays than nonrural counties.

We may appraise the relative effects of the independent variables in the gay male equation by examining their standardized regression coefficients (shown in Table 2.3 in parentheses below the metric coefficients). Although there is a problem in the interpretation of the meaning of standardized coefficients when the independent variable is a dummy variable (cf. Long, 1997), the standardized values nevertheless indicate the relative effects of the ecological variables on the gay male prevalence rate. The rural variable has the greatest relative effect on the prevalence of gay male partnering, followed by the retirement variable.

The multiple regression results for the lesbian equation are similar to those for the gay male equation. As was the case with the gay male equation, in the lesbian equation the farming, retirement, and rural variables are all positive and significant, and the Republican variable is negative and significant.

The most influential ecological variable in the lesbian equation is the rural variable followed by the retirement variable and the farm-dependent variable; these were also the three most important predictors in the gay male equation. The mining variable is the next most influential, followed by the Republican variable. Among the nonmetropolitan counties, for every one standard deviation increase in the percentage of residents voting Republican, there is a .07 standard deviation decrease in the lesbian partnering rate.

The multiple regression equations reported in Table 2.3 were estimated for those 1,221 nonmetropolitan counties with at least 20 partnered gay men (the gay male equation), and for those 1,313 nonmetropolitan counties with at least 20 partnered lesbians (the lesbian equation). In other research we conducted when

TABLE 2.3. Metric and Standardized Regression Coefficients from Multiple Regression Equations of Gay Male and Lesbian Partnering Rates on Eight Ecological Correlates: Nonmetropolitan Counties of the United States, 2000

Ecological Correlate	Gay Rate	Lesbian Rate
Farm-dependent (+)	3.201*	6.086*
	(.081)	(.092)
Mining-dependent (+)	1.516	5.448*
	(.034)	(.073)
Retirement (+)	7.578*	12.995*
	(.176)	(.248)
Rural (+)	7.794*	11.987*
	(.265)	(.252)
Percent w/ College Education (+)	−3.756*	−4.010*
	(−.203)	(−.130)
Percent Voting for Dole (−)	−0.047*	−0.108*
	(−.047)	(−.065)
Adjacent to Metropolitan Area (+)	−1.152*	0.187
	(−.057)	(.006)
Constant	27.837*	40.570*
R^2 (adjusted)	.203	.179
Number of nonmetropolitan counties	1,221	1,313

*Coefficient statistically significant at $P < .05$, one-tail.

Standardized coefficients reported in parentheses.

writing this chapter, we also estimated the same regression equations for counties with at least nine partnered gay males (or lesbians), with at least 29 partnered gay males (or lesbians), and with at least 39 partnered gay males (or lesbians). The results are remarkably similar to those reported in Table 2.3. We turn now to a discussion of the above analyses for the metropolitan areas and nonmetropolitan counties.

Discussion and Conclusion

In this chapter we used census data to develop rates of the relative presence of partnered gay males and partnered lesbians residing in the metropolitan areas and nonmetropolitan counties of the United States in 2000. These are likely the best metropolitan area and nonmetropolitan county estimates available on gay male and lesbian prevalence. The prevalence index we developed, moreover, was itself robust. Other research we have conducted in writing this chapter has shown that it does not seem to matter whether persons or households are used as the numerator, or whether ever married, never married, or all persons of age 18 and over, or same-sex households or all households, are used as the denominator. The rates developed and used in this chapter are highly correlated with rates using alternative numerators and denominators.

We first described the settlement patterns of gay male and lesbian partners. Among the metropolitan areas in 2000, gay male partners in San Francisco have the highest level of concentration, and lesbian partners in Santa Rosa have the highest concentration. The highest gay male and lesbian rates in the nonmetropolitan counties are in Lyon County, Florida, and in Pushmataha County, Oklahoma. There are high correlations between the gay male rates and the lesbian rates, which indicate that gay male and lesbian couples tend to settle in similar metropolitan and nonmetropolitan areas, although not necessarily at the same levels.

Indeed we showed that in over 92 percent of the metropolitan areas, and in almost 90 percent of the nonmetropolitan counties, the levels of lesbian prevalence are higher than the levels of gay prevalence. Among the metropolitan areas, we reported that partnered gay men tend to favor a few MSAs, namely, San Francisco; Atlanta; Los Angeles–Long Beach; Miami; Jersey City; Washington, DC; New York; and Fort Lauderdale, where their prevalence rates surpass those of lesbians. Partnered lesbians, on the other hand, tend to have concentrations that are greater than those of gay men in most of the metropolitan areas, tending not to prefer certain areas to the degree they are preferred by gay men.

Second, we asked about the kinds of ecological characteristics that might be argued to influence and be related to the geographical locations of gay male and lesbian partners. Drawing on sociological human ecology and a more limited literature on gay male and lesbian settlement patterns, we identified characteristics of metropolitan areas argued to be related to levels of gay male and lesbian concentration. Among the metropolitan areas, the variables that were most influential in predicting levels of gay male and lesbian concentration were a physical temperature index, the poverty rate, and the heterosexual cohabitation rate. Variables focusing on characteristics of the metropolitan areas that are of relevance mainly to gay men and lesbians, such as those dealing with sodomy and antidiscrimination laws, as well as the presence of political and religious conservatism, were either not statistically important predictors or exhibited only minimal influence.

One can see the influence of some of these variables in the metropolitan areas that exhibit the highest prevalence of same-sex partners. For instance, the San Francisco Bay Area, including Sonoma County, has one of the most temperate climates in the nation. Consequently, the relationship between the temperature variable and the high concentrations of gay men and lesbians in these climates can be easily gleaned. Although legislation did not have the anticipated effects on the prevalence of same-sex partners, this could be attributable in part to the lack of awareness of such policies and/or the enforcement of the laws; this applies to both sodomy and antidiscrimination laws, both of which are rarely enforced.

Among the nonmetropolitan counties, the variables that we find to be most influential are whether the counties were retirement counties and whether they were rural; also significant was whether they were farming-dependent. These findings indicate that gay men and lesbians are more highly concentrated in nonmetropolitan communities that are more isolated and quiet, rather than closer to cities. The nonmetropolitan counties with the highest concentrations of gay males and lesbians support these findings, as both Lyon County, Kentucky and Pushmataha County, Oklahoma are rural counties.

This chapter is a quantitative examination of the prevalence of partnered gay men and lesbians in the metropolitan areas and nonmetropolitan counties of the United States in 2000. The next three chapters of this book continue to examine how and why same-sex unmarried partners vary in residential patterns across the nation. Chapter 3 is a quantitative examination of the patterns of residential segregation of gay men and lesbians from heterosexuals. Chapter 4 is a primarily qualitative assessment of the location and characteristics of gay male and lesbian enclaves in the greater San Francisco Bay Area. And Chapter 5 focuses specifically on migration and seeks to determine quantitatively the degree to which sexual orientation affects an individual's migration decision. Together these four chapters extend considerably the largely qualitative analyses of gay men and lesbians that have been so prominent in the social science literature and that were reviewed earlier in this book.

CHAPTER 3

♔

The Residential Segregation of Gay Males and Lesbians from Heterosexuals

Residential segregation has long been a central area of research in sociology. One of the first sociological analyses of residential segregation was Park's (1925, 1926) study of the relationship between physical distance and social distance, later replicated by Duncan and Duncan (1955). Much of this research has focused on the residential segregation of racial and ethnic minorities from the majority race/ethnic group in the United States, as well as segregation between minority racial and ethnic groups (see Lieberson 1963; Farley 1977; Massey 1979; Massey and Denton 1987, 1988, 1989, 1993; Farley and Frey 1994; Alba et al. 1999; Alba and Nee 2003; among many other studies).[1] Fewer analyses have been conducted on the spatial segregation of nonracial/ethnic minorities from the majority.

Indeed there are no systematic analyses of which we are aware that examine the extent to which homosexual individuals are residentially segregated from heterosexuals. There are several studies of "gay spaces" and enclaves (Weightman 1981; Castells and Murphy 1982; Lauria and Knopp 1985; Knopp 1990; Valentine 1993; Gates and Ost 2004), but most of these are either case studies of single cities (e.g., San Francisco [Murray 1992]) or analyses of gay enclaves and political forces and activism. There are no systematic quantitative empirical studies of cities in the United States (or elsewhere) of the degree to which homosexuals are residentially segregated from heterosexuals. This chapter addresses this void, using the same-sex partnering data from the 2000 Census for the 40 U.S. cities with the largest populations of gay men and lesbians (see the cities listed in appendix table 3.1).

Background and Hypotheses

Racial, ethnic, and other minority populations are residentially segregated from the majority population for a host of reasons, some voluntary and others

59

involuntary. Many social scientists believe that the primary reason for spatial segregation between racial minority populations and the majority population is economic. Frisbie and Kasarda (1988: 640) suggest that segregation is attributable to "the inequalities that constitute the overall system of stratification. . . . Greater affluence allows some persons to acquire housing in more desirable areas, leaving other locales for the less wealthy." The residential segregation of minorities from the majority is lessened when minorities become economically and culturally assimilated with the majority (Massey 1985; Massey and Denton 1987). This spatial assimilation argument thus views the segregation of minorities from the majority as largely involuntary.

In contrast, others theorize that residential segregation tends to be more voluntary than involuntary. Some ethnic neighborhoods are maintained despite the economic and cultural assimilation of their members. Alba and his associates (1997), for instance, show the persistence of certain white ethnic neighborhoods, particularly Italian, in the Greater New York region in the 1980s, despite the assimilation of these ethnic groups into the white majority (see also Alba and Nee 2003: Chapter 3).

Any existing residential segregation of gay men and lesbians from heterosexuals, we hold, could be both involuntary and voluntary. Mondimore (1996) notes that, with the possible exception of prisoners, gay men and lesbians are considered by many to be so different from "normal" people that they must be avoided. Acknowledging that "homosexuality is much less stigmatized than it was only a few years ago," Mondimore (1996: 171) nevertheless cautions that "much stigmatization remains." Indeed until the U.S. Supreme Court ruling in 2003 overturned the sodomy law in Texas (*Lawrence et al. v. Texas* 2003), consensual sexual activity of homosexual persons was defined by statutes in 18 states as criminal (see also Knopp 1990). Also, many religions condemn homosexuality, and others condemn homosexual behavior. Thus, "homosexuality continues to be viewed as undesirable by many in our society" (Mondimore 1996: 171), suggesting that heterosexuals might be expected to avoid contact with gay men and lesbians, especially living in the same neighborhoods with them.

Studies of racial and ethnic segregation indicate that the majority group will avoid spatial contact with minorities they perceive as undesirable, and will take action to prevent them from moving into the majority group neighborhood (Fong and Shibuya 2000). Much of the racial segregation literature documents that blacks have been unable to move into choice neighborhoods because of discomfort expressed by whites (Fong and Shibuya 2000; Farley and Frey 1994; Krysan 2002). These findings, therefore, tend to support the notion that any existing residential segregation between homosexual and heterosexual individuals is attributable to gay men and lesbians involuntarily living apart from heterosexuals.

On the other hand, the stigma of homosexuality may lead to the voluntary segregation of gay men and lesbians from heterosexuals. Mondimore

(1996: 172–173) observes that as gay men and lesbians "become more comfortable with their homosexuality, they move into a stage where they do not merely tolerate their homosexual identity but begin to accept this view of themselves as a valid, meaningful, and fulfilling self-identity. . . . Where once the only homosexual 'culture' was that of the gay bar, now entire communities of gay and lesbian people . . . can be found in larger cities." Murray (1992: 112) argues that "contemporary gay and lesbian urban North American enclaves differ from those of ethnic immigrant [enclaves] in several ways." Whereas immigrants tend to be relatively impoverished and speak a language other than English, homosexuals are relatively well integrated socioeconomic ally, with a native command of English. As a result, gay men and lesbians who live in gay neighborhoods might choose voluntarily to live alongside other homosexual individuals, rather than, as is the case with new immigrants, "being restricted to [living alongside] those who speak the same minority language" (Murray 1992: 112).

Whether involuntary or voluntary, there is a basis for expecting gay men and lesbians to be residentially segregated from heterosexuals. But, as already noted, to date there have been no systematic quantitative investigations of the degree to which they are segregated from heterosexuals. One reason for this neglect is the lack of available data on the residential distributions of homosexual and heterosexual men and women. There have been a "few sizable surveys completed on the homosexual population, but many have been convenience samples" (Black et al. 2000: 139). As noted earlier in this book, until the conduct of the 1990 Census, the use of spatial data for the analysis of the homosexual community was only possible through indirect means.

How might cities be expected to vary in their levels of segregation of homosexual from heterosexual individuals? The racial and ethnic residential segregation literature suggests that the size of the minority group should be associated with the level of segregation. The larger the minority group, the greater its level of segregation from the majority. This owes in part to the role of assimilation, which, as noted above, should tend to reduce levels of segregation. In this context, assimilation refers to "the process whereby distinct populations merge into one social structure and become indistinguishable" (Fossett and Cready 1998: 174). Ecologists argue that assimilation is more likely to occur for smaller populations who will accept inferior economic roles and have fewer cultural and physiological differences compared to the dominant group (Fossett and Cready 1998). This suggests that cities with larger numbers of gay men and lesbians will have higher levels of homosexual-heterosexual segregation than cities with smaller numbers.

There are other ecological factors that help to explain why segregation levels would be expected to vary from city to city. Some factors assist in explaining residential choice for all persons, such as a city's level of sustenance-producing activities and overall general quality of life, whereas other factors, like a city's social, political, and religious attitudes, apply specifically to gay men and lesbians. We hypothesize that cities with higher rates of poverty and crime will have higher levels of segregation in general, as compared to cities with lower rates of poverty and crime. This is partially attributable to the fact that poorer cities and those with high rates of crime may not be as accepting of minorities, be they racial or sexual. Thus the majority populations will not want to intermingle and coreside with gay men or lesbians, resulting in higher levels of segregation.

An argument for less segregation could also be made with regard to crime. In a city with a higher crime rate, the overall population may view gay men and lesbians as less threatening or dangerous than other groups who may be more stereotypically associated with crime. Nevertheless, we believe that there will be greater segregation with higher poverty and crime rates, especially if enclaves are the outcome of involuntary segregation.

We have also included a number of factors that might specifically explain residential choices for gay men and lesbians. First, we hypothesize that there will be greater segregation in cities with a political climate that is more conservative than progressive. Cities with large proportions of Republican voters should be more likely to have an antihomosexual climate, leading to more segregation between heterosexual and homosexual individuals, than cities with a small proportion. We noted earlier that there is evidence that, rightly or wrongly, the Republican Party is associated with an antihomosexual orientation and anti-homosexual policies (O'Reilly and Webster 1998). Also, cities located in states with sodomy laws should be characterized by a more conservative climate than cities in states without such laws, resulting in greater amounts of segregation based on sexual orientation. Thus, we hypothesize that greater segregation should occur in more Republican areas and in those with sodomy laws.

In this chapter, we examine both the degree of segregation of gay men from heterosexuals and the segregation of lesbians from heterosexuals. Should we expect one of these homosexual groups to be more segregated from heterosexuals than the other? There is reason to expect that lesbians should be less segregated from heterosexuals than gay men. Lesbian households are more likely than gay male households to contain children (Bellafante 2004; see also Chapter 6). Thus, lesbian families are expected to place more of a premium on such amenities as schools, safe streets and neighborhoods, and low-density environments than are gay male families. Lesbian families should desire many of the same residential amenities as heterosexual families with children, and would hence be more inclined than gay male families to seek housing in heterosexual neighborhoods. There is also an economic aspect to consider. On average, lesbian households report lower earnings than gay male households (Smith and Gates 2001; Klawitter and Flatt 1998), which may give lesbians less of a choice regarding places to live. Lesbians may not be able to afford trendy, gay male enclaves. We thus expect that the levels of segregation of lesbians from heterosexuals will be lower than the corresponding levels of segregation of gay men from heterosexuals. We turn next to a discussion of the data.

Data and Methods

In this chapter we develop one residential segregation index for gay male households and one for lesbian households. Our indexes are based on census tract data on same-sex unmarried partners from Summary File 2 (Table PCT 22) from the 2000 U.S. Census tabulations. To obtain the number of partnered gay males in each census tract of the 40 cities in our study (see the cities in Appendix Table 3.1), we multiplied by two the number of male-male households in the census tract; we followed the same strategy to obtain the number of partnered lesbians. We have thus obtained data on the number of same-sex male and female partners in each of the census tracts in each of the 40 most highly populated homosexual cities in the United States.

Appendix Table 3.1 lists the forty cities with the largest numbers of partnered gay males and lesbians in the United States in 2000. They are ranked according to the number of partnered gay males. New York has the largest number of partnered gay males, over 30,000, which comprises more than 17 percent of all the partnered gay males in the 40 cities. New York also has the largest number of partnered lesbians of all 40 cities, almost 22,000 lesbians, comprising over 17 percent of all partnered lesbians in the 40 cities. Similar kinds of data have been obtained for the married and unmarried heterosexual populations in the census tracts of each of the 40 cities.

We opted to focus on these 40 cities because they contain over 25 percent of all same-sex unmarried partners enumerated in the 2000 U.S. census, with a total of 173,681 gay male partners and 124,188 lesbian partners. As shown in Appendix Table 3.1, the first 20 cities make up approximately 78 percent of our sample and 19 percent of all same-sex unmarried partners in the nation, while the next 20 cities make up 24 percent of our sample and only 6 percent of all same-sex unmarried partners in the nation. Thus, a majority of the sample is located in the first 20 cities. In addition, it should be noted that more male same-sex unmarried partnered couples are represented than female same-sex unmarried partnered couples, with 29 percent of all male same-sex unmarried partners in the nation represented in the 40 cities and 21 percent of all female same-sex unmarried partners. This is consistent with the findings from Chapter 2 of this book where we showed that male same-sex partners tend to favor a few selected cities, which are mostly included among our 40 cities, whereas female same-sex partners are more likely to favor metropolitan areas in general. As a result, it makes sense that men are slightly overrepresented in our sample. It should also be noted that these cities are located throughout the United States, allowing for what we believe to be a good representation of American cities, geographic and otherwise.

The Measurement of Residential Segregation

There are many ways to conceptualize and measure residential segregation (Massey and Denton 1988). In this chapter we use one measure, namely, the exposure index, which gauges the extent to which one group is exposed to another group. Massey and Denton (1988) observe that although the exposure index is usually correlated with other segregation indexes, it is conceptually distinct from them. To illustrate if one compares the isolation index with another popular segregation index, namely, the dissimilarity index, the two are related but are "conceptually distinct because the former depends on the relative size of the groups being compared, while the latter does not. Minority members can be evenly distributed among residential areas of a city, but at the same time experience little exposure to majority members if they are a relatively large proportion of the city" (Massey and Denton 1988: 287), and vice versa.

The exposure index (E) measures the degree to which gay males or lesbians are exposed to the other members of their residential areas. The index for a city is the following:

$$E = (\sum_{i}^{n} (HOM_i / HOM) \ (HET_i / TOT_i)$$

where HOM_i and HET_i are the numbers of homosexuals and heterosexuals living in the ith census tract of a city, TOT_i is the total number of persons living in the ith census tract, and HOM is the total numbers of homosexuals in the city. We calculate four exposure indexes for gay male partners, and four for lesbian partners. The four indexes for the gay male partners represent their degree of exposure, respectively, to married heterosexual cohabiters, to unmarried heterosexual cohabiters, to all heterosexual cohabiters (both married and unmarried), and to lesbian partners. Four analogous E indexes are calculated for lesbians, except that the eighth index represents the degree of exposure of lesbian partners to gay male partners. When we calculate the E index of gay males to lesbians, we treat the gay males as the "HOM" group and the lesbians as the "HET" group. Similarly, when we develop the E index for lesbians to gay males, we classify the lesbian as the "HOM" group and the gay males as the "HET" group.

The E index varies between 0 and 1. To illustrate, in the case of the four gay male indexes, each may be interpreted as the likelihood that a randomly drawn gay man shares a residential area with a heterosexual (the first index), with a married heterosexual (the second index), with an unmarried heterosexual (the third index), or with a lesbian (the fourth index). The higher the value of the E index, the greater the exposure of the gay male group to the other group, and thus the lower the degree of residential segregation of the gay male group from the other group. The last three gay male indexes listed above, plus another gay male index that measures their exposure to other gay males (which we do not report in this chapter), sum to 1.0. Because the E indexes depend on the relative population size of the groups being compared, they are asymmetric; thus the E index comparing gay males with lesbians need not be the same as the E index comparing lesbians with gay males. As Massey and Denton (1988: 288–89) note, "only when two groups comprise the same proportion of the population will the indexes equal one another."

Results

Exposure indexes are calculated for each of the 40 cities for the following eight different kinds of segregation: (1) the degree to which gay male partners are exposed to all heterosexual partners, (2) the degree to which lesbian partners are exposed to all heterosexual partners, (3) the degree to which gay male partners are exposed to married heterosexual partners, (4) the degree to which gay male partners are exposed to unmarried heterosexual partners, (5) the degree to which gay male partners are exposed to lesbian partners, (6) the degree to which lesbian partners are exposed to married heterosexual partners, (7) the degree to which lesbian partners are exposed to unmarried heterosexual partners, and (8) the degree to which lesbian partners are exposed to gay male partners.

Appendix Table 3.2 shows the values of the eight exposure indexes for each of the 40 cities in the year 2000. Table 3.1 presents descriptive information for the eight indexes. The index values in Appendix Table 3.2 and the descriptive data in Table 3.1 show clearly that there are varying degrees of exposure of same-sex unmarried partners to heterosexual partners across cities.

Table 3.1 reports that on average across the 40 cities, there is a .95 probability, or 95 percent chance, that a randomly drawn gay male will share a residential area with a heterosexual. Gay males have the lowest probability of sharing an area with heterosexuals in San Francisco, with an exposure index of .82, and the highest probability in Orange, with an exposure index of .99. This means that in San Francisco there is an 82 percent chance that a gay male will share an area with a heterosexual and a 99 percent chance in Orange. Other cities with lower probabilities of interaction between gay male households and heterosexual households are New York (.87), Atlanta and Dallas (.88), and Boston (.90). Once again, the higher the value of the exposure index, the less the segregation. Therefore, in the above examples, gay males are more segregated in San Francisco than in Orange.

Looking next at the interaction between lesbian households and heterosexual households, the average probability that a randomly drawn lesbian shares an area with a heterosexual across all 40 cities is .96 (Table 3.1). Among the 40 cities, the index values range from a low of .86 in San Francisco to a high of .99 in Orange. Other cities with lower probabilities of interaction, that is, higher levels of segregation, between lesbian households and heterosexual households are New York (.88), Atlanta (.91), Dallas (.93), and Boston (.94).

TABLE 3.1. Means, Standard Deviations, and Minimum and Maximum Scores: Exposure Indexes of Homosexual-Heterosexual Segregation, in 40 U.S. Cities, 2000

Variable	Mean	Std. Dev.	Minimum	Maximum
Gays to All Heterosexuals	0.948	0.036	0.821 (San Francisco)	0.989 (Orange)
Lesbians to All Heterosexuals	0.961	0.026	0.867 (San Francisco)	0.989 (Orange)
Gays to Married Heterosexuals	0.797	0.055	0.677 (San Francisco)	0.918 (Orange)
Gays to Unmarried Heterosexuals	0.151	0.033	0.071 (San Jose)	0.206 (Detroit)
Gays to Lesbians	0.014	0.007	0.005 (Orange)	0.035 (San Francisco)
Lesbians to Married Heterosexuals	0.816	0.046	0.722 (San Francisco)	0.92 (Orange)
Lesbians to Unmarried Heterosexuals	0.145	0.033	0.069 (Orange)	0.211 (Detroit)
Lesbians to Gays	0.023	0.022	0.005 (Orange)	0.111 (New York)

We hypothesized that gay males should have less interaction with heterosexuals than should lesbians. Our results support this expectation. As can be seen in table 3.1, across all 40 cities, gay males have lower mean exposure scores for comparisons to all heterosexuals and to married heterosexuals; gay males, however, have a higher mean exposure score than lesbians for the comparison with unmarried partners. In only five of the 40 cities are lesbians less exposed to married partners than are gay males (Detroit, Newark, Oakland, Las Vegas, and Riverside). However in 30 of the 40 cities, lesbians are less exposed to unmarried partners than are gay men. The 10 cities where lesbians are more exposed to unmarried partners than gay men are Atlanta; Washington, DC; Detroit; Ft. Lauderdale; Las Vegas; Miami; Newark; Oakland; Orlando; and Tampa.

These findings are due in part to the small size of the homosexual (gay male or lesbian) population. Recall that the exposure index, unlike some other segregation indexes, for example, the dissimilarity index, is influenced by the size of the minority group. If the group is small compared to the majority, it will have a greater likelihood of being exposed to the majority. If it is large, there will be less interaction with the majority.

In addition, we provide evidence that gay male partners and lesbian partners do not necessarily share the same residential spaces with one another. We find that the average probability that a randomly drawn gay male household shares an area with a lesbian household across all forty cities is .01 (Table 3.1). Among the 40 cities, the index scores range from a low in Orange of .01 to a high in San Francisco of almost .04. In looking at the interaction between lesbian households and gay male households, we find that, on average, there is a .02 probability that a randomly drawn lesbian household shares an area with a gay male household across all 40 cities.

Ecological Correlates of Homosexual Residential Segregation

We now examine various factors hypothesized to be associated with segregation based on sexual orientation. First, we explore the effects of population size variables. The racial and ethnic segregation literature suggests that the larger the size of the minority group, the greater its level of segregation from the majority. We have five measures of the size of the homosexual population in each of the 40 cities: two are relative numbers, namely, the number of partnered gay males in the city per 1,000 unmarried males, and the number of partnered lesbians in the city per 1,000 unmarried females; and three are absolute numbers, namely, the absolute number of partnered gay males, partnered lesbians, and total partnered homosexuals in the city. We also include the total population size of the city as a sixth measure of size. Zero-order correlations between each of the six size variables and the two exposure indexes measuring homosexual-heterosexual segregation are shown in Table 3.2.

We hypothesized that the size of the homosexual community should be positively associated with the amount of segregation of homosexual individuals from heterosexual individuals and thus negatively associated with the indexes. All of the statistically significant coefficients shown in Table 3.2 between the measures of size and residential segregation are negative as expected; this indicates that as the population of gay men or lesbians increases, the likelihood of being exposed to heterosexuals decreases. The absolute and relative numbers of gay men are more

TABLE 3.2. Zero-Order Correlations Between Exposure Indexes and Explanatory Variables in 40 Cities of the U.S., 2000

	E Indexes	
	Gays to All Hets	Lesbians to All Hets
Gay Prevalence Rate	−0.658*	−0.642*
Lesbian Prevalence Rate	−0.189	−0.244
Number of Gay Males	−0.580*	−0.641*
Number of Lesbians	−0.419*	−0.516*
Number of Homosexual Persons	−0.520*	−0.596*
City Population Size	−0.306*	−0.393*
Crime Rate	−0.07	−0.025
Poverty Rate	0.011	0.062
Presence of Sodomy Law	0.121	0.152
Percent Voting Republican	0.399	0.498

*indicates a significance level of .05, one-tailed test.

associated with levels of segregation than are the absolute and relative numbers of lesbians. Both the gay male prevalence rate and the absolute number of gay men are significantly correlated with all four of the segregation indexes. In contrast, the lesbian prevalence rate is not significantly associated with any of the four segregation indexes. However, the absolute number of lesbians in the city is significantly correlated with all of the segregation scores, except the total number of homosexual individuals in the city and city population size.

These findings might indicate that gay males are perceived as more different from heterosexuals than are lesbians, and perhaps appear to be more of a threat to the heterosexual community, resulting in greater levels of segregation. This would be a reasonable interpretation if homosexual-heterosexual segregation is involuntary. On the other hand, if the segregation tends to be more voluntary than involuntary, gay males more so than lesbians might choose to be segregated from heterosexuals. This may occur largely for economic and family considerations.

We next consider four more explanatory variables in order to better understand the variation in homosexual to heterosexual residential segregation across the 40 cities. These are the city's crime rate, defined as the number of serious crimes known to police per 100,000 in 1995; the city's poverty rate, defined as the percent of persons below the poverty level in 1993; whether or not the city is in a state that has sodomy laws against homosexuals; and a measure of political conservatism defined as the percent of the voting age population who voted for Robert Dole in the 1996 presidential election. The crime rate and poverty rate were chosen because, as mentioned in Chapter 2, they represent the negative side of an overall general quality of life that would be unattractive to all persons, not just to homosexuals.

In contrast, the sodomy law variable and the Republican variable reflect social attitudes and political characteristics that may reflect the political and religious climate of the city. Cities without sodomy laws and with lower percentages voting Republican should be more open to gay men and lesbians, and thus, should have lower levels of segregation, and vice versa. All of the statistically significant coefficients shown in Table 3.2 are appropriately signed. However, these variables not related to size, namely, the crime rate, poverty, sodomy law, and Republican variables, are statistically insignificant.

We next estimated two ordinary least squares multiple regression equations to model the variation in homosexual-heterosexual segregation among the 40 U.S. cities in 2000. The dependent variables for the equations are (1) the gay male to all heterosexuals exposure index, and (2) the lesbian to all heterosexuals exposure index. The five independent variables are the gay male prevalence rate,[2] the city crime rate, the city poverty rate, the sodomy law variable, and the Republican variable.[3] Table 3.3 shows the multiple regression equation results. We have entered positive or negative signs after the name of the independent variable to indicate the direction of the variable's hypothesized relationship with the two gay/lesbian indexes.[4]

The results of the regression analyses show that the most influential predictor of variation in homosexual-heterosexual segregation for cities is the relative size of the gay male population in the city. This supports the racial and ethnic segregation literature suggesting that the size of the minority population will affect the degree of segregation between the majority and minority group.

The ecological variables not related to population size, such as crime and poverty rate, do not seem to account much for the variation in segregation levels across cities. These are variables drawn from the literature on race and ethnic segregation. This is very interesting in that it suggests that homosexual-heterosexual residential segregation in U.S. cities may be a somewhat different phenomenon from racial and ethnic residential segregation. Sociologists and demographers, therefore, will need to develop a different theoretical framework for understanding homosexual-heterosexual residential segregation, rather than relying on the race and ethnic models.

In addition, we found no statistically significant effect for the variables that we included to capture segregation effects unique to sexual orientation. Neither

TABLE 3.3. Metric and Standardized Regression Coefficients from Multiple Regression Equations of Homosexual-Heterosexual Segregation on Five Ecological Variables in 40 U.S. Cities, 2000

| | Exposure Indexes | | | |
| | Gays to All Hets | | Lesbians to All Hets | |
Independent Variables	Metric	Std	Metric	Std
Gay Prevalence Rate	−0.003*	−0.669	−0.002*	−0.6256
Crime Rate	0.000	0.194	0.000	0.192
Poverty Rate	−0.001	−0.169	−0.001	−0.115
Presence of Sodomy Law	−0.007	−0.067	−0.006	−0.081
Percent Voting Republican	0.002	0.264	0.001	0.375
Constant	0.978		0.960	
R-squared (adj.)	0.444		0.495	

*indicates a significance level of .05, one-tailed test.

the percent voting Republican nor the presence of a law prohibiting sodomy resulted in a significant increase in the segregation between heterosexual and homosexual individuals. These particular measures of a conservative environment, therefore, did not support our hypotheses that gay men and lesbians would be less segregated from heterosexuals in a more liberal climate.

Conclusion

The analyses undertaken in this chapter have only begun to address issues of concern pertaining to the residential segregation of homosexual individuals from heterosexuals. While we have accomplished what we set out to do, namely, to measure levels of residential segregation based on sexual orientation, a great deal remains to be done. We have only begun to lay the foundation for discovering possible causes of the variation in the residential segregation of gay men and lesbians from heterosexuals. For one thing, we need to develop and test more ecologically based hypotheses.

What are some of the other city characteristics that may be influencing segregation? Are there differences in income between gay men and lesbians that would explain their differential spatial segregation from heterosexuals? Is the political, economic, and physical climate of the city associated with the levels of segregation? Other research has indicated that more politically conservative areas tend to have a greater prevalence of same-sex partners than less conservative areas (see chapter 2; Walther and Poston 2004). If these findings may be extended to segregation, one would expect that politically and religiously conservative cities would have higher levels of segregation than would less conservative cities. The preliminary work shown here, however, does not support this expectation.

We also need to address more thoroughly the issue of whether segregation between homosexual and heterosexual individuals is more voluntary than involuntary. Do gay male and lesbian couples tend to seek to live near others like themselves, or are they being avoided and shunned by heterosexuals? The sociological and demographic analysis of homosexual residential segregation is new, and there is a great deal of work that remains to be done.

CHAPTER 4

⚜

Gay Male and Lesbian Enclaves in the San Francisco Bay Area

In earlier chapters of this book, we used 2000 Census data to provide quantifiable evidence of a fact already well-known and observed: Gay men and lesbians are not evenly distributed throughout the country. Rather, there are several areas in the United States with a particularly high prevalence of gay men and lesbians. One of the most notable is the San Francisco Bay Area, and its several "enclaves," such as the Castro Valley District. Although many of the so-called enclaves, like the Castro, have been identified and examined extensively, the motivation for gay men and lesbians to reside in these areas remains a debated issue. Some assert that gay men and lesbians are drawn to enclaves because of uniquely "homosexual" factors, such as the presence of other gay men and lesbians, or an open-minded political climate (see, i.e., Collins 2004; Sibalis 2004; Murray 1996; Weightman 1986). Others argue that gay men and lesbians tend to base their residential choices on the same kinds of amenities as heterosexuals, such as nice weather, beautiful nature, or the availability of a strong arts community; gay men and lesbians are, arguably, clustered in particular areas due to their enhanced ability to afford living in these high-amenity areas (Black et al. 2002).

In this chapter, we build on the findings of the first two chapters of this book by engaging in a more in-depth analysis of *why* gay men and lesbians select particular residential locations. We explore this issue through a quantitative and qualitative examination of four gay male and lesbian enclaves[1] in the Greater San Francisco Bay Area. We consider the Castro and Mission Districts of San Francisco, along with Oakland, and parts of Sonoma County, and attempt to accomplish two primary tasks. First, we use 2000 Census data to highlight, both graphically and descriptively, enclaves with the highest prevalence rates of same-sex unmarried partners in the nation. In particular, we show the locations of these enclaves, as well as the variation in them that exists due to differences in race, gender, age, and class. Second, we engage in field research and gather interview data to address questions concerning why gay men and lesbians live in high-prevalence areas. Are gay men and lesbians drawn to these enclaves due to factors based on sexual orientation, or are their residential choices grounded in factors common to all, regardless of orientation?

Introduction to the Enclaves

In this section, we provide a brief description of each of the enclaves explored in the Greater San Francisco Bay Area. Figures 4.1–4.4 are maps of each county according to either its gay male or lesbian prevalence rate to show the location of the enclaves and the specific census tracts on which we have focused. These four enclaves were chosen primarily because of their high prevalence rates of same-sex unmarried partners and/or their reputations as gay male or lesbian enclaves. They were also selected to show that gay men and lesbians do not necessarily live in the same areas, that "gay spaces" or enclaves are not only found in metropolitan areas, and that race can play a factor in choice of enclave. Overall, we find that there is more than one type of gay male and lesbian enclave.

San Francisco: The Castro and the Mission Enclaves

We chose to study the Castro Valley and Mission Districts of San Francisco because they are "the largest and the institutionally and commercially most complete gay and lesbian enclaves" in the nation according to much of the qualitative literature (Abrahamson 1995: 103; see also Murray 1992). Likewise, these enclaves are well known in the gay and lesbian communities for having either a heavy concentration of gay men, in the case of the Castro, or lesbians, in the case of the Mission. Further, according to 2000 Census data on same-sex unmarried partners, San Francisco has the largest prevalence of gay men and lesbians of any major metropolitan area in the United States (Chapter 2; see also Gates and Ost 2004). In addition, the City and County of San Francisco ranks first among all U.S. cities and counties for the highest prevalence of gay males, and among the top five for lesbians (Gates and Ost 2004).

On closer examination of the census data for San Francisco County, we found that the three census tracts with the highest gay male prevalence rates are all in the Castro Valley District (see Figure 4.1). Likewise, two of the three census tracts with the highest lesbian prevalence rates are in the Mission District (see Figure 4.2). Thus, the reputation of these communities as gay male and lesbian, coupled with the high census data prevalence rates, make the Castro Valley and Mission Districts essential enclaves to include in this study.

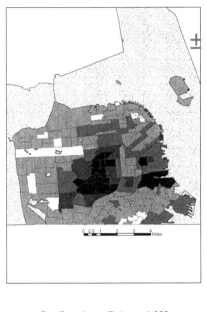

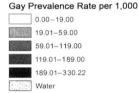

Gay Prevalence Rate per 1,000

	0.00–19.00
	19.01–59.00
	59.01–119.00
	119.01–189.00
	189.01–330.22
	Water

FIGURE 4.1. San Francisco County by Gay Prevalence Rate

Oakland

East of San Francisco, on the other side of the San Francisco Bay, lies Oakland (in Alameda County), a city less well known for having gay male and lesbian enclaves. In fact, there is an absence of literature on gay and lesbian enclaves in Oakland. However, according to data from the 2000 Census, Oakland is ranked second only to San Francisco as the city with the largest prevalence rate of gay men and lesbians in the United States (Gates and Ost 2004). Our primary reason for selecting this city, however, is that it boasts the highest prevalence rate of female same-sex unmarried partners in the nation, according to some prevalence measures. Indeed, the census tract with the highest prevalence rate of female unmarried partners in Oakland is nearly two and a half times higher than the census tract in San Francisco with the highest lesbian prevalence rate. Although this information may be unexpected to some, many of our subjects asserted that it is well known in the Oakland lesbian community. In fact, one respondent in Oakland observed that the city's status as the "number one" lesbian community is repeatedly emphasized at local events.

In addition to public announcements concerning the prevalence of lesbians in the city, there has been a movement by a member of the Oakland City Council to establish a gay male and lesbian district in the city, to the consternation of some of our subjects, and the appreciation of others.[2] Perhaps contributing to this movement to create a defined gay male and lesbian space is the lack of stringent boundaries and the low visibility of the Oakland community, compared to the other enclaves explored (Zamora 2004; Figures 4.1–4.4). This distinguishing characteristic of the Oakland community, coupled with its large working-class and minority presence, provides an interesting contrast to the other three enclaves included in our study.

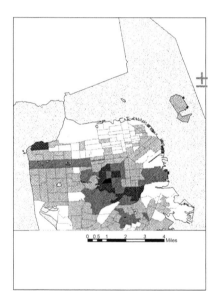

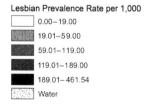

Lesbian Prevalence Rate per 1,000

FIGURE 4.2. San Francisco County by Lesbian Prevalence Rate

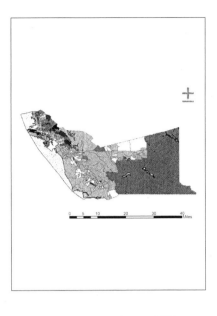

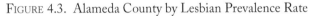

Lesbian Prevalence Rate per 1,000

- 0.00–19.00
- 19.01–59.00
- 59.01–119.00
- 119.01–189.00
- 189.01–461.54
- Water

FIGURE 4.3. Alameda County by Lesbian Prevalence Rate

Sonoma County

The fourth area we explored is Sonoma County, California. Much like Oakland, Sonoma County is not generally identified by most Americans as a gay male or lesbian area. Originally, recreational sites in Sonoma County, particularly those on and nearby the Russian River, were weekend and seasonal attractions for individuals from the San Francisco Bay Area. In fact, Guerneville, a small town in Sonoma County on the Russian River, became in the 1970s a gay male and lesbian resort community with bars, restaurants, bookstores, and a gay and lesbian business association (Sorrells 1999). Prior to that time, Guerneville and most of the other small towns on the Russian River were weekend and resort locations for the Bay Area's heterosexual population. Although Guerneville's surrounding areas still draw on weekend and resort visitors, more and more people are deciding to stay and live in the county year round (Sorrells 1999).

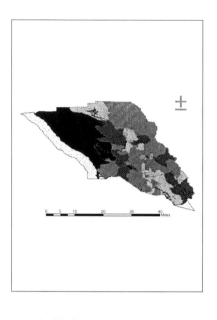

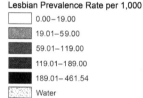

Lesbian Prevalence Rate per 1,000

	0.00–19.00
	19.01–59.00
	59.01–119.00
	119.01–189.00
	189.01–461.54
	Water

FIGURE 4.4. Sonoma County by Lesbian Prevalence Rate

With regard to the gay male and lesbian population, the 2000 census data show that the Santa Rosa Metropolitan Statistical Area (MSA), which is coterminous with Sonoma County, has the highest gay male and lesbian prevalence rates in the United States among MSAs with populations between 200,000 and 500,000 (Gates and Ost 2004). It also is the MSA with the highest prevalence of female same-sex couples of all MSAs in the United States (Chapter 2; Gates and Ost 2004; Poston et al. 2003).[3] In addition to containing the MSA with the highest prevalence of female same-sex couples, we selected Sonoma County due to our desire to examine a more rural area that could be compared with the decidedly more metropolitan lesbian enclaves of the Mission District and Oakland.

Quantitative Analysis of Enclaves

Methods

For the quantitative analysis, we have drawn on the same-sex partnering data of the 2000 Census described in earlier chapters of this book. For the three counties in which our enclaves exist, we obtained the number of two-person households in which (1) both persons were age 18 and over, (2) the second person in the household self-identified as the "unmarried partner" of the householder, and (3) both householder and partner are the same sex. These data comprise our sample of same-sex unmarried partners (gay male and lesbian) for the census tracts within our counties.

We used the same gay male (lesbian) prevalence rate employed in Chapter 2, which we found in related research to be based on the statistically best population from which partnered lesbians and gays are drawn. This prevalence rate is defined as:

$$GAY(LESBIAN)\ RATE =$$

$$\left(\frac{\#\ of\ Gay\ (Lesbian)\ Partners}{\#\ of\ Never\text{-}Married\ Males\ (Females)\ of\ age\ 18+} \right) \times 1,000$$

With this index, descriptive maps of San Francisco County, Alameda County, and Sonoma County were generated shape files downloaded directly from the Census Bureau Web site (see Figures 4.1–4.4). The maps illustrate the prevalence of gay male (or lesbian) unmarried partners in each census tract in each county. For example, among all metropolitan areas in the United States, the average gay male prevalence rate is 20/1,000, and the average lesbian prevalence rate is almost 27/1,000 (see Chapter 2). This means that among all metropolitan areas of the United States in 2000, there was an average of 20 gay male partners for every 1,000 never-married males of age 18 and older, and an average of just under 27 lesbian partners for every 1,000 never married females of age 18 and older.

Results and Discussion

In this section, as well as in our earlier introduction to the enclaves, we draw on the census data to calculate the prevalence rates of same-sex unmarried partners in the three counties, and to graphically illustrate this prevalence using GIS mapping software (Figures 4.1–4.4). We then use the same-sex unmarried partner data to present general descriptive characteristics of the census tracts with the highest prevalence rates of gay male (or lesbian) unmarried partners in the three counties.

Figures 4.1–4.4 show graphically the prevalence of gay men or lesbian partners in the census tracts in our three counties. Census tracts colored black on the maps illustrate a very high prevalence rate of 189/1,000 and above. Thus, tracts colored black are, at the very least, nine and one-half times larger than the national metropolitan average for gay male unmarried partners (i.e., 20), and about seven times larger than the national metropolitan average for lesbian unmarried partners (i.e., 27).

As can be seen in Table 4.1, our three counties overall have prevalence rates of same-sex unmarried partners that are above the national metropolitan average, as would be expected for most counties in the state with the largest population of same-sex unmarried partners (Gates and Ost 2004). San Francisco County has the largest overall gay male prevalence rate of 72.3. Further, its top three gay male tracts, all located in the Castro District, are more than 14–17 times above the national MSA gay male prevalence rate, and 4 times the county average. Likewise, the three top lesbian tracts in San Francisco County are about 6 to 7 times above the national MSA lesbian prevalence rate and 4 times the county average. In Alameda County, the top three lesbian census tracts range from 7 to 17 times higher than the national MSA prevalence rate for female same-sex unmarried partners and 4 to 9 times higher than the average for the county. Sonoma County has the highest overall lesbian prevalence rate of 79/1,000, and its top three lesbian tracts are about 3 times higher than the county average.

Further examination of the descriptive data from the 2000 census demonstrates some interesting differences among the enclave areas that should be highlighted, although they may not all be entirely unexpected (Table 4.1). For example, the Castro area is predominantly white, and men in the selected census tracts earn significantly more money on average than women in the Castro or Mission Districts. The median income for men in the Castro is the highest median income of all enclaves examined. With regard to the Mission District, it should be pointed out that although it is predominantly white, there is a large population of Hispanics and, in some areas, Asians. Overall, the Mission District appears to be the most racially diverse of the four areas we examined. However, the census tracts in Oakland contain a more significant presence of African-Americans, although there is less of an Asian presence compared to the Mission. Further, in one high-prevalence census tract in Oakland, over half of the population is Hispanic. There also appears to be less mixing of gay men and lesbians in Oakland, as compared to San Francisco and Sonoma County. For example, the tract in Oakland with the highest rate of lesbian prevalence has no gay male unmarried partners residing in it. Furthermore, Oakland has the youngest population of our enclaves, whereas Sonoma County has the oldest. Last, women in Sonoma County have a lower median income compared to the women in the San Francisco and Oakland enclaves.

TABLE 4.1. Characteristics of Top Gay and Lesbian Tracts in Four Enclaves

Tract #	Gay Rate	Lesb Rate	Race[b]					Avg. Age	Median Income[c]
			% White	% Black	% Asian	% Hispanic	% Other		
San Francisco County	72.3	41.4							Men
Top Gay Tracts									
170	330.2	142.6	89.3	a	5.0	5.4	0.3	41.4	69,375
205	311.0	107.0	87.4	a	5.1	5.7	1.8	39.5	57,578
206	293.6	149.9	84.8	2.1	5.8	8.0	a	37.6	60,160
									Women
Top Lesbian Tracts									
212	251.1	191.9	87.4	a	5.8	6.4	0.4	38.2	49,474
252	157.1	188.6	65.3	3.7	9.8	28.5	a	36.4	36,625
254.02	105.7	167.4	44.3	7.4	28.1	28.9	a	36.9	32,195
Alameda County	34.6	52.1							Women
Top Lesbian Tracts									
4,274	0.0	461.5	72.9	11.6	a	12.2	3.3	23.4	33,571
4,047	158.9	269.2	79.1	10.8	7.0	0.0	3.1	43.7	59,773
4,019	52.6	210.5	24.7	23.9	a	52.4	a	29.3	38,875
Sonoma County	40.2	79							Women
Top Lesbian Tracts									
1,534.04	29.9	251.3	90.4	a	a	4.5	5.1	42.4	39,920
1,543.01	140.0	244.1	86.4	a	a	11.2	2.4	48.4	29,911
1,537.04	189.9	235.6	89.5	a	a	10.2	0.3	41.0	29,539

[a]Signifies that there were less than 100 people in this category and thus not presented in the tables on www.census.gov.

[b]This percentage is based on persons giving a single race response for the categories of "White," "Black," "Asian," or "Other"; the Hispanic category, however, includes persons of any race who responded as "Hispanic."

[c]This value reflects the median earnings for (fe)male full-time, year-round workers.

TABLE 4.2. Summary Characteristics of Respondents

	Average Age	Percent White	Percent Partnered
Sonoma	52	100%	100%
Oakland	25	0%	60%
Mission	40	100%	100%
Castro	40	100%	25%

The data on the characteristics of the subjects we interviewed are fairly in line with those reflected by the census data (see Table 4.2). Although the average age of our respondents in Sonoma County is above the average age of those in the highest prevalence census tracts, our Sonoma County respondents are nonetheless the oldest of our respondents, as the census data indicate they should be.

Qualitative Examination of Enclaves

Methods

Through ethnographic field research and in-depth interviews, we continued to explore the characteristics of these enclaves and the individuals who reside within them. In this work, we paid particular attention to the articulated reasons for moving to, and staying in, the chosen enclave. We made two trips, four months apart, to the Greater San Francisco Bay Area to collect our data for the field research and to conduct the majority of our interviews. During each trip, we made detailed observations of the enclave areas, including noting what types of businesses and institutions were in operation and whether a gay and lesbian population was especially apparent. In addition, we visited numerous lesbian and gay outreach centers and organizations, and took a historical tour of the Castro district.[4]

In addition to field research, we conducted in-depth interviews with 20[5] gay men and lesbians who were either currently residing in our main areas of focus or were residents there during the 2000 U.S. Census. Specifically, we interviewed eight individuals from the Castro and Mission Districts, five from Oakland, and seven from Sonoma County. Given the nature of the study, a random sample of the population would have been an onerous undertaking. In most areas (other than, perhaps, the Castro District) it would be difficult to obtain a random sample of gay men, lesbians, or both given that this is a relatively small subpopulation—even in the specific enclaves. Consequently, we relied primarily on a snowball sampling method to obtain our sample, given that this method is best-suited for situations in which the population under study has unique characteristics and is difficult to locate in order to conduct a random sample (Babbie 2006; Kalton 1983). We located our primary informants principally through acquaintances or during our field research, by informing some individuals of our study and distributing business cards and consent forms with relevant descriptions of the project. These individuals, in turn, sometimes provided contact information for other individuals who were interested in participating in the study.

Descriptive statistics about our respondents are contained in Table 4.2. On average, respondents in Oakland were younger and more racially diverse; respondents in the Mission and Castro were white and slightly older; and respondents in Sonoma County were all white and significantly older. All of the respondents in Sonoma County and the Mission were in self-identified "partnered" relationships, whereas 60 percent of those in Oakland, and only 25 percent of those in the Castro were currently partnered.

Interviews took place via three means: in person, over the phone, and through e-mail. We attempted to make the interview process as convenient as possible for the participants, and allowed them to elect the means by which the interview would occur.[6] Regardless of the format, the interviews covered the same topics. After acquiring general background information, we began with an open-ended question that allowed the subjects to describe their primary reasons for moving to or staying in the particular enclave area. We then moved on to more focused questions that probed the subjects to consider whether specific issues played any role in their decision to move to/remain in the area, including: moving with or moving to family, friends, or partners; environmental and cultural attractions; political climate of the enclave; political climate of the place of origin; the presence of gay men and/or lesbians (attractions of dating partners, culture); acceptance from the heterosexual community; gay and lesbian businesses; and employment and/or gay-friendly employment policies.

We then explored a number of general questions relating to the enclave, including perceptions of the enclave as a large gay or lesbian community, evidence of presence of gay men and/or lesbians, and so forth. We also asked the subject questions related to his or her desire to remain located in the enclave, as well as areas that might hold more or less attraction as a residential choice. Finally, we examined issues related to the same-sex unmarried partner category on the U.S. Census, including: determining whether the subjects were partnered in 2000; if they used the unmarried partner response; if they received promotional materials about this new category from advocacy groups; and whether they would be hypothetically willing to answer a question that asked directly about sexual orientation on the census.

Once the interviews were conducted, we compiled our separate field notes and interview notes. We reviewed the data for common themes, utilizing coding schemas generated based on our analytic framework (Lofland and Lofland 1995). Patterns emerged via the coding process that shed light on both enclave traits, as well as the forces that compelled individuals to move to and remain in enclaves. The interview data were evaluated against both our field research and the census data to ascertain similarities and inconsistencies. Most of the information from our field research and census data was consistent with the interviews; however, the interviews were more descriptive and revealing regarding the motivations for residing in these enclaves.

Motivations for Moving to an Enclave

Much of the research conducted to date on gay enclaves has tended to subscribe to the notion that gay men and lesbians move to particular areas because of elements unique to the gay lifestyle. They might move due to the presence of other gay men and lesbians; a desire to be close to gay and lesbian institutions or organizations; a wish to reside in a more liberal, accepting environment; concerns about safety; and/or a need for anonymity or personal growth that can be provided by a fresh start in a large city (Collins 2004; Sibalis 2004; Murray 1996; Weightman 1986). An alternative theory is that gay men and lesbians move to certain locations for the same reasons as heterosexuals—for the local amenities (Black et al. 2002). Black and his colleagues (2002) argue that gay men and lesbians face physical, legal, and social constraints that make it more difficult for them to have children; as a result, they have more available lifetime resources and less demand for large housing, which enables them to allocate their resources toward living in more desirable and costly areas, such as in San Francisco.

In testing this contention, Black and colleagues (2002) used census data and mortgage prices and showed a very strong correlation between mortgage prices and the concentration of gay male couples, and a weaker correlation between mortgage prices and the concentrations of lesbian couples and middle-age childless heterosexual couples. Although acknowledging that negative attitudes toward homosexuality do indeed play a role in the spatial distribution of gay men and lesbians, they concluded that homosexual individuals are not special, with idiosyncratic preferences that uniquely determine their location decisions; rather, simple economic motivations can better explain their distribution among cities.

If gay men and lesbians do actually have more free resources than heterosexuals, they are more capable of acting on their desire to live in particular locations than are heterosexuals. We hypothesized, however, that unique motivations nonetheless guide their choice of a residential location—motivations that are very different from those considered by heterosexuals when selecting a particular community.

In the following discussion, we examine the reasons proffered by gay men and lesbians in the San Francisco Bay Area for their choice of residence. We explore the literature to date that has suggested a number of factors unique to gay men and lesbians in choosing a place of residence, and we highlight our findings from the San Francisco Bay Area communities that both support and contradict the earlier literature. As demonstrated by Table 4.3 and our discussion below, respondents primarily enumerate "homosexual-specific" factors when discussing their residential choices.

TABLE 4.3. Reasons for Moving to, or Remaining in, Enclave, by Percentage Responding "Yes"

	Weather	Nature	Community	Political Climate	Lesiglation	Institutions
Sonoma	29%	100%	100%	100%	57%	43%
Oakland	20%	40%	100%	100%	60%	80%
Mission	25%	25%	100%	100%	25%	75%
Castro	50%	25%	100%	100%	0%	100%
TOTAL	30%	55%	100%	100%	40%	70%

Safety/Community

Issues surrounding safety and a sense of community have been found to be important in drawing gay men and lesbians to enclave environments. Gay men and lesbians face a heightened potential of being victims of hate crimes, as well as the possibility of discrimination both in public spaces and in their places of employment (Collins 2004). These threats can be alleviated by residing in an enclave community because of the decreased likelihood of socializing with those hostile to gay men and lesbians and the sense of safety created by being surrounded by others who are supportive of their lifestyle. Black and his colleagues (2002) found some support for this notion, determining that the concentration of gay men and lesbians in metropolitan areas decreased as negative attitudes about homosexuality increased. As a result, it is possible to conclude that homosexual individuals would be drawn to enclave environments, because negative attitudes toward gay men and lesbians would likely be at a minimum in such neighborhoods.

The presence of other gay and lesbian individuals is one of the top two responses provided by members of all the communities we surveyed when they were questioned as to their reasons for moving to, or remaining in, their respective enclaves. Indeed, 100 percent of our subjects cited this reason (see Table 4.3). When one man was asked why he selected the Castro in particular, he replied in a matter-of-fact tone, "It's gay!" In particular, he was drawn to the ability to be outwardly gay in the Castro, observing that "you could walk down the street holding hands. You just couldn't do that anywhere else." Another man living in the Castro noted that this community was "one of the deciding factors in moving to San Francisco," stating that when you have a larger gay community, "the lifestyle is a little more accepted."

In the Mission, women were also drawn to the city because of the sense of community and safety that it could provide a gay individual. One woman noted that when she came to the area, she "couldn't believe how many gay people were here, and how up front you could be, as a gay person—kissing or holding hands on the street, tons of bars to hang out, dance and socialize in." She stated "I wanted to live in that kind of freedom, rather than just visit it." Another woman appreciated both the community and safety benefits associated with living in the Mission, observing that "I stayed as part of finding the queer community and feeling safe here. . . . Most of the individuals I know who stay here do so because they feel safer here."

In Oakland, the presence of not only a lesbian community, but a lesbian community of color, appears to have served as a primary draw for women to move to, and remain in, the city. One woman explained the attraction of the lesbian community, observing, "When I first moved here, it was gay pride—on the televisions and everywhere. . . . And I thought, I am in the promised land. . . . Everyone around me was gay." Another subject told a similar story, stating that "when I came to visit, it was the week of Dyke March and Pride and that is what I did all weekend, and I was in love—I was ready to move." One respondent noted that the acceptance that accompanies the large community makes it "really easy to be gay here"; in contemplating moving elsewhere, she asks "how easy is it to be gay there? . . . I don't want to figure out how to be gay somewhere else." The Oakland climate is unique compared to others, in that it is focused on women of color, and is less visible than in some of the other communities. One woman observed that, "I know there're queer people, but they're not necessarily visible." A woman in the Mission who had previously lived in Oakland, echoed this observation, stating that "there are probably fewer organizations. . . . It is a little less organized and less visible."

In Sonoma County, women also took note of the importance of having a strong lesbian community drawing them to the area. One woman observed that all of her friends in the area are lesbians, and indicated that it was comfortable to be out in Sonoma County. She stated that "I know I look like a big dyke—I don't think about that here, but sometimes I feel nervous when we go elsewhere." Another woman echoed this sentiment, stating that in Sonoma County, "I feel more normal. More like I can fit in. More like I can be myself." When she visited Sonoma County prior to her move, she observed that "there was a sense that this was a good place to be gay." Another subject agreed, noting that "one good reason to stay here is because there is a huge community here and it is considered a very gay and lesbian place." In fact, the presence of lesbians was the defining draw for one woman, who learned about Sonoma County from a friend; she was told that Santa Rosa boasted a "really great women's community," and she quickly determined that this "is where I am going to move."

Politics

Coupled with the notion of tolerance is the presence of an accepting political climate in the surrounding area. This differs from tolerance only in the gay enclave because it includes acceptance from heterosexuals who perhaps reside outside of the enclave itself. Murray (1996) notes that in the United States, an important consideration in a gay man's choice of residence is the political climate of the city, primarily as it relates to gay men and lesbians. At the same time, however, empirical research attempting to link political views and the presence of gay men and lesbians has had mixed results. In Chapter 2, we explored the relationship between political climate and the spatial distribution of gay men and lesbians in metropolitan cities. Our results indicated that gay men and lesbians residing in metropolitan areas might seek to avoid those areas where a higher percentage of the population had voted Republican. The presence or absence of specific laws concerning homosexual individuals (such as sodomy laws, or laws prohibiting discrimination against gay men and lesbians) did not seem to have a clear effect on the presence of gay men or lesbians in a city. Thus, how the political dynamic plays out might well depend more on the overall political climate, rather than on demonstrable policies in support of gay and lesbian concerns.

Our respondents' statements supported this hypothesis. Although 100 percent named the liberal political climate as a major factor in their move to the San Francisco Bay Area, only 40 percent referenced particular legislative policies relevant to gay men and lesbians that affected their residential choice (see Table 4.3). In the Castro, for instance, one man observed that he moved to San Francisco from an area in the Northeast that would be considered "a lot more conservative than here." The liberal political climate played an important factor in his remaining in the area. When asked about legislation, however, he stated that "I wouldn't say it wouldn't be a consideration, because I have thought about Vermont because they do have the civil unions, but it would definitely be more how many gay people live in the area that would be a consideration for me." Thus, an overall liberal atmosphere and a high concentration of gay individuals in the area were more significant factors in his decision of where to live, than gay-friendly legislation.

The women in the Mission tended to echo this sentiment, emphasizing the importance of living in a liberal atmosphere. One woman observed, "I think if it were a conservative environment, I would go crazy." Another woman stated that she moved to the Mission from a less progressive area of California because she wanted to live in a more liberal environment to pursue many of her political interests. One respondent observed that the liberal political atmosphere makes it very accepted to be gay, so much so that there are "many gay and lesbian politicians and leaders" in the community. Although gay-friendly legislation was not necessarily a top concern for some of the women, one did note that she would consider "negative freedoms" in making a decision as to where to live. If legislation was in place that denied rights to gay people, rather than granted rights, she "would hesitate to go there. I would avoid places where the law reflects the will of the people in that way."

Women in Oakland repeatedly cited the liberal political climate as a significant factor in their decision to move to, or remain in the area. One respondent said about her move to Oakland that "I found a political community and a political home." If she were to move to another location, she told us that the progressiveness of the community would play an important factor. Another woman noted that the results of the 2004 election emphasized the importance to her of remaining in a liberal community; she stated, "[The election] has limited my feeling that I could move to other areas in the country and enjoy the same privileges that straight people enjoy." Another subject echoed this sentiment, observing "we do have some privilege here and I think it is very Bay Area, like if you go outside the Bay Area you won't see it. . . . We have our own bubble, but if you go outside of it, it is business as usual." At the same time, however, many of the Oakland respondents did not place gay-friendly legislation as a high priority in their residential choice (Table 4.3). Some of the women specifically stated that, although they were aware of the marriage debate, they were not necessarily concerned with, or active in, the debate. Instead, their political concerns seemed to be founded in issues that were more centered on race, the environment, or crime.

The women in Sonoma County also reported that a liberal atmosphere played an important role in their choice of residence. One woman observed that "the combination of a liberal lifestyle and a rural environment was attractive"; there are few places in which one could choose country living and have it coincide with a progressive environment. Yet another respondent was drawn to the female-dominated political atmosphere, observing that "every single person who represents me is a woman except one." She noted that the liberal political climate was important to her in making a residential choice, contending that she "would not move to a small town in Kansas." Many of the subjects in Sonoma County cited the extensive support of gay-oriented legislation in the area: the county provides domestic partnership benefits, there were city proclamations in Sebastopol (a town in Sonoma County) in favor of gay marriage, Sonoma County was one of the first counties in California to have an antidiscrimination law based on sexual orientation, and there is an out lesbian mayor in Sebastopol. The community as a whole is very supportive of gay rights. For instance, when the Briggs Initiative was introduced, which attempted to prohibit gay individuals from teaching children, the community united in opposition against it. One woman observed that this "is one of the most important things about living here. There is political response against that kind of insanity."

Institutions and Organizations
The presence of gay male and lesbian institutions and organizations has been found to be one of the fundamental characteristics of a gay enclave (Weightman 1981). These institutions include gay bars, baths, bookstores, theaters, churches, community centers, hotels, and clothing and retail stores. In addition, political and social organizations centered around the gay male and lesbian community also tend to dominate enclaves. These institutions and organizations serve as both a draw to the community, as well as a factor encouraging individuals to remain once they arrive there.

Almost three-quarters of our subjects in the Castro, Mission, Oakland, and Sonoma County areas confirmed the importance of gay institutions and organizations to their residential choice, although the *type* of institutions and organizations that was valued differed among the communities (Table 4.3). All of the subjects living in the Castro stressed the importance of gay bars and dance clubs. One man recalled that the gay bars and clubs were an important draw for him to the area, stating that "of course it was the bars, the bars and the discos and everything. . . . Not that I was a disco bunny. That was gay life." Although the nightlife was an important factor for Castro men, one subject observed that bars are not the only gay institutions that hold attraction in the area; he also frequents gay shops and businesses, noting that these businesses "definitely cater to gay people." As one subject stated, "just about anything a gay person could want in life can be found in the Castro."

In the Mission, just a few blocks away, there is less emphasis on bars or gay businesses than in the Castro. Although there have been many attempts to create lesbian bars and spaces in the Mission, these attempts seem to have failed over the years. One woman observed that "there are no women-only spaces. There was an attempt in the late 1990s to make this kind of space. . . . The idea was that it was going to be a women-only safe space. . . . a place you could go and hang out." This venue, however, failed. She observed that bars owned by lesbians were more successful, but most of these eventually failed or were taken over by the gay men in the area. Other subjects echoed the notion of the vanishing lesbian venue, with one woman commenting that "I expect those places to close because they're owned by women and women have less money." Lesbian-owned businesses, other than bars and clubs, do seem somewhat more prevalent in the Mission. One respondent noted that "everybody on Valencia [Street] is a lesbian. . . . the people who work there are mostly lesbians." When discovering the number of lesbian-owned businesses, she stated that "I was blown away." These businesses serve as more of an attraction for the women in the area, including women's bookstores, restaurants, and a women's bathhouse located in the Mission—this bathhouse is the only women's-only bathhouse in San Francisco.

Looking across the San Francisco Bay to Oakland, however, there is a different picture when it comes to gay institutions and organizations. None of our subjects was aware of the presence of lesbian-only bars in Oakland. Nonetheless, there were lesbian events held at other clubs. One woman noted that the lesbian events were held at gay clubs or gay-friendly clubs, but not at lesbian-only clubs. Another woman echoed other subjects in emphasizing the lack of lesbian bars in the area, noting that "[i]n the Bay Area in general, it is very hard to find women-centered space. San Francisco is very male-centered." Although there is an absence of lesbian bars in Oakland, all of the Oakland subjects were aware of places to go for lesbian events, and emphasized the importance of there being gathering places for lesbians of color. They noted that the existence of events for lesbians of color was an important factor in their moving to, and/or remaining in, Oakland. In addition to the lesbian nightlife, women in Oakland were aware of, and frequented, lesbian and gay businesses. One woman noted that there are restaurants and hotels that are lesbian-owned that she and her friends frequent; in addition there are some restaurants that are just known as lesbian hangouts, such as the "queer Denny's."

Northward, in Sonoma County, subjects not only report an absence of lesbian bars, but few emphasize gay male or lesbian institutions as a reason for moving to, or remaining in, the community. None of the respondents was able to name a single lesbian bar in the area, and few knew of any gay bars, other than those in Guerneville. The failures of prior attempts to establish lesbian bars led one woman to observe that the area "can't support a women's gathering place."[7] Two main suggestions were offered for why there was a lack of gay male and lesbian bars in the area: financial constraints, as well as the notion that "women in general are [not] as drawn to [bars]—women are looking for a connection." Instead, one respondent suggested that lesbians are more likely to participate in group activities or to attend churches in order to interact with the community. In Sebastopol, however, there are some known lesbian venues, such as a lesbian café and a gift store. Further, there are at least two churches in the Santa Rosa/Sebastopol area of Sonoma County that are considered to be gay and lesbian friendly, operated, or dominated.

Conclusion

In this chapter, we have described the characteristics of four gay male and lesbian enclaves located in the San Francisco Bay Area, an area that boasts the highest prevalence rates for both male and female same-sex partners in the nation. Despite the variation in the gender, race, and income of residents in the enclaves, we found that the top reasons articulated for living in an enclave were (1) the presence of other gay men, lesbians, or both and (2) a liberal political climate. These findings differ from those of Black and his colleagues (2003) that the residential choices of gay men and lesbians are founded primarily in concerns about amenities, such as climate, nature, and access to artistic attractions. Indeed, none of our respondents listed artistic or tourist attractions as a motivation for residing in an enclave, although two individuals claimed that they had grown to appreciate such offerings after moving to the area.

Natural attractions, such as access to the mountains, ocean, or other outdoor activities, were either disregarded or viewed as a "bonus" by most respondents, save those in Sonoma County where all of the respondents cited this as a primary reason for moving there. For one of the women living in Sonoma County, the "country atmosphere, bucolic setting, slower pace" were named as primary attractions; this sentiment was echoed by others. While the draw of the natural beauty of the area was an attraction, these amenities were nearly always listed in tandem with the liberal climate of the area. For instance, one woman observed, "It is so beautiful, open-minded, and wonderful. That is why I live here." Another woman in the Mission echoed the secondary nature of the natural attractions in motivating her residential choice, stating that "in addition to the primary reason I described in the first question [the open-mindedness and presence of other gay individuals], the rampant natural beauty of the area and proximity to the ocean were big draws for me." Comments such as these emphasize that even for those who select their residence due to natural amenities, the acceptance of the gay lifestyle and the presence of other gay men and lesbians, serve as at least as important determining factors, if not more so.

Respondents varied widely in regard to whether the climate of their respective enclaves was a positive attraction, or a negative one. One woman in the Mission observed that "the Mission is great, it's sunny. . . . But not warm enough for shorts." She labeled the weather as one of the things she liked least about living in San Francisco, and noted that she would prefer to move to Berkeley or Oakland because the weather is somewhat warmer there. Another woman in the Mission noted that the weather "is just fine," stating that she would prefer to live somewhere with more rain; this type of sentiment was echoed by one man from the Castro who stated that the weather was "not at all" an attraction, and noted that he "missed the snow." Similarly, one woman in Oakland labeled the weather as more of a deterrent than an attraction, stating "I think it is really cold."

Approximately 30 percent of the respondents did cite the weather as a reason to move to, or remain in, the area. Of those who appreciated the weather, many seemed to believe that the benefits of attractive weather must be weighed against other concerns peculiar to the gay male and lesbian community. For example, one woman in Sonoma County noted that when she considered the option of one day moving to Canada, she concluded that "the weather is not as good in Canada, but is that as important as safety?" In a similar comment, a woman in Oakland observed that while the weather was attractive and important, it was a "secondary concern. If this community had been inland and landlocked in New Mexico, I would have moved there too. *I moved for the people*" (emphasis added). These observations are representative of many of the comments made by other individuals concerning the attraction of the type of amenities described by Black and his colleagues; for some, these amenities are not viewed as attractive in the least, whereas for others they are secondary. Independent of the presence of other gay men and lesbians and the open-minded, liberal climate, these "high-amenity" factors would likely not serve as a sufficient draw for many of those who reside in the area.

Perhaps one way to reconcile the findings from this research with that of Black and his colleagues is by viewing the presence of gay men and lesbians, a liberal climate, gay institutions, and safety concerns as "amenities" in and of themselves. Collins (2004) makes the argument that a large gay population can be understood as a valued amenity to the gay male and lesbian population, one which serves to draw other gay individuals to an enclave environment. With this in mind, it becomes possible to assert that gay men and lesbians, like heterosexual individuals, apply their available economic resources toward the cost of living in an area replete with the amenities that they value. For gay men and lesbians, however, these amenities appear to differ from those of heterosexuals, yet they are willing to "pay the price" to live in the communities that provide these attractions.

CHAPTER 5

❦

Factors Affecting the Migration Decision of Gay Men and Lesbians

In the first four chapters of this book, we have shown that sexual orientation affects the spatial distribution of gay men and lesbians in the United States. If sexual orientation was not a factor in residential choice, we would expect to see an even distribution of same-sex unmarried partners. However, gay men and lesbians are not evenly distributed throughout the United States; some geographic areas contain high concentrations and others low concentrations of same-sex partners. This suggests that there are characteristics about those locations that serve to draw or to discourage partnered gay men and lesbians. Our prior chapters have explored some of the ways in which characteristics of the place of destination and, to some extent, the place of origin, affect the residential choices of gay men and lesbians. In this chapter, we attempt to assess the effects of *individual characteristics* on the interstate migration decision for same-sex and different-sex partnered individuals. Specifically, we examine whether sexual orientation is a significant factor affecting the odds of making an interstate move.

Demographers have long recognized that an individual's decision to migrate is affected by such individual characteristics as age, sex, and education, as well as the characteristics of the place of origin and the place of destination, including region, political climate, and labor market characteristics. In other words, individuals take into consideration their own personal characteristics, in addition to the characteristics of the places of origin and destination, when weighing the costs and benefits of a move (Lee 1966). But is sexual orientation one of the factors that affects an individual's likelihood to engage in interstate migration? Although social scientists have determined that a number of factors are particularly important for predicting interstate migration, there has been no systematic evaluation of whether gay men and lesbians are more or less likely to migrate than heterosexuals.

Just as the interstate migration decision often differs for individuals of different races and for females and males, one's sexual orientation could well affect the manner in which the costs and benefits of a move are viewed and, ultimately, the outcome of the migration decision. For example, gay men and lesbians might be more likely than heterosexuals to engage in interstate moves because of a desire to live in a more accepting political and social climate, and/or an area with a higher concentration of dating partners (see Chapter 4).

We take up this question here and explore the manner in which sexual orientation affects the odds of engaging in interstate migration. We also evaluate the interaction of sexual orientation with several demographic, social, and human capital characteristics of the individual. Through this process, we are able to assess whether factors that are known to affect migration decisions, such as education level or the presence of children in the household, perhaps shape the migration decisions of gay men and lesbians in a manner different from that of heterosexuals. Our findings indicate that sexual orientation, like many other individual characteristics long viewed central to migration studies, does indeed play a role in predicting one's likelihood of engaging in interstate migration. Further, the manner in which sexual orientation interacts with other individual characteristics is affected by sex.

Background: Sexual Orientation and Interstate Migration

There are a few analyses that explore the manner in which gay men and lesbians are concentrated in metropolitan areas throughout the United States (see chapter 2 in this book; also see Walther and Poston 2004; Black et al. 2002). To our knowledge, however, demographers have not examined the manner in which sexual orientation might interact with the migration decision. Consequently, our discussion is necessarily limited to reviewing both theoretical and empirical findings concerning the manner in which the individual-level variables included in this analysis have been found to affect the migration decision in general, as well as some of the studies concerning prevalence rates of same-sex partners that may have bearing on the migration question.

As noted by Lee (1966), a number of individual characteristics can affect the decision to make an interstate move. A particularly strong relationship has been found between the demographic variables of age and sex and the migration decision. As age increases, the probability of migrating tends to decrease; this is attributable to the fact that migrants are likely to be individuals in their late teens or young adults who are entering college or the labor force, getting married, or making other life changes (White and Lindstrom 2005; Tienda and Wilson 1992; Lee 1966). Further, younger migrants have a greater likelihood of recovering the costs of migrating over their lifetimes and are, as a result, more likely to move in response to new employment opportunities (White and Lindstrom 2005). Rural to urban migration is also more likely to occur than urban to rural migration (Greenwood 1997). Consequently, one's status as a metropolitan or nonmetropolitan resident could be an important factor in predicting interstate migration.

Sex is also correlated with migration behavior, as males tend to make more long-distance moves, whereas females appear to make more short-distance moves (Lee 1966). This relationship is especially strong in developing countries. However, with increases in the degree of gender equity in a society, the migration rates of females tend to approximate those of males (Poston 2005). Nonetheless one still might expect to see males making slightly more interstate moves than females. In part, demographers have attributed the sex difference in migration patterns to the repercussions of sex-typed occupations which result in fewer job opportunities for women in many labor markets (White and Lindstrom 2005). Further, women tend to have less influence in terms of making important household decisions relevant to moves (Jacobsen and Levin 1997; Cooke and Bailey 1996). The presence of children in the household can also serve as a deterrent in making an interstate move, because those who have established family households are less likely to disrupt them in order to make a move (White and Lindstrom 2005).

Research also indicates that one's race and ethnicity can influence migration behavior. Findings indicate, for instance, that African-Americans engage in different migration patterns than non-African-Americans (Burr et al. 1992; Sandefur 1991). According to 2000 census data, African-Americans had an age-adjusted interstate migration rate of 71.1 compared to a rate of 93.9 for whites (Saenz and Morales 2005). However, other racial minorities, such as Asian Indians, Koreans, and Chinese engage in more interstate migration than whites (Saenz and Morales 2005). In contrast, individuals of Hispanic origin tend to have lower rates of interstate migration. They are less likely to migrate than non-Hispanics for an assortment of reasons (Saenz and Morales 2005; Saenz and Davila 1992; Saenz 1991), including human capital limitations. Because of these findings regarding the effects of race and ethnicity on migration patterns, incorporating a measure of race and Hispanic ethnicity into a model assessing the probability of making an interstate move makes theoretical sense and is supported by empirical findings.

In addition to demographic and social characteristics, human capital characteristics also play a role in predicting the probability of migrating. One's education level, in particular, has been found to increase the odds of making an interstate move; that is, as education increases, the odds of moving increase (Greenwood 1997; Tienda and Wilson 1992). This is likely due to a number of factors, including the availability of increased wealth, the enhanced capability of securing employment, and an added knowledge base regarding opportunities in other locations. Likewise, the ability to speak English has also been shown to increase interstate migration (Tienda and Wilson 1992); possessing this skill increases one's desirability in other labor markets.

Consequently, researchers have established that demographic, social, and human capital characteristics all affect the probability that an individual will migrate. But is there any evidence that the relationship between these characteristics and the migration decision would be different for homosexual individuals than for heterosexuals? Black and colleagues (2003) attempted to determine whether gay men and lesbians are concentrated in certain cities such as San Francisco because these cities are "gay enclaves" (see Chapter 4 in this book), or whether they live in the cities for the same reasons as would heterosexuals, that is, for the local amenities. They argued that gay men and lesbians face physical, legal, and social constraints that make it more difficult for them to have children. As a consequence of not having children, homosexual individuals have more available lifetime resources and less demand for large housing enabling them to allocate their resources toward living in more desirable and costly areas, such as San Francisco. Thus, Black and his colleagues contend that gay men and lesbians do not choose to live in San Francisco or other "gay hot spots" because they are gay enclaves, but do so for pretty much the same reasons as do heterosexuals; they are simply more able to live in these areas due to additional free resources.

In addition, Black and colleagues assert that as education increases (and income, correspondingly, increases) and the number of children decreases, individuals will be more likely to locate in high amenity areas, regardless of sexual orientation. They, therefore, argue that the personal characteristics of education and number of children are among those that determine free resources which, in turn, affect place of residence. One might argue, however, that if gay men and lesbians have fewer children because of their sexual orientation and, as some contend, seek higher education to combat discrimination against homosexuality, then perhaps their distribution in these areas is in fact directly linked to their sexual orientation.

Black and colleagues focused on spatial distribution, rather than on the migration decision itself, but nonetheless concluded that the personal characteristics of education and number of children might play an important role in the location decisions of homosexual individuals. They argued, however, that these characteristics should not have differential effects for individuals of varying sexual orientation. The analysis we undertake in this chapter examines whether the same finding holds true for the migration decision: Do the personal characteristics of gay men and lesbians affect their migration decision in the same manner as they do for heterosexuals?

Methods

In order to examine migration decisions by sexual orientation, we draw on data collected by the U.S. Census Bureau in the 2000 long-form questionnaire, as assembled in the 5 percent Public Use Microdata Sample (PUMS) file. To assess whether the determinants of interstate migration vary by sexual orientation, separate models are constructed by sex: one model contains all partnered men, including same-sex unmarried partners, heterosexual unmarried partners, and married men; a similar model is estimated for women.

The dependent variable for the analysis is a dichotomous variable measuring whether an individual engaged in interstate migration between 1995 and 2000. This variable is captured by questions on the census long-form questionnaire that ask the respondent whether he or she resides in the same residence in 2000 as in 1995 and, if not, to provide information about the 1995 residence. From these data, one can determine whether an individual has migrated from the 1995 residence to a different residence in 2000; if this residence is in a different state, the individual has engaged in interstate migration. The interstate migration dependent variable is assigned a value of one if the state of residence in 2000 differs from that of 1995, and zero if otherwise.

The use of census data to measure migration is problematic in a number of respects. Individuals who perhaps engaged in interstate migration between 1995 and 2000, but returned to the 1995 place of residence by the year 2000, are not coded as interstate migrants (Saenz and Davila 1992). They are thus excluded from the analysis, despite their having engaged in interstate migration. In addition, the census questionnaire collects data on most individual characteristics for the year 2000, but the decision to migrate as measured by the census question occurs some time between 1995 and 2000. As a result, the use in analyses of many individual characteristics that are viewed as strong theoretical predictors of migration behavior is problematic due to temporality concerns (Saenz and Davila 1992; Sandefur 1991; Shryock, Siegel and Associates 1976). For instance, income level might be a strong predictor of whether an individual is able to make an interstate move. The census data contain information only on an individual's income in the year of 1999, however, which almost always will reflect income earned *after* the move. Since a move is often made in pursuit of income gain, using postmigration income to predict the migration decision is problematic. As a result, many researchers choose to include only variables that are less likely to be affected by, or to be endogenous to, the migration process (Sandefur 1991). Nonetheless, the census five-year question is the dominant measure of migration and, due to lack of alternative data, the only feasible measure of migration for studies involving sexual orientation.

Although we opted not to use income due to this temporality problem, we have included some variables in our analyses that could change after a move, including education and the number of children. We believe these variables are less likely to be endogenous to an interstate move and/or to change within the time period at issue in the census question. It is also likely that were we to have data on these characteristics from 1995 or earlier, they would vary in pretty much the same way as the census data we have available to us for the year 2000. The fact that the variation should be similar is important to keep in mind because it is the variation in a variable that is important in a regression model.

We ran two separate models for both partnered males and partnered females in order to estimate the effects of sexual orientation on interstate migration. Model 1 contains nine independent variables, including demographic, social, and human capital characteristics of the individuals (see Table 5.1). To assess the effect of sexual orientation on the migration decision, an independent variable was included for couple-type, using three categories: (1) married heterosexual (reference category); (2) heterosexual unmarried partner; and (3) same-sex unmarried partner.

TABLE 5.1. Variables in Models 1 and 2

Variable Name	Description
Model 1	
Migrant (Dependent Variable)	Interstate Migration, 0 = nonmigrant, 1 = migrant
Couple Type	Couple Type: Married, heterosexual unmarried, and same-sex unmarried; reference category married
Age	Age, measured in years 18–100
Race	Race, 0 = nonwhite, 1 = white
Education	Education, 0 = less than college degree, 1 = college degree or higher
Metro	Metropolitan residence, 0 = nonmetropolitan, 1 = metropolitan
Child	Presence of child in the home, 0 = no, 1 = yes
Citizen	Citizen, 0 = no, 1 = yes
Speaks English	Speaks English well or only English, 0 = no, 1 = yes
Hispanic	Hispanic, 0 = no, 1 = yes
Model 2[a]	
Orientation*Age	Interaction of orientation and age
Orientation*Race	Interaction of orientation and race
Orientation*Education	Interaction of orientation and education
Orientation*Child	Interaction of orientation and presence of child in the home
Orientation*Hispanic	Interaction of orientation and Hispanic identity

[a]Model 2 includes all of the variables of Model 1, as well as the additional interaction terms.

A variable measuring the demographic characteristic of age was included, with age measured in years. The presence of children in the household was also included, measured as a dummy variable (with 1 indicating the presence of a child). The race variable was measured as a dummy variable, as well, indicating whether individuals are nonwhite or white. Ethnicity is assessed by a variable indicating whether an individual is Hispanic or non-Hispanic (with 1 indicating Hispanic).

Although variables measuring income and occupation were not included in this analysis due to the previously mentioned problems with temporality, the human capital characteristics of education and speaking English were included. We have incorporated a measure of the level of education, coded 1 if the individual has earned a college degree or higher. The variable for speaking English is measured as a dummy variable assessing whether an individual speaks English well, only English, or both (coded 1), versus not speaking English well or at all (coded 0).

We have theorized that a number of these variables may well interact with sexual orientation in order to create migration outcomes that are different for same-sex partners than for heterosexuals. For example, a lesbian with the same education level as a heterosexual woman might be more likely to move if she were seeking to improve her employment and income situation. As we show later in chapter 8, lesbians have the greatest likelihood of all couple types to be in the labor force, which is probably attributable to the pressures of the gender wage gap; that is, lesbians do not have a relatively high-earning male partner for support. Consequently, in Model 2 we retain the independent variables from Model 1, and also introduce variables which measure interactions between sexual orientation and a number of those variables.[1]

Specifically, we include interaction terms for sexual orientation and education; sexual orientation and the number of children in a household; sexual orientation and race; sexual orientation and Hispanic identity; and sexual orientation and age. Gay men and lesbians with children may be more likely to engage in an interstate move because they might either (1) be experiencing a divorce or separation from their opposite-sex partner with whom they parented the children, or (2) be in search of a friendly environment for their children. We predicted that gay men and lesbians who are minorities might be less likely to make an interstate move because these individuals perhaps would experience double-discrimination in the workplace, resulting in lower levels of income. Since higher levels of income usually result in greater odds of migrating, we believe that minority same-sex partners will have lower odds of engaging in interstate migration. On the other hand, those gay men and lesbians with a college degree or higher will perhaps gain added workplace benefits and protection, resulting in higher income and increased odds of interstate migration. Finally, gay men and lesbians might be more likely to continue moving as they age, if Black and colleagues (2002) are correct in suggesting that they possess greater disposable income due to fewer familial demands.

Using the dependent variable and the fourteen independent variables, the probability of engaging in interstate migration was estimated separately for partnered males and partnered females using logistic regression. Logistic regression was used due to the dichotomous nature of the dependent variable of the migration decision.

Results

The results of the two logistic regressions, one for partnered males and one for partnered females, are presented in Table 5.2 (Model 1) and Table 5.3 (Model 2). We have chosen to present the results in terms of odds ratios, rather than logit coefficients, due to the ease of interpretation. After controlling for many of the factors that could affect interstate migration,[2] it is evident that sexual orientation plays an important role in interstate migration (Table 5.2). The odds ratio for men who are in same-sex unmarried partner relationships is 1.08, indicating that the odds of engaging in an interstate move are 8 percent higher when a man is in a same-sex unmarried partnership compared to being married, holding constant the other variables in the equation. In contrast, the odds of migrating are 6 percent higher for a man in a cohabiting partnership with a woman versus for a married man. These results indicate that married men are less mobile than same-sex or heterosexual unmarried partners, perhaps indicating that marriage imbues a sense of residential stability. Notably, however, partnered gay men are 2 percent more likely to engage in an interstate move than partnered heterosexual men compared to married men. Thus, although

TABLE 5.2. Logistic Regression Results for Model 1

	Men		Women	
Variable	Odds Ratio	Prob	Odds Ratio	Prob
Heterosexual Unmarried	1.06	.00	1.03	.00
Same-sex Unmarried	1.08	.00	1.04	.00
Age	.96	.00	.96	.00
Race	.92	.00	.96	.00
Education	1.93	.00	1.62	.00
Metro	.97	.00	1.02	.00
Child	.67	.00	.65	.00
Citizen	1.03	.02	1.09	.00
Speaks English	1.13	.00	1.31	.00
Hispanic	.81	.00	.77	.00

TABLE 5.3. Logistic Regression Results for Model 2[a]

	Men		Women	
Variable	Odds Ratio	Prob	Odds Ratio	Prob
Orientation*Age	1.00	.32	1.00	.26
Orientation*Race	1.26	.00	1.08	.17
Orientation*Education	.97	.49	1.22	.00
Orientation*Child	.95	.42	1.05	.37
Orientation*Hispanic	.85	.02	1.01	.89

[a]Model 2 also includes all independent variables incorporated into Model 1.

married men are less migratory than those in unmarried partnerships, it is men who are in same-sex partnerships who are the *most* likely to migrate. We discuss the possible implications of this finding in the conclusion to this chapter.

In Model 2, we have added variables assessing the interactions between sexual orientation and many of the other independent variables (Table 5.3). Specifically, we included interactions between sexual orientation and age, presence of children in the household, education, race, and Hispanic identity. Out of these five variables, only two proved to be statistically significant: the interactions of sexual orientation with race and with Hispanic identity. Men who are both white and gay are approximately 26 percent more likely to engage in interstate migration than men who do not possess both of these characteristics (i.e., black gay men and heterosexual men). On the other hand, being both Hispanic and gay decreases a man's likelihood of engaging in interstate migration by approximately 15 percent compared to other men. Thus, it appears that, although gay men are more likely, on average, to migrate than heterosexual men, the addition of a racial or ethnic minority status to a homosexual identity decreases gay men's odds of engaging in interstate migration.

These results highlight emerging differences in migration patterns based on sexual orientation. We turn now to an examination of the manner in which sexual orientation might affect the migration patterns of women. As in the preceding analyses of male migration patterns, Table 5.2 also demonstrates that women who are in unmarried partner relationships are more likely to engage in interstate migration than are those who are married. That is, both lesbians and cohabiting heterosexual women are more likely to migrate than married women.

The interaction terms included in Model 2 tell a different story for women than for men (Table 5.3). For women, and not for men, the interactions of sexual orientation with race and Hispanic identity were not statistically significant. Rather, only the education interaction was statistically significant. Lesbians who have earned a college degree, or higher, are approximately 22 percent more likely to engage in interstate migration than other women (lesbians without a college degree or heterosexual women). It appears, therefore, that the acquisition of additional education provides a special boost to the mobility of lesbians that is not the case for all heterosexual women.

Discussion and Conclusion

Our examination of the role that sexual orientation plays in the interstate migration decision indicates that sexual orientation is a pertinent factor. Countless studies have explored the effects of age, race, ethnicity, and the presence of children in a household in determining migration behaviors; in contrast, little to no quantitative research has been conducted examining sexual orientation's role in this process. Given our finding that being in a same-sex partner relationship has a statistically significant effect on the odds of interstate migration, it is clear that this is an area in the migration literature that needs more attention.

For both men and women, we find that individuals who are in unmarried partner relationships are more likely to engage in interstate migration than those who are married. These findings are in line with previous research indicating that married individuals are less likely to migrate than unmarried individuals (Jacobson and Levin 1997; Polachek and Horvath 1977; Mincer 1978). This is thought to be attributable to the fact that committed families consider moves in light of their long-term consequences for the family's well-being (Polachek and Horvath 1977). In contrast, single individuals or persons in partnered relationships without the symbolic permanence of marriage are more likely to move when doing so is beneficial for the individual.

Although our findings support prior research concerning married individuals being less likely to migrate than unmarried, we have highlighted a previously unanalyzed difference between the migration propensities of heterosexual and same-sex unmarried partners. Particularly in the case of men, same-sex unmarried partners are more likely to engage in interstate migration than are heterosexual unmarried partners. There are a number of possible explanations for this phenomenon.

First, it is possible that same-sex partners are more likely than heterosexuals to engage in interstate migration because they are drawn to particular states with friendly social or political climates. As we have explored in the first three chapters of this book, many high concentrations of gay men and lesbians are in fact located in areas with more accepting social and political climates. Moreover, all of our respondents in the qualitative interviews we reported on in Chapter 4 indicated that a liberal political atmosphere and the presence of a gay and lesbian community drew them to their current residence. Further, gay men and lesbians might be more likely to make an interstate move than heterosexuals in order to escape their home state, region, or family in search of a place where their sexuality is more accepted. After making such an exodus, gay men and lesbians are then provided with new chances to develop a sense of collective belonging (Ramirez 2003).

Consequently, a desire for amenities such as these that are concentrated in certain states could result in same-sex partners making more interstate moves than heterosexuals. One way to assess the influence of these factors on the migration decision would be to conduct a multilevel analysis, introducing state-level characteristics into the equation. As previously mentioned, we opted to focus on individual-level characteristics in this chapter because we feel the first three chapters devote extensive time to examining the role of state-level characteristics in determining the residential choices of gay men and lesbians. Future research in this area, however, is encouraged.

In addition to the possibility that state-level characteristics are boosting the migration rates of gay men and lesbians, it is also possible that same-sex partners, particularly male same-sex partners, are better able to find employment for both partners in a new labor market. We noted that prior research has attributed the sex difference in migration patterns to fewer job opportunities for women in many labor markets that result, in part, from employer discrimination and occupational segregation (White and Lindstrom 2000). This can be especially problematic for heterosexual partners who are seeking to secure employment in a local labor market that might be beneficial to a man's career, but not the woman's (Costa and Kahn 2000). As a result, migration for heterosexual couples—both married and unmarried—can be problematic, because it might prove more challenging for both individuals to find employment in the same labor market. This situation results in one member of the couple (the tied-stayer) often declining employment opportunities because of the limited employment opportunities for the other (Mincer 1978).

Even though heterosexual unmarried partners are more likely to migrate than partners who are married, employment considerations are bound to affect many of these couples. The term "unmarried partner" is indicative of a marriage-like relationship, suggesting that these couples view themselves as committed and indeed take their economic future into consideration when making decisions about a move. For same-sex partners, on the other hand, moving into local labor markets that are dominated by sex-segregated occupations would pose less of a hindrance. Assuming that both partners work in occupations dominated by their sex,[3] these couples might find coemployment less of a problem. Further, male same-sex couples might be more likely to engage in interstate migration than females due to the greater availability of labor market opportunities for men, as compared to women (White and Lindstrom 2000).

Turning to the insights revealed by the interaction terms (Table 5.3), we found that men who are both gay and black or gay and Hispanic have lower odds of engaging in interstate migration. This finding supported our original hypothesis that being gay coupled with being a racial or ethnic minority, could lower one's odds of migrating. Prior research has found that both Hispanics and many other racial minorities have lower odds of engaging in migration, controlling for other individual characteristics. Although gay males have higher odds of engaging in interstate migration, those who are minorities, as is the case for heterosexual minorities, are less likely to migrate. A portion of these differences could be due to unaccounted for income differences. Being black and being unmarried can reduce one's income; consequently both white gay men and white married men likely have higher incomes than minority gay men. Without a measure of income in 1995, though, a control for income could not be included in the analysis. When 2000 income level was added to the model, however, the race and ethnicity differences did not significantly change; the differences were sustained and were statistically significant. Despite the lack of a control for income differences, the model does contain two controls for human capital differences (education and ability to speak English) that should assist in alleviating some of the problems associated with the lack of an income variable.

We found that the interaction of one of these human capital variables, education, with sexual orientation resulted in increased odds of migration for lesbians. This finding supported our original hypothesis that same-sex partners who have a higher level of education will be more likely to engage in interstate migration. Women, overall, are less likely to migrate than are men. As we have repeatedly noted, this has been attributed in part to more restricted economic opportunities and demands for women's labor. However, women who have attained a college degree or higher, have improved their odds of acquiring a position in other labor markets. Perhaps lesbians, in particular, benefit from this added education due to the insulation it provides from discrimination directed at them on the basis of sexual orientation. Or, it is possible that lesbians are more likely to act on the market advantages provided by additional education than are heterosexual women.

In this chapter, we attempted to answer the following question: Does one's sexual orientation affect one's decision to make an interstate move? We have found the answer to be in the affirmative. Gay men and, to a lesser extent lesbians, have greater odds of engaging in interstate migration than heterosexual couples. We have examined some interactions between sexual orientation and individual characteristics and found that race, ethnicity, and education appear to interplay with sexual orientation in important ways in determining migration outcomes. This chapter reveals the importance of sexual orientation in the migration decision.

Our empirical results, however, have enabled us to only begin to understand the ways that sexual orientation affects migration. Its effect on the migration decision of unpartnered gay men and lesbians should be examined, when and if an appropriate data-set is developed to permit such analyses. It is possible that unpartnered gay men and lesbians will have even greater odds of interstate migration than will heterosexuals, due to their desire to seek out gay populations for community and dating purposes. Finally, additional research examining the relationships among individual and contextual characteristics, as well as exploring the role of sexual orientation in international migration, is definitely needed.

PART II

SAME-SEX UNMARRIED PARTNERS AND THE FAMILY

CHAPTER 6

⚜

Characteristics of Same-Sex Families

Families play an important role in society and are one of the most active agents of socialization. It is in our families where we learn how to participate in society and where we spend most of our lives. Likewise, the family is where we generally have our strongest social and emotional attachments. However, like individuals, families are diverse, and their construction and organization reflect a great deal about the larger social frameworks in which they are nested. For example, urbanization, market economies, education structures, and the move toward individualism, have all had an effect on how families are defined and organized (Waite 2005). Additional factors including, but not limited to, governmental politics, legislation, and civil rights movements have a strong influence over who is allowed to marry, when individuals are likely to marry, and who is expected to make decisions in the family.

Just as with heterosexual families, same-sex families are arranged in a variety of shapes and sizes, and they are influenced by similar kinds of contextual factors, such as education and workplace expectations. However, same-sex families may face issues that are not always confronted by heterosexual families. For example, since in most jurisdictions same-sex couples cannot legally marry, they do not share many of the same legal rights and protections as married heterosexual couples, nor do their children (Demo et al. 2000; Cahill et al. 2002). Moreover, there are many state-level laws, policies, and practices concerning the regulation of adoption, foster care, and child custody and visitation issues which are biased in favor of heterosexual people, their relationships, and their families (Cahill et al. 2002).

In addition, same-sex relationships and families often face more social biases; they are frequently taken less seriously and are less accepted than heterosexual relationships and families. Same-sex partners may feel less free to show affection toward one another in public or to talk about their home-life while at work. Also, compared to heterosexual couples, they are less likely to be extended "couple" privileges with respect to invitations, occupational benefits, and so forth, or to be viewed as authentic couples (Baca Zinn and Eitzen 1999). Such factors may well have an influence on the organization of families and relationships.

The effects of these interactions between sexual orientation and the family lead to important questions for social scientists wishing to examine issues of same-sex families. (For example, many who object to the marriage of same-sex individuals argue that marriage is a necessary environment for the raising of children. Since homosexuals cannot procreate naturally, they should not be permitted to marry. Nonetheless, many same-sex partners are raising children despite these "biological" limitations. The presence of children in same-sex households then raises questions such as the following: Where do these children come from? Are these children from previous heterosexual relationships? Are same-sex partners adopting or employing other means to have children biologically?)

In this chapter we will not be able to answer all of these questions, but we do hope to begin to lay a foundation and present a more complete picture about same-sex families. Unlike other chapters in this book, in this chapter we go beyond looking only at same-sex unmarried partners and also include other members of the household. In addition, we give special attention to the children in same-sex households, including their relationship to the householder, and whether they are biological or adopted. We also consider the probability that a child is present in a same-sex unmarried partner household. Finally, we discuss some of the issues about same-sex families that cannot be directly apprised because of the limitations of the census data.

What Is a Same-Sex Family?

Past literature defines a family as individuals having either biological or marital associations that are culturally recognized (Waite 2005; Baca Zinn and Eitzen 1999). Families have also been described as being responsible for the bearing and the raising of children, for comprising the structure within which individuals reside, and for being the means by which property is shared and passed down (Waite 2005; Baca Zinn and Eitzen 1999). However, others have asserted that these sorts of definitions, often based on legal or structural terms, tend to be too narrow and leave out some of the increasingly common "alternative" family styles, including cohabiting couples living alone, "families of choice,"[1] and GLBT families[2] (Weston 1991; Cahill et al. 2002; Waite 2005).

Beginning in the 1970s, a shift occurred in the understanding of the definitions and roles of the family and, consequently, how scholars studied the family. This was due in part to secular changes such as increases in age at first marriage and in the percentage of single-headed households. Researchers thus began to focus more on variation in household form that resulted in part from these changes (Seidman 1993; Weston 1991). This new way of looking at the family has resulted in changing definitions of family and, thus, the greater visibility of gay male and lesbian families. In the book *Families We Choose,* anthropologist Kath Weston (1991) asserts that the major challenge for gay male and lesbian families is confronting the ideology of dominant American culture. Homosexuality tends for many to be associated with deviance, singleness, and unnaturalness, all of which directly counter the traditional image of the family which encompasses heterosexuality, morality, and nature (Weston 1991; see also Seidman 1993).

Thus, same-sex families do not fit many of the definitions of family in that relationships between two adults of the same sex are often not socially or legally recognized relationships. However, when families are defined in the broader sense, and by the more current definitions of family, gay male and lesbian relationships are, in fact, understood as families. This often involves emotional relationships, living together, the pooling of resources, the specialization of household duties, the coordination of various activities, and a connection to the greater society as a single entity (Weston 1991; Patterson 2000; Cahill et al. 2002). Moreover, same-sex couples frequently undertake many of the same behaviors as heterosexual couples to indicate their commitment and love, including the public announcement of their relationship to friends, family, and coworkers; being economically interdependent on one another; having legal documents which recognize their relationship; marrying within their church; exchanging rings as a symbol of commitment; and having and raising children with one another (Cahill et al. 2002).

Although definitions of the family increasingly incorporate the families of gay men and lesbians, Weston (1991) observes that the language of kinship has only recently been employed by and applied to gay men and lesbians. The relative newness of this trend may account at least in part for the lack of available data on gay male and lesbian families.

In this chapter, we define a same-sex family as a household headed by same-sex unmarried partners. A couple is considered to be a family irrespective of whether a child is present. This definition is a subset of gay male and lesbian families, as a whole, because most definitions of a family would also include gay male and lesbian single parents. Given the inability of census data to identify single gay men or lesbians, our definition of a same-sex family must be limited to households with unmarried partners.

Past Research on Same-Sex Families

Overall, little quantitative research has been conducted on same-sex couples and their families. Starbuck (2002) suggests that the primary reason is the relatively small population of gay, lesbian, bisexual, and transgender (GLBT) people.[3] It has been noted in this book and elsewhere, however, that the size of this population is not insignificant (see Chapter 1; see also Smith and Gates 2001).[4] Some have estimated that gay male and lesbian families in the United States account for as much as 5 percent of all families (Baca Zinn and Eitzen 1999). In a review of over 8,000 articles from leading sociology and psychology journals, Demo and Allen (1995) find that even when broadly defined, families of gay men and lesbians have been practically ignored by family researchers (Demo and Allen 1995).

Past studies in the family literature tend to concentrate primarily on individuals within same-sex families—their attributes, feelings, and actions. Research has also examined the social and emotional effects on children of growing up in GLBT families (Allen and Demo 1995; Stacey and Biblarz 2001). Although there are many reasons to study same-sex families and relationships, it could be argued that the literature has tended to focus in areas that have also been the center of the "family values" debate in mainstream America. Many of the research questions posed often endeavor to prove or disprove elements of this debate (such as examining the effects of these relationships on children), or to assess the manner in which same-sex families affect heterosexual society.

In addition, most of what is known about same-sex couples and families has come from a few large-scale family studies (e.g., Blumstein and Schwartz [1983] or the Lawrence Kurdek series [1987, 1992]), and various other small-scale studies, all of which used convenience samples consisting of respondents who were overwhelmingly white, middle-class, young adults with higher levels of education than the average public (Blumstein and Schwartz 1983; Kurdek 1987, 1992). Once again, this could be due to the social stigma attached to homosexuality and the lack of good representative data.

Nonetheless, it should be noted that findings and conclusions from prior research overwhelmingly indicate that gay male and lesbian parents are just as capable of raising children as are their heterosexual counterparts (Stacey and Biblarz 2001; Cianciotto and Cahill 2003). Likewise, most of the major child advocacy organizations[5] recognize "gay and lesbian parents as good parents, and assert that children can and do thrive in gay and lesbian families" (Cahill et al 2002: 69).

Same-Sex Parents and Their Children

As with the family literature, there have been very few demographic studies of same-sex families, and of the children of gay male and lesbian parents.[6] Once again, we believe this is largely due to the lack of quality data addressing this subject. Badgett (2001) notes that there are only a handful of good surveys with which to estimate the number of children with gay male and lesbian parents. However, since many of them are not based on representative samples, it is difficult to draw reliable conclusions. In a review of research drawing on the Voter Research and Surveys (VRS) and the Yankelovich Monitor, Badgett (2001) finds that the percentage of children in lesbian households is roughly equal to that in heterosexual women's households. However, gay male households are only about half as likely as heterosexual male households to have children.

The General Social Survey/National Health and Social Science Life Survey (GSS/NHSLS) and the 1990 Census suggest that there are slightly fewer children in same-sex households. According to work done by Black and his associates (2000), the GSS/NHSLS data indicate that 28 percent of lesbians and 14 percent of gay men have children in their households (Black et al. 2000). Data from the 1990 U.S. Census indicate lower percentages of children in same-sex, as compared to heterosexual, households. According to the 1990 Census, only 20 percent of female same-sex households and 5 percent of male same-sex households have children, compared to 57 percent of married households (Black et al. 2000; Badgett 2001). Badgett asserts that the sizable difference in the census data between homosexual and heterosexual families is most likely a reflection of the exclusion of single-parent households, or a bias in reporting patterns for same-sex households where couples with children may be less likely to disclose their relationship on the census questionnaire (Badgett 2001).

Recent work has estimated that there are between 2 and 8 million gay and lesbian parents in the United States (Cianciotto and Cahill 2003). With respect to the number of children with one or more gay, lesbian, or bisexual parents, a range of from 1 to 14 million has been estimated (Cianciotto and Cahill 2003). A poll conducted in 2000 by the Kaiser Family Foundation indicates that 8 percent of the 405 self-identified gay, lesbian, and bisexual respondents had children under 18 in their households (Cianciotto and Cahill 2003). The Black Pride Survey 2000 indicates that 21 percent of black gay, lesbian, bisexual, or transgendered participants reported being biological parents, while 2.2 percent reported being adoptive or foster parents (Cahill et al. 2002). Moreover, 12 percent reported currently living with children, while 25 percent had at least one child (Cahill et al. 2002).

Drawing on the 600,000 same-sex unmarried partners enumerated in the 2000 U.S. Census, Simmons and O'Connell (2003) find that 34 percent of the female same-sex unmarried partner households and 22 percent of the male same-sex unmarried partner households contained at least one child under 18. Cianciotto and Cahill (2003: 1) assert that for female same-sex unmarried partner households this rate "is not that much lower than the percentage of married opposite-sex households with children (46 percent) or the percentage of unmarried opposite-sex households with children (43 percent)." They observe, however, that male same-sex partner households "parent at about half the rate of married couples (22 percent vs. 46 percent)" (Cianciotto and Cahill 2003:1).

Another question we explore in this chapter is the effect of family laws and regulations on same-sex unmarried partner households. Specifically, how do state-level legislation and policies that prohibit or restrict adoption and/or foster care placement affect the presence of children in same-sex unmarried partnered households? While one might expect that more barriers to parenting or gaining access to children would reduce the probability of children in a given household, the actual effect of such laws and policies on same-sex unmarried partner households is unclear. Badgett (2001: 163) asserts that laws "determine who is considered a parent in allocating legal parental rights and obligations" and that "the legal institution of parenthood seems likely to influence lesbian, gay, and bisexual's people's decisions about becoming a parent." In addition, uncertainty about the legal system, including legal rights, definitions, and processes, may also reduce the willingness of same-sex partners to produce or raise children (Badgett 2001). Moreover, the adoption of restrictive parenting legislation by a state could be indicative of negative public sentiment toward homosexuality and issues of sexual minorities. This sentiment could well influence whether same-sex couples decide to have children, not to mention their accessibility to children and family services. Overall, we expect that antigay parenting legislation at the state level should have a negative effect on the presence of children in same-sex households.

Thus far, most demographic research analyzing same-sex families and their children has been limited to summations of various parenting rates. In addition, we are not aware of any previous, nationally representative quantitative studies that examine the effect of various individual and state characteristics on the probability of children being present in same-sex households. Instead, most nationally representative research that discusses same-sex partners and their children has been largely descriptive in approach (Smith and Gates 2001; Cahill et al. 2002; Simmons and O'Connell 2003).

Results

Demographics of Same-Sex Families

The data used in this chapter are from the five percent Public Use Microdata Sample of the 2000 U.S. Census. The sample is limited only to same-sex unmarried partnered households. The households are comprised of 64,728 same-sex unmarried partners (31,972 male and 32,756 female) and 30,973 other members in the household, including 21,111 individuals under the age of 18; we have identified 20,868 of these individuals as children (in the next section we discuss these issues in more detail).

The male and female same-sex partners in our sample are predominantly white, as one would expect. The male partners are, on average, 45 years old, and the female partners, 43 years old. Most of the gay male and lesbian couples have attended at least some college. On average the gay males have a household income of $79,000 and the lesbians, $67,000. Over 57 percent of the male unmarried partners, and 50 percent of the female unmarried partners, are categorized as "never married." With regard to children in the household, 85 percent of the male households, and 78 percent of the female households, report having no children.

Table 6.1 shows the relationship of all individuals in the household to the head of household. Excluding the unmarried partners, the next five largest

TABLE 6.1. Relationship to Head of Household of Same-Sex Households

Relationship to Head	All Ages		Under 18	
	Frequency	Percent	Frequency	Percent
Head/Householder	32,364	33.8%	33	0.2%
Child	20,167	21.1%	16,169	76.6%
Adopted Child	867	0.9%	723	3.4%
Stepchild	1,490	1.6%	1,200	5.7%
Child-in-law	291	0.3%	11	0.1%
Parent	675	0.7%	0	0.0%
Parent-in-law	216	0.2%	0	0.0%
Sibling	994	1.0%	137	0.6%
Sibling-in-law	244	0.3%	19	0.1%
Grandchild	1,436	1.5%	1,279	6.1%
Other Relative	255	0.3%	101	0.5%
Grandparent	31	0.0%	0	0.0%
Aunt or Uncle	69	0.1%	0	0.0%
Nephew or Niece	555	0.6%	358	1.7%
Cousin	187	0.2%	33	0.2%
Unmarried Partner	32,364	33.8%	111	0.5%
Housemate/Roommate	1,073	1.1%	27	0.1%
Roomers/Boarders/Lodgers	691	0.7%	72	0.3%
Foster Children	156	0.2%	156	0.7%
Other Nonrelatives	1,576	1.6%	682	3.2%
TOTAL	95,701	100.0%	21,111	100.0%

categories of people in the households are "children," 21 percent; "other non-relatives," 1.6 percent; "stepchildren," 1.6 percent; "grandchildren," 1.5 percent; and "housemates/roommates," just over 1 percent.

Demographic Characteristics of Children in Same-Sex Families

In the preceding section, we mentioned some of the descriptive characteristics of individuals residing in same-sex households. We now turn to a closer analysis of the children who are present in same-sex households. Specifically, we wish to determine whether these children are identified on the census questionnaire as being the biological or the adopted children of the same-sex partners, or if they are identified by some other relationship status. One challenge with analyzing these relationships using census data is that the census question about children is not phrased in a way that permits a distinction between biological or adopted children; further one cannot determine whether the children belong to another member in the household (Badgett 2001). These data limitations restrict somewhat our ability to analyze fully the relationships within the families of gay men and lesbians. Although we are unable to determine definitively to whom the children belong in the household, or whether they are biological or adopted, we are able to illustrate how children are identified *in relation to the head of household*. We are able to determine how many children have been categorized as being an adopted child or a natural-born child of the head of household, and we are able to assess some other relationships for individuals in the household who are under the age of 18.

As previously mentioned, there are 20,868 children in our sample. Although the 5 percent PUMS data include 21,111 individuals under the age of 18, we have opted to drop 243 individuals whose indicated relationships were inconsistent with that of a parent-child relationship. These individuals appeared to fall outside the "child" category, either because (1) they were living as adults, as indicated by their assignment to the "head/householder" or "unmarried partner" relationship categories, or (2) their relationship to the head of household was indicated as "housemates/roommates" or "roomers/boarders/lodgers," suggesting the lack of parental relationship. However, we opted to keep the "other nonrelatives" category due to its size and the ambiguity of the category in association with a parental relationship. For example, we believe this may be a logical choice for categorizing children who have been informally adopted by the head of household. This leaves us with a total of 20,868 children in same-sex households, with 8,381 in gay male partnered households and 12,487 in lesbian partnered households (see table 6.2).

The majority of the children in our sample are white. But the racial and ethnic breakdown of children is quite a bit more diverse when compared to the racial and ethnic breakdown of the same-sex unmarried partners in the sample. Also, the children are, on average, eight years old with an education level between the first and fourth grades.

As reflected in Table 6.2, "children," "adopted children," "stepchildren," "grandchildren," and "other nonrelatives" comprise the top five relationships for children to the head of same-sex households; these categories account for just over 96 percent of all the children in these households. Those children identified as the children of the heads of household likely include children who are the biological offspring of the heads. This category might also be used by gay men and lesbians who used artificial reproductive technologies, surrogacy, or both to have children. Thus, even if the head of household did not contribute biologically to the birth of the child, he or she still might consider the child to be his or her "natural child."

The "adopted child" category is likely used by an individual who has engaged in the formal legal adoption of the child of their partner. This child

TABLE 6.2. Relationship of Children to Head of Household of Same-Sex Households

Relationship to Head	Frequency in Gay Male Households	Frequency in Lesbian Households	Total	Percent of Children
Child	6,657	9,512	16,169	77.5%
Adopted Child	258	465	723	3.5%
Stepchild	472	728	1,200	5.8%
Child-in-law	6	5	11	0.1%
Sibling	68	69	137	0.7%
Sibling-in-law	11	8	19	0.1%
Grandchild	494	785	1,279	6.1%
Other Relative	36	65	101	0.5%
Nephew or Niece	149	209	358	1.7%
Cousin	17	16	33	0.2%
Foster Children	40	116	156	0.7%
Other Nonrelatives	173	509	682	3.3%
TOTAL	8,381	12,487	20,868	100.0%

could be the natural-born child from a previous heterosexual relationship, or could be a child resulting from artificial reproductive technologies (i.e., in the case of a female same-sex couple, one woman might bear the child and the other might formally adopt the child). The "stepchild" category is perhaps most often used by same-sex partners who have entered into some form of commitment ceremony, marriage, or domestic partner registration, and where there are children present from prior relationships.

Although we can more easily reason about the use of the relationship categories just discussed, the "other nonrelatives" category poses more of a challenge. We are unable to ascertain the actual relationship between children in the "other nonrelatives" category and the same-sex unmarried partners. One should note, however, that the "adopted child" category and the "other nonrelatives" category are fairly similar in frequency and are both substantial in size compared to the other categories. Perhaps the "other nonrelatives" category is a logical category for children who have been informally adopted by the head of household.

Factors Predicting the Presence of Children in the Household

Although there is a great deal of speculation regarding children's actual relationships to the same-sex partners, it is evident that children are certainly present in same-sex households. The census data allow us to examine how same-sex households with children differ demographically from those without children. In other words, what factors contribute to the presence of children in a same-sex household?

To answer this question we estimate a logistic regression to predict the probability of a child being present in a same-sex household. The results are shown in Table 6.3. Our dependent variable is a dichotomous variable indicating whether or not a child is present in the household. We use several independent variables, including race and ethnicity, sex, household income, age, and region of residence. Age and household income are treated as interval variables, while the race (white/nonwhite), ethnicity (non-Hispanic/Hispanic), sex (male/female), and region of residence (non-South/South) are measured as dummy variables. We also include a "previous heterosexual relationship" variable and an "antigay parenting" variable, both of which will be discussed in more detail below.[7]

As may be seen in table 6.3, we find that female same-sex partners are 1.4 times more likely to have a child in their household than are male same-sex partners. In other words, the odds of having a child present in the household are 40 percent higher for lesbians compared to gay men. Also, racial or ethnic

TABLE 6.3. Results of Logistic Regression Predicting the Odds of Children Being Present in Same-Sex Households

	Child Present in Household (odds ratio)	Percent Change in Odds Ratio
Female	1.40*	40%
Racial Minority	1.73*	73%
Hispanic Minority	1.57*	57%
Household Income	.95*	−5%
Age	.97*	−2.6%
South	1.03	2.9%
Previous Heterosexual Relationship*	2.74*	174%
Antigay Parenting Laws and Regulations†	.84*	−16%

*Coefficient is statistically significant at P<.05 (one-tailed).

†See text for discussion of different results for this variable in a multilevel model.

minorities are more likely to have children present in their households. The odds of having a child in the household are 73 percent higher for nonwhite individuals, compared to white individuals. Similarly, the odds of having a child in the household are 57 percent higher for Hispanics compared to non-Hispanics. With regard to household income, we find that partners in households where children are present earn about 5 percent less than those who live in households where there are no children present. However, whether or not individuals live in the South does not have a statistically significant effect on the presence of children in their household.

In addition to the effects of these social demographic factors in predicting the presence of children in the household, we also attempt to discern whether children in same-sex households are the biological children of one or both of the partners. More specifically, are the children a product of previous heterosexual relationships or the current relationship via reproductive alternatives? While we are unable to determine with complete certainty how children came to be in the household, we are able to speculate whether they are from a previous formal heterosexual relationship, that is, marriage.

Using data from the marital status question on the census, we created a dichotomous independent variable where persons identifying as "separated," "divorced," or "widowed" are categorized as "having a previous heterosexual relationship" and scored 1, and those identifying as "never married" or "not applicable" are categorized as "not having a previous heterosexual relationship" and coded zero.[8] More than half of the same-sex unmarried partners may be categorized as not having a previous heterosexual relationship.

We find that individuals who indicated a previous heterosexual relationship on the census are 2.7 times more likely to have a child in their household than those who marked the "never married" or "not applicable" category. This means that the odds of having a child present in the household are nearly three times greater for those who have had a heterosexual marital relationship in the past, compared to those who have not. While this result does not speak to how the children come to be in same-sex households, it does give support to the notion that children present in same-sex households are likely from previous heterosexual marriages.

We also examine the effect of state-level parenting laws on the presence of children in same-sex unmarried partner households. As mentioned before, we expect that laws and policies which prohibit adoption and foster-care placement based on sexual orientation will have a negative effect on the presence of children in same-sex households. Our "antigay parenting" variable indicates whether a same-sex household is in one of the three states in which there were antigay parenting laws or policies regarding adoption and foster-care placement before 2000, or whether it is in a state without such legislation. As of January 2000, only five states (Arkansas, Florida, Nebraska, New Hampshire, and

Oklahoma) had any sort of antigay parenting laws or policies (Lambda Legal 2006; NGLTF 2006; Soulforce 2006).

In the logistic regression, we find that state-level legislation has a statistically significant effect on the likelihood of the presence of children in same-sex households. Individuals living in states where there were antigay parenting laws prior to 2000 are less likely to have a child in their household than those living in states where there were no laws or regulations restricting adoption and foster-care placement. However, there are methodological issues concerning the appropriateness of including both individual-level and contextual (state-level) characteristics in a single logistic model where individuals are the units of analysis.[9] We thus estimated a second model, specifically, a statistically correct multilevel model. In this analysis, we find that the antigay parenting variable has no statistically significant effect on the presence of children in the household.[10] Contrary to our expectations, it appears that state-level laws do not have a statistically significant influence on the likelihood of gay men and lesbians having children in their homes.

Discussion and Conclusion

To date, the 2000 U.S. Census provides the largest nationally representative dataset available for analyzing the characteristics of same-sex households and families. The data are nonetheless still limited for the study of same-sex families. We are still unable to answer some of the most basic questions about these families. For example, we are unable to determine with certainty how children come to be in same-sex households and whether they are biologically related to one of the partners. There is no way to tell how many of the children are products of previous relationships (heterosexual or homosexual), their current relationship with the household head (whether through adoption, artificial insemination, surrogate birthing, and so forth), or whether they belong to another member of the household.

Likewise, we are unable to ascertain to which of the same-sex partners the children are related, when they do come from a previous relationship. In addition, there are many ways the heads of household can identify children who are not their children through biology or through formal adoption, via the "other nonrelative" and "other relative" categories. Furthermore, we have no way of knowing about children who exist outside of the household, although this is also true of heterosexual partners.

There are also numerous issues with regard to the marital status variable. The census uses a very formal, and narrow, definition of marriage that is based on the federal definition of marriage as being between a man and a woman. This means that the marital status categories are defined and the data are processed under a definition in which unmarried partners are not able to indicate "married" on the census questionnaire. While we know that just over half (52 percent) of same-sex partners were allocated by the census into the "Never married/Not Applicable" category, we do not know if this was because they indicated that they were "married" or because they did not respond to the question. This has the potential to greatly affect the "previous relationship" variable. On the one hand, if a large proportion of people allocated to the "never married/not applicable" category originally selected "married" on the marital status question, then our analysis would have failed to most appropriately categorize those who had been in a previous heterosexual relationship from those who had not. However, if individuals are selecting "married" to indicate that they are married to their same-sex partners, then the allocation procedure would work in a satisfactory way for our analysis.

Likewise, if a large proportion of people allocated to the "never married/ not applicable" category had originally not responded to the question, this too could affect the analysis. Perhaps same-sex partners fail to answer the question if they recognize the legal definition of "married" as being heterosexually married or if they see the question as being not politically inclusive with respect to their relationship or sexual orientation and thus skipped it. In either case, we are unable to differentiate all of those who have been in a previous heterosexual relationship from those who did not respond to the marital status question.

While we may not be able to identify all the partners who have had a previous heterosexual relationship, we are able to at least differentiate between those who have self-identified as having a had a previous relationship due to their election of "divorced," "separated," or "widowed," from those who have not or have not so indicated. Thus, in spite of the marital status allocation procedure, we are confident about our findings which suggest that children are more likely to be present with partners who have indicated previous heterosexual relationships.

With regard to the effect of state-level legislation on same-sex families, our multilevel analysis revealed that antigay parenting laws and regulations do not seem to result in a statistically significant decrease in the odds of gay men and lesbians having children in their households. Perhaps this occurs because of the high likelihood that children in these families are coming from previous heterosexual relationships. Or, perhaps the lack of statistical significance is a consequence of the lack of enforcement of the existing restrictive parenting laws. Furthermore, it is possible that other laws and forms of legislation have a stronger effect on same-sex families than the antigay parenting variable used here. While we employed a very broad variable that included legislation and policies related to adoption and foster-care placement, it is possible that surrogacy laws and regulations concerning child custody have a stronger effect on families since so few children in same-sex households are categorized as "adopted" children.

Overall, the findings presented in this chapter support the notion that there are children present in same-sex households and that they have diverse relationships with the same-sex unmarried partners. Most of these children are categorized as "children" of the head of household, which is logical given that "child" is the most generic term and also encompasses significant emotional and parental attachment. With regard to our analysis assessing factors predicting the presence of a child in the household, the results support the notion that it is easier for a gay man or lesbian to have a child when he or she has been in a prior relationship with a person of the opposite sex, compared to those who have not. External barriers and added financial resources may render it challenging for two individuals of the same sex to have children, absent a prior heterosexual relationship. However, we did not find a notable difference between households with children and those without regarding household income, indicating that financial differences might not play as notable a role as one would predict.

Furthermore, given that individuals who have previously had heterosexual relationships are overwhelmingly more likely to have children in their households, it would also follow that children in the households would be categorized as "children" on the census if they are the biological children from that relationship. This would, thus, further explain the clear popularity of "child" as the chosen relationship on the census for children in same-sex households (see Table 6.2).

For future study, we believe these findings indicate the importance of analyzing the effects of other forms of legislation on the presence of children in the home, such as child custody and surrogacy laws and practices; these types of laws would potentially have a stronger effect on the presence of biological children. In addition, we hope our analyses illustrate the need for better data on gay male and lesbian families as a whole, including single households, single-headed GLBT families, and GLBT children. Perhaps other datasets and data from qualitative studies may be employed to help supplement the current limitations of the census data and to aid in answering the many questions that still exist about the social demography of same-sex families.

CHAPTER 7

The Effects of Sexual Orientation on Dimensions of Family Attachment

In recent debates about the legality and morality of same-sex marriages, some have argued that permitting gay men and lesbians to enter into legally recognized marriages is unnecessary because marriage provides no real benefits that cannot be gleaned through contractual nonmarital agreements. Past research in family studies, however, has shown that the institution of marriage does indeed provide added securities that enhance relationship stability, commitment, and living standards (Waite and Gallagher 2000). Some scholars have questioned the stability of same-sex relationships, viewing them generally as less stable and less attached or involved than relationships where individuals are legally married (Starbuck 2002; Sarantakos 1996). In this chapter, we use data from the 2000 U.S. Census and examine the validity of these and related claims.

We first analyze the characteristics of four types of couples, namely, gay male unmarried partners, lesbian unmarried partners, heterosexual unmarried partners, that is, cohabiting partners, and heterosexual married partners. We examine the manner in which these four couple types vary across several social and economic indicators of relationship attachment. We particularly seek to determine whether the characteristics of persons in same-sex relationships are similar to those of cohabiting partners and to married partners and to assess the degree to which same-sex partnerships are comparable to heterosexual and unmarried partnerships.

Past Research on Same-Sex Relationships

Past family studies suggest that lesbians and gay men, like most heterosexuals, seek and desire secure, intimate relationships. Same-sex partners tend to look for the same relationship qualities as heterosexual men and women, such as spending time together, sharing intimate feelings, having equal power in their relationships, and being monogamous (Starbuck 2002; Kurdek 1992).

Most current research indicates that there is little difference between same-sex partners and heterosexual cohabiting couples when it comes to issues of stability, conflict, problem-solving, decision-making, interpersonal violence, and the division of household labor (Demo et al. 2000; Sarantakos 1996; Carrington 2000). Likewise, rates of relationship dissolution are about the same for gay men, lesbians, and cohabiting heterosexuals, all of which are higher than those for married heterosexuals (Starbuck 2002). These findings support the notion that same-sex households and families are similar to unmarried heterosexual households and families.

Also, some have argued that same-sex partners and their families may be more stable than has been suggested in the family literature (Gottman et al. 2002). The National Gay and Lesbian Task Force has asserted that not only do same-sex partners exist in large numbers, they are also "stable, productive households and have many of the same needs as do opposite sex couples" (Bradford et al. 2002: iv). There have been no clear explanations provided in the current literature that would account for the lower levels of stability of same-sex unmarried partners compared to married partners. For instance, dissimilarities in rates of stability between heterosexual married couples and same-sex couples cannot be definitively attributed directly to sexual orientation. Instead, additional factors, such as external stresses stemming from heterosexist norms, lack of social privileges, legal rights, and other issues may also be contributing to the observed instability.

Methodological issues in family research may also be contributing to the inflated instability measures for gay male and lesbian families. As mentioned in the previous chapter, most of what is known about same-sex couples and families has come from a few large-scale family studies (e.g., Blumstein and Schwartz [1983]; Kurdek [1987, 1992]), and various other small-scale studies, all of which used convenience samples comprised of mainly white, middle-class, young adult respondents with higher than average levels of education (Blumstein and Schwartz 1983; Kurdek 1987, 1992). This literature relies heavily, or in some cases solely, on data that are often well over 10 years old and are not nationally representative.

Also most past research has been based on the traditional marriage construct as the ideal. This may well affect the manner in which researchers have undertaken their analyses (Brines and Joyner 1999). Frequently, they have tended to view cohabitation as a form of "trial marriage" rather than as its own form of relationship, with unique attributes and characteristics (Brines and Joyner 1999). These views are likely to affect how surveys are developed and how behaviors are interpreted. For example, it is often assumed that married couples have a higher level of attachment to one another and to their relationship by the mere fact that they are married. In contrast, unmarried cohabiters are viewed as less attached and as less serious about their relationships compared to married couples. This has implications for same-sex couples who cannot legally marry and whose relationships often go unrecognized.

Benefits of Marriage

From a demographic point of view, there are many benefits that are unique to marital relationships. Married individuals are healthier, live longer, have more satisfying sexual relationships, and tend to have more assets and wealth than individuals who are not married (Waite 1995; Waite and Gallagher 1999; Blumstein and Schwartz 1983). Past studies that have focused on such economic issues as Social Security wealth, wealth from real and financial assets, and the value of primary residence have all found that married households are better off than other households (Waite 1995). Likewise, married couples tend to have higher household incomes than couples in other kinds of households (Waite 1995). Further, married individuals are more likely than cohabiting and single individuals to earn higher wages, controlling for other relevant characteristics (Waite 1995).[1]

So, how and why does marriage increase wealth and lead to other beneficial outcomes? One answer focuses on marital selectivity, in which it is argued that individuals who are healthier and have greater access to earnings and assets are more likely to get married, to be viewed as desirable in the marriage market, and to maintain a marriage (Waite 1995; Lillard and Waite 1995). But the marital selectivity argument leaves a great deal unexplained. Waite (1995: 498) asserts that "perhaps we have been too quick to assign all the responsibility to selectivity and not quick enough to consider the possibility that marriage *causes* some of the better outcomes." Rather, she believes that the institution of marriage indeed provides some portion of the benefits on at least four fronts.

First, marriage assumes a long-term contract. The notion of permanence allows partners to make choices that over time tend to bring greater benefits. Likewise the institution of marriage, itself, further supports couples in maintaining long-term commitments by providing them with social support and imposing both social and economic costs on those who end their contract (Waite 1995). Second, Waite states that marriage assumes the sharing of social and economic resources. This also serves as a form of insurance for married individuals because those who do not pool resources have to carry all the financial costs and assume the economic setbacks (Waite 1995). Third, "married individuals benefit—as do cohabiting couples—from economies of scale," meaning that two can live for the price of one or one-and-a-half (Waite 1995: 498). Last, marriage attaches individuals socially to other individuals, such as the spouse and the spouse's social network, as well as to other social institutions. Not only does marriage provide an individual with a source of pride, it also gives "life meaning beyond oneself" (Waite 1995: 498). For example, should a single person decide to quit a job without any other source of income, it is only one life that would be inconvenienced. However, if a person is married, then the person's life, the life of the spouse, and their life together may be inconvenienced by the lack of income. Further, marriage connects individuals to one another and to other social institutions, hence providing additional social, emotional, and financial support.

Cohabitation certainly has the potential to provide some of the above benefits. However, it does not provide all of them. Waite (1995) suggests that this occurs because cohabitation does not usually signify a lifetime commitment. As a result, individuals who cohabit are less likely than married individuals to pool financial resources and to invest with their partner. Furthermore, marriage represents a social attachment to a significant other, where social attachments are defined "as a sequence of increasing commitments in adult relationships," including emotional, social, and economic commitments (Ross 1995:131). According to this interpretation, married individuals are the ideal type and are attached to one another across these realms. Not only do they have a significant other with whom they live, they also are viewed as being further committed by the mere fact that they are married.

In examining the differences between marriage and cohabitation among heterosexuals, the ways the relationships are organized tend to vary. For example, marriage is often associated with a collective mentality and a specialization/division of labor, whereas cohabitation is more likely to be associated with individualism and an egalitarian approach to task assignment (Brines and Joyner 1999). These differences in organization tend to contribute to differences in levels of stability and living standards between the two couple-types. But it is unclear whether this is an outcome of the characteristics of the individuals in the relationship, the type of relationship itself, the lack of a formal commitment by the cohabiters, or a combination of these factors.

Without Officially Recognized Unions

So, what does this mean for gay male and lesbian couples who, by law, are not allowed to marry and, therefore, do not have access to marriage and to its benefits? It has been suggested that same-sex relationships are built on the same principles as heterosexual relationships (Gottman et al. 2002). Many same-sex couples thus try to replicate the social side of marriage. However, the status as a member of a permanent and sexually bounded couple is often absent, hidden, and/or ignored for same-sex couples, whereas with married heterosexual couples it is assumed (Waite and Gallagher 2000). Likewise, since same-sex couples are not allowed to marry, they have fewer barriers prohibiting them from exiting a relationship (Gottman et al. 2002).

The above observations have interesting implications for same-sex couples. On the one hand, it is a mistake to assume that same-sex couples may not be as emotionally and economically attached to their partners as married individuals simply because they are not married. On the other hand, without the legitimization that marriage provides to same-sex couples, they are less likely to reap the benefits of marriage and may in fact have less enduring and meaningful relationships.

In addition, it is unclear how other forms of legislation, such as nondiscrimination policies and civil unions, affect couples. Likewise, it is not clear whether it is possible to achieve that which marriage provides to individuals by other contractual or legal means. As already noted, some have argued that it is unnecessary to provide legally sanctioned marriages to gay men and lesbians because marriage provides no real benefits that cannot be gleaned through a simple contractual agreement (Badgett 2001). This notion goes against much of the family literature that states that marriage indeed provides unique features to couples, both privately and publicly (Waite and Gallagher 2000). Moreover, gay-friendly legislation is a sign of social support and an indicator of whether society regards same-sex relationships as authentic and significant. This, in turn, may also affect how same-sex couples regard and negotiate their relationships.

In this chapter, we use data from the 2000 U.S. Census and examine the validity of these and related claims. We examine the manner in which social and economic attachments vary by couple type. Particularly, we seek to determine whether the characteristics of same-sex relationships are similar to those of cohabiting partners and to married partners, and to assess the degree to which same-sex partnerships are comparable to heterosexual married and unmarried partnerships along four measures of attachment: household income, home ownership, presence of children, and employment.

In the sociology of family literature, such variables are often used as measures of relationship "commitment" (Waite 1995; Waite and Gallagher 1999; Blumstein and Schwartz 1983). For example, those who have had children together or own a home together are considered to be more likely to rate higher on stability and commitment indexes (meaning that they are likely to continue their relationship) than those who do not possess these traits. The idea is that these traits contribute to familial obligations or responsibilities and also create more barriers to exiting a relationship. However, since "commitment" often denotes an emotional tie between individuals, we refrain from using this term as our data do not permit us to make assumptions about the emotional ties among heterosexual couples, gay couples, or both within our sample. Consequently, we have chosen to use the phrase "measures of attachment," which, for the purposes of this chapter, is intended to suggest the degree of familial interdependence for couples as expressed via our four variables: household income, home ownership, presence of children, and employment. Sadly, we are unable to draw on other more intuitive variables due to the design and make up of the census data.

While there have been a few economic analyses of same-sex couples using 1990 census data (Klawitter and Flatt 1998; Allegretto and Artur 2001), no large-scale studies to our knowledge have compared various measures of family attachment across heterosexual married households, cohabiting households, gay male households, and lesbian households. Further, although the census data do not allow us to determine whether being legally married affects same-sex couples and their relationships, the data do allow us to examine the effects of current legislation on the social and economic characteristics of couples.

Results

Demographic Characteristics of the Couples

The data used in this analysis were collected in the 2000 U.S. Census and assembled in the 5 percent Public Use Microdata Sample (PUMS). The sample is limited to all married and unmarried households. Table 7.1 shows the general characteristics of the sample. There were 13,407 male same-sex households, 14,046 female same-sex households, 202,815 heterosexual unmarried households, and 2,284,782 heterosexual married households. The married households tend to be somewhat older with an average age of 44 for the partners, followed by lesbian households at 40, and gay male households and heterosexual unmarried households at 35.

TABLE 7.1. Descriptive Characteristics of the Sample, by Household Type

Demographic Characteristics	Gay Households	Lesbian Households	Heterosexual Unmarried	Heterosexual Married
Frequency	13,407	14,046	202,815	2,284,782
Average Age	35.3	40	35	44
% White	75.1	75.1	70.8	81.5
Education	Some College, No Degree	Associates Degree	Some College, No Degree	Some College, No Degree
Household Income	$84,578	$71,151	55,798	$77,669
% Home Owners	65.8	68.2	46	81.5
% w/Children	31.9	45.3	46.3	63
% Dual-Income Households	71.2	71.5	73.6	63.9

As reflected in Table 7.1, heterosexual unmarried partners are slightly more racially diverse than the other couple types. Married individuals are the most likely to be white out of all couple types, with heterosexual unmarried partners having the lowest percentage of whites, and same-sex unmarried partners falling roughly in between. The average level of education for all couple types is "some college," with the exception of lesbians; lesbian partners are slightly more educated than the other couple types, having an average level of education of an associate's degree.

Measures of Attachment

In order to ascertain whether same-sex partners are similar to, or different from, married heterosexual partners and unmarried heterosexual partners, we compare gay male and lesbian partners with the two groups of heterosexual partners along three primary dimensions of family: household assets and wealth, the presence of children, and employment; these are our "measures of attachment."

In our sample, gay male households have the highest household incomes, with an average of $84,578, followed by married households at $77,669, lesbian households at $71,151, and lastly unmarried partners at $55,798 (Table 7.1). On the surface, it appears that gay male and lesbian households do make more money, on average, than heterosexual unmarried partners. Turning to home ownership, one can see that married couples are the most likely to own their home, at over 81 percent; lesbians and gay men follow, at 68 percent and 66 percent, respectively; and heterosexual cohabiters are the least likely to own a home, with only 46 percent (Table 7.1). These descriptive results suggest, then, that lesbians and gay men fall between married and cohabiting heterosexuals on the home ownership measure. The regression analyses, however, enable us to move beyond simply comparing the averages on both the household income and home ownership variables.

Our analysis of the first dimension of household assets and wealth consists of estimating two regression analyses, one with the dependent variable of household income and the other where the dependent variable assesses whether or not one of the members of the couple owns the home. As previously mentioned, married individuals tend to have more income and more assets than other individuals. Further, they are more likely to pool resources and to make long-term, financial commitments, such as purchasing a home together (Waite 2000). Consequently, these variables provide some measure of attachment of the two individuals, as indicated by higher earnings and financial acquisitions.

Table 7.2 presents selected results from 16 different regression equations. Four different dependent variables are examined, namely, household income, home ownership, presence of children, and whether the household has two earners. Each of these four dependent variables is estimated in four different

regression equations pertaining to (1) gay male unmarried partnered households and heterosexual married households; (2) lesbian unmarried partnered
households and heterosexual married households; (3) gay male unmarried partnered households and heterosexual unmarried partnered households; and (4)
lesbian unmarried partnered households and heterosexual unmarried partnered
households. The unit of analysis in each of the sixteen equations is the household. Each of the four regression equations predicting each of the four dependent variables employs household type as the primary independent variable, as
follows: equation 1, whether the household is a gay male partnered household
(versus a heterosexual married household); equation 2, whether the household
is a lesbian partnered household (versus a heterosexual married household);
equation 3, whether the household is a gay male partnered household (versus a
heterosexual unmarried household); and equation 4, whether the household is
a lesbian partnered household (versus a heterosexual unmarried household).
Each equation also includes additional independent variables that control for
race, age, education, and region of residence. Only the coefficient for the "couple-type" variable is shown in Table 7.2, as this is our focus in this analysis.

The top row of Table 7.2 presents the slope coefficients for the "couple type"
dummy variable from the four OLS regression equations where household income is the dependent variable. In each case, the gay male or lesbian household

TABLE 7.2. Selected Results from 16 Regression Equations,[a] Predicting
Indicators of Attachment, by Couple Type

Dimension of Attachment	Gay Men vs. Married	Gay Men vs. Unmarried	Lesbian vs. Married	Lesbian vs. Unmarried
Household Assets & Wealth				
Household Income (OLS Regression)	.061*	.165*	−.102*	.006
Home Ownership (Logistic Regression)	.469*	1.479*	.555*	1.763*
Children Dimension				
Child Present (Logistic Regression)	.158*	.719*	.297*	1.480*
Employment Dimension				
Dual-income Households (Logistic Regression)	1.350*	.869*	1.296*	.821*

[a]All equations include control variables for race, age, education, and region of residence.

*Coefficient is statistically significant at P<.05 (one-tailed).

is coded 1, and the heterosexual married or unmarried household is coded 0. The four equations predict the natural log of household income for each of the four different populations, as mentioned in the preceding paragraph.

The coefficient of .061 reported in the first equation (first number, top row, table 7.2) is statistically significant and informs us that gay male households earn more income than married households. Since the dependent variable is the natural log of household income, we may convert the slope coefficient into a percent income score, using this formula, $(e^b - 1) \times 100$. We may interpret this coefficient as indicating that, on average, gay male households earn about 6.2 percent more income than married households, controlling for race, age, education, and region of residence. In the comparison of gay male households with heterosexual unmarried households, the coefficient is .165, indicating that gay households earn 17.9 percent more income, holding other things equal. In the equation comparing the lesbian households versus married households, the coefficient is $-.102$, which means that lesbian households earn 9.7 percent less than married heterosexual households. There is no difference in the amount of household income earned by lesbian households compared to unmarried heterosexual households; the coefficient of .006 is not statistically significant.

These results indicate that even after controlling for important household-level characteristics and region of residence, the households of gay male unmarried partners earn more than those of heterosexual married and unmarried partners.[2] But lesbian households earn less than married households. It appears that gender plays a role in the comparisons of same-sex unmarried partner households with married households; gay households earn more than married households, and lesbian households earn less compared to married households. Perhaps, this result may be attributed in part to the female wage penalty.[3]

In the next set of regression equation results on the second row of Table 7.2, we have changed the dependent variable to whether or not the couple owns their home. Logistic regression equations are estimated, and we report on the second row of Table 7.2 the odds ratios for the couple-type variable for each of the four logistic regression equations. For ease of interpretation, we convert these odds ratios into percent change in odds ratios, using this formula, (Odds ratio -1) $\times 100$. The results in Table 7.2 indicate that the odds of a gay male couple owning a home are .469 times those of a married couple, or we can say that gay unmarried partners are about 53 percent less likely to own their homes as married couples. However, in comparison to heterosexual unmarried partners, gay male couples are 1.48 times as likely to own their home, or 48 percent (i.e., $(1.479 - 1)$ $\times 100 = 48$) more likely, holding all else equal. With regard to lesbian couples, they are .56 times less likely to own their homes as are married couples and 1.76 times more likely to own compared to heterosexual unmarried partners. Overall, these results indicate that same-sex partners are less likely to own a home than married individuals, but more likely to own a home than heterosexual unmarried partners.

Regarding household wealth and assets, it appears that for the most part gay male and lesbian households fall between heterosexual married and heterosexual unmarried households. The one exception is that gay male households tend to earn more on average than married households. This "wage advantage," however, is likely attributable to the fact that the gender wage gap has a negative effect on heterosexual households, whereas gay male households have the benefit of two male wage earners. As we show in Chapter 8, when income is analyzed at the individual, rather than the household level, a different picture emerges in the comparison of the earnings of gay men with those of married men.

The next dimension of family addressed in the regression equations is the presence of children in the household. As already mentioned, the family literature often employs the presence of children in a household as an indicator of social attachment because children act as an additional barrier to the entering or exiting of a relationship. The data in Table 7.1 show the percentage of homes with children for each of the four types of households. Gay male and lesbian households have the lowest percentages of children present; only 32 percent of gay male households and 45 percent of lesbian households have children present. Approximately 46 percent of cohabiting heterosexuals have children present, which is very similar to that of lesbian households. Heterosexual married households have the highest percentage, at 63 percent.

In the third row of data in Table 7.2, we appraise the effect of couple-type on the presence of children in the household; the dependent variable in this set of four equations is whether or not children are present in the household, scored 1 if yes. We find that the odds of gay men having children in their households are .16 those of heterosexual married persons; in other words, the odds of gay male partners having children in their households are 84 percent less than those of heterosexual married partners. However, comparing gay male partners with heterosexual unmarried partners, the odds ratio of the effect of couple type on the presence of children in the household increases to .72, indicating that the odds of gay male partners having children in their households are 28 percent less than those of heterosexual unmarried partners. When we compare lesbian households with married households, we find that the odds of lesbian households having children are 70 percent less than those of heterosexual married households, but 48 percent greater than those of heterosexual unmarried households.

These findings show that the odds of gay male partners having children are less than those of both married and unmarried heterosexual partners. Lesbian partners, on the other hand, have greater odds of having children in the household than unmarried heterosexual partners, but lower odds than those of married heterosexual partners.

We turn finally to an examination of the effect of couple-type on employment, specifically, whether both partners in the household are gainfully employed. The literature indicates that unmarried heterosexual partners are more likely to have both partners working full-time and, therefore, less likely to specialize in a household division of labor, such as the breadwinner/homemaker stratagem (Waite and Gallagher 2000; Brines and Joyner 1999). Married households, on the other hand, are found to be more likely to organize their relationship around household areas of specialization, with one partner less likely to be employed (Waite and Gallagher 2000).

Our descriptive data (Table 7.1) do indeed show that married heterosexual households have the lowest percentage of dual-income households, with less than two-thirds of them having two wage earners. In contrast, over 70 percent of the other three couple types, namely, gay male households, lesbian households, and heterosexual unmarried households, have both partners employed. The data in Table 7.2, fourth row, allow us to appraise this relationship within a multivariate context.

We estimated four logistic regressions, appraising the effect of couple-type on the log odds of the household having both partners gainfully employed. As with the other regression equations, we also controlled here for race, education, and region of residence. The odds ratios reported in Table 7.2 indicate that the odds of gay male households, as well as lesbian households, having dual earners are 35 percent, and 30 percent, respectively, greater than those of heterosexual married households. In contrast, the odds of gay male and lesbian households having dual earners are 13 percent and 18 percent, respectively, less than those of heterosexual unmarried households. Thus, both gay male and lesbian households are less likely than heterosexual unmarried households to have both partners employed, but are more likely than heterosexual married households to be so classified.

Our regression results suggest that same-sex unmarried partners are themselves more diverse than previously reflected by the literature; in some cases they are more like heterosexual unmarried partners, and in other cases more like married partners. This is not unexpected, and in fact is why we have argued throughout this book about the importance of including both married persons and heterosexual unmarried persons as groups to compare with same-sex unmarried partners. Also, it is unclear how much of this effect may be attributed to issues of discrimination or to the lack of certain privileges or advantages, legal and otherwise, that accompany marriage; these are benefits and privileges that same-sex partners cannot, at this time, legally achieve.

Discussion and Conclusion

It has been estimated that gay male and lesbian families "make up at least 5 percent of families in the United States" (Baca Zinn and Eitzen 1999). However, in demographic literature based on 2000 census data and the current debates on homosexuality, there has been relatively little attention given to same-sex couples and their families beyond that of descriptive statistics and their residential locations or concentrations (Bradford et al. 2002). This chapter examined whether same-sex households are demographically more like married households or heterosexual unmarried households by comparing couple types across measures of social attachment. Findings indicate that, on the whole, same-sex households fall between the two types of heterosexual couples on the majority of our measures, rendering them not entirely comparable to either heterosexual couple type. For instance, it appears that same-sex couples have greater financial attachment and dependence on one another than do heterosexual unmarried partners, although these appear to be less than those of married households. On average, they appear to be better-off financially than unmarried heterosexual households.

In addition to the individual-level factors considered in this chapter, one might also expect contextual factors to affect the social and economic attachment levels of same-sex and heterosexual couples. In other work, we used multilevel modeling[4] to assess the influence of several state-level factors on the measures of attachment examined in this chapter (i.e., household assets and wealth, children, and employment). Specifically, we explored whether couple-types differed on the measures of attachment depending on whether they resided in a state that was a red (Republican) state or a blue (Democratic) state in the 2000 presidential election, a state that had a Defense of Marriage Act in 2000, and a state had a law prohibiting discrimination based on sexual orientation in 2000. We found that the three state-level variables did not have consistent or noteworthy effects on the relationship between couple-type and our measures. We suspect that due to the high levels of aggregation of the data, the state-level effects are not as revealing as they might be at lower levels of aggregation, say, among counties or cities or neighborhoods. Future studies need to introduce these kinds of contextual effects at lower levels of aggregation for a more revealing picture of the effects of politics or legislation. Likewise, we suspect that much of the legislation may still be too recent or has not yet been fully implemented consistently to be able to reveal significant effects.

In considering the findings presented in this chapter, it is important to note that the census data provide only a rough indication of social and economic attachments and that methodological issues and the survey design of the census may complicate attempts to compare these couple types. In a study on the current editing process of the U.S. Census, Fields and Clark (1999) found that same-sex couples who self-identified as married in the census were different from those that self-identified as unmarried partners on numerous characteristics. Respondents who identified as married were more likely to be older (above 40), white, have children as coresidents in the household, and to have indicated that they lived in the same house five years ago, while those who identified as unmarried were more likely to have had some college and to have both partners currently employed (Fields and Clark 1999). This suggests that editing procedures may be combining heterogeneous groups of same-sex couples.

It is possible, then, that the single same-sex unmarried census category that captures both types of same-sex relationships, committed and cohabiting, contributes in part to our findings that same-sex partners fall between married heterosexual partners and unmarried heterosexual partners on many measures of attachment. If this is the case, same-sex couples who identify themselves as "married" might be very similar to heterosexual married couples, whereas those who identify themselves as cohabiting might have characteristics more similar to heterosexual unmarried partners. Thus, the differences we observed between the couple-types could be attributable, in whole or in part, to this methodological problem, rather than to a true difference in couple characteristics based on sexual orientation.

Despite these methodological limitations, we believe that this analysis sheds light on the relationships of same-sex unmarried partners. As previously mentioned, prior studies have suggested that gay male and lesbian partners have relationship qualities that are more like those of cohabiting heterosexuals. Our findings do not support this assertion. Rather, individuals who identify as same-sex unmarried partners on the census have qualities, as measured by our measures of attachment, which fall between those of married and cohabiting heterosexuals. These findings suggest, at the very least, that gay male and lesbian partners do not organize their relationships in an identical fashion to those of heterosexual unmarried partners. Our results indicate that same-sex couples exhibit a greater degree of financial attachment to one another than do unmarried heterosexual couples and, for lesbian couples, they equal unmarried heterosexual couples when it comes to having children in the household. Future research assessing other dimensions of the family are needed to further understand these differences among couple types.

PART III

SAME-SEX UNMARRIED PARTNERS IN THE LABOR MARKET

CHAPTER 8

The Economic Cost of Homosexuality

Is there an economic "cost" associated with one's sexual orientation? Specifically, do gay men and lesbians earn more or less than heterosexuals? This question has generated substantial popular debate and a modest academic literature. Gay men and lesbians are not generally portrayed as a "disadvantaged class," economically speaking. Much of the popular and political discourse is based on stereotypes or convenience studies (Badgett 2001; Black et al. 2000). Some of these images depict gay men and lesbians as professionals who earn more money than the average individual. Indeed some policy makers take this view to defend both their stance against a federal law prohibiting sexual orientation discrimination in employment, and to support their position against gay marriage. However, most empirical studies and analyses show that gay males, at the very least, earn significantly less than heterosexual males (Black et al. 2003; Berg and Lien 2002; Allegretto and Arthur 2001; Klawitter et al. 1998; Badgett 1995). Because of the attention this question has received both in academic and political circles, as well as conflicting results reported in some of the quantitative studies, additional research is needed to tease out the relationship between sexual orientation and income.

This chapter explores the results of past studies and then builds and extends on them using data from the 2000 U.S. Census. Some of the earlier studies dealing with sexual orientation and earnings have used 1990 U.S. Census data, but none to our knowledge have used 2000 data. This is important for a number of reasons. First, the Census Bureau used a different method for handling inconsistent responses on the marriage and sex questions in 2000 than was employed in 1990, as discussed in Chapter 1. Suffice it to say that the 2000 data provide a larger sample and a more accurate count of same-sex unmarried partners than do the 1990 data (U.S. Census Bureau 2001). In addition, using the 2000 data provides new insight into the debate over income inequality since yet another decade has passed, during which time significant strides have been made implementing state-level legislation intended to ban employment discrimination.

In our analysis of the 2000 data, we uncover results that stand in contrast to findings in many of the previous studies about the relationships between sexual orientation and income. In particular, our results show that gay males have a wage *advantage* over heterosexual cohabiting males; this is the first study in which an income advantage has been shown for gay men. Further, our findings emphasize that the cost of being a gay man differs greatly from that of being a lesbian, a finding that emphasizes the interactions between gender and sexual orientation that produce income differentials. Finally, our results have important implications concerning not only the cost of being a gay man or lesbian, but also the cost of being unmarried, underscoring the important interplay between these characteristics and income.

Exploring the "Cost of Being Homosexual"

In the debate about "the cost of being homosexual," some have advocated that gay men and lesbians have a wage advantage over heterosexuals, and others that they have a disadvantage. Both groups of researchers have drawn on data gathered in surveys of convenience, such as those obtained from readers of magazines and newspapers (for a discussion, see Badgett 2001; and Black et al. 2000). Due to the biases inherent in such data, no definitive conclusions can be reached concerning the true economic consequences of homosexuality.

Beginning in the mid-1990s, social scientists, led primarily by economists, began to draw on data from nationally representative samples to quantify the income differences between homosexual and heterosexual individuals. They relied principally on two data sources: the General Social Survey (GSS) and the U.S. Census.[1] We first present some brief background about these two data sources, including their strengths and weaknesses, along with a discussion of the major studies of income differences and sexual orientation using these data.

Income Studies Using General Social Survey Data

The General Social Survey (GSS) is a representative sample of the United States population, and presumably, a representative sample of the homosexual population. Consequently, it is has been frequently employed in studies of income and sexual orientation (Table 8.1). As we discussed in the Introduction to this book, the definition and specification of one's sexual orientation is one of the more problematic aspects of research attempting to study any differences based on this characteristic. When using data from the GSS, however, this decision is partially remedied by the fact that the GSS does not ask respondents about sexual desire or to self-identify their sexual orientation. Rather, they are only asked about sexual activity. The researcher must decide on the *amount* of same-sex sexual activity that renders an individual gay or lesbian.

TABLE 8.1. Summary of Results of Prior Research Regarding the Economic Cost of Being Homosexual

Data Source and Study	Gay Men Compared to Heterosexual Men	Lesbians Compared to Heterosexual Women
General Social Survey Data		
Badgett (1995)	−24%	Negative, not statistically significant
Berg and Lien (2002)	−22%	+30%
Black et al. (2003)	−14%	+20%
1990 Census Data		
Klawitter and Flatt (1998)	−26% compared to married	0% compared to married (when full time)
Klawitter (1998)		0% (when full time and children)
Allegretto and Arthur (2001)	−15.6% compared to married; −2.4% compared to unmarried	

Using GSS data in economic analyses, however, may be problematic because it could be more important to capture individuals who *self-identify* as gay men and lesbians, rather than to classify individuals based on same-sex sexual behavior. Those who self-identify should be more likely to disclose their sexual orientation in the workplace and, in turn, may be more likely to be subject to discrimination (Badgett 2001).[2]

In addition to this definitional challenge, even if one employs the broadest definition of homosexuality and pools years of GSS data, the sample will still be fairly small, particularly if the researcher wishes to control for occupational and other differences. Further, respondents' residences in the GSS are identified only by region, so state or local variables, such as the presence of antidiscrimination laws, cannot be incorporated into the analyses.

Despite these weaknesses, a number of researchers have employed GSS data to examine income differences based on sexual orientation, and have obtained varying results; we summarize the results of this prior research in Table 8.1.

Badgett (1995) used GSS data to conduct what we believe to be the first published study of sexual orientation and wage discrimination using nationally representative data. She combined GSS data from 1989 to 1991 and categorized an individual as behaviorally gay, lesbian, or bisexual if the person had at least one same-sex partner since the age of 18. Using Ordinary Least Squares regression, Badgett found that, when controls were introduced, being behaviorally lesbian/bisexual for women had no statistically significant effect on income.[3] For men, the income penalty for being gay/bisexual was found to be as much as 24.4 percent, depending on the definition of homosexuality employed.[4]

Badgett hypothesized that the effect of sexual orientation on income differed for men and women for three primary reasons. First, behavior might not be as good a proxy for homosexual identity for lesbians, and identification might incur a greater penalty than behavior since those who identify as gay men or lesbians might be more likely to disclose their identity in the workplace. Second, gay men might face greater discrimination than lesbians because of an association with HIV and AIDS. Finally, lesbians might be more occupationally segregated than gay men and, therefore, the penalty for being a homosexual individual might take a different form.

Two additional studies have used GSS data to examine the effect of sexual orientation on income, attempting to improve on Badgett's (1995) research both methodologically and theoretically. Berg and Lien (2002) pooled the GSS data for 1991 to 1996, the six years after Badgett's study, and used a more stringent definition of homosexuality and a different measure of income. They reported that gay men earned 22 percent less than heterosexual men, and lesbians earned 30 percent more than heterosexual women. They theorized that different preferences concerning leisure activities and income could well explain why gay men earned less and lesbians earned more than their heterosexual counterparts. If lesbians were more hesitant than heterosexual females to interrupt their careers to raise children, then their earnings should be higher than those of heterosexuals. The authors noted, however, that correlations of parenthood and homosexuality suggest that lesbians are not necessarily less likely to be parents than heterosexuals.

Berg and Lien suggested, then, that employers may use homosexuality as a proxy for information about future career trajectories, and might interpret homosexuality differently according to gender. Lesbians might be perceived as being more similar to heterosexual men by employers, and perhaps viewed as less likely to take leaves of absence than heterosexual women; as a result, they would earn more than heterosexual women. Homosexuality, however, may not imbue gay men with the same "beneficial" workplace stereotypes. Finally, Berg and Lien suggested that gay men may simply face more discrimination in the workplace than lesbians.

Black and his colleagues (2003) pooled GSS data from 1989 to 1996 to replicate and extend Badgett's work, with some modifications, including applying a more stringent definition of homosexuality and using income categories rather than median values. They found that depending on the definition of homosexuality used, gay male/bisexual behavior *reduced* earnings by 14–16 percent, whereas lesbian/bisexual behavior *raised* them by about 20–24 percent.

Researchers using GSS data have produced consistent findings indicating that being a behaviorally gay man results in being paid less than being a heterosexual man. However, the results have been less consistent when it comes to income differences between lesbians and heterosexual women. These inconsistencies may be due to problems with how to define homosexual status, as well as other methodological and theoretical concerns tied to the GSS. Some researchers have thus turned to U.S. Census data to examine the effect of sexual orientation on income. These studies, however, have produced yet another set of mixed results.

Income Studies Using U.S. Census Data

Compared to GSS data, U.S. Census data have a number of attractive qualities for studies of sexual orientation and income, including the size of the sample and the self-identification of individuals as being in same-sex unmarried partnerships with another person. As previously noted, however, these data are limited compared to GSS data in at least one aspect: only individuals who choose to identify as unmarried partners are captured, and unpartnered gay men and lesbians are unaccounted for.

At least four studies have been conducted using 1990 Census data to examine the effect of sexual orientation on income (Table 8.1). Klawitter and Flatt (1998) used 1990 data to examine not only whether sexual orientation affected income, but also whether state laws prohibiting discrimination on the basis of sexual orientation had an effect on income. Using multivariate regression analyses of income for both individuals and households, they found no evidence that public or private employment protections significantly improved earnings or household income for same-sex male or female couples. They determined, however, that couple type significantly affected earnings and income levels, with male same-sex couples earning approximately 26 percent less than married men. In addition, income for female same-sex couples was actually higher than that of married women by about 18 percent, but the difference disappeared when the sample was limited to women who worked full-time, year round.[5]

Klawitter (1998) conducted another analysis using 1990 Census data that focused on the income differences between lesbians and heterosexual women. She found that the average earnings for partnered lesbians were higher due to differences in individual characteristics, as well as unexplained effects she attributed to discrimination. In particular, she found that higher levels of human capital and living in urban locations provided the largest boosts to the incomes of same-sex coupled women.[6] Finally, when Klawitter added controls for the presence of children under 6 and ages 6 to 17, almost all of the earnings gap between same-sex and different-sex couples was attributed to individual characteristics rather than to unexplained effects. Thus, Klawitter found that the appearance of higher earnings of lesbians compared to heterosexual women may be attributed to differences in individual characteristics pertaining to human capital and the presence of children, rather than to discrimination in favor of lesbians.

While Klawitter focused on income differences between women, Allegretto and Arthur (2001) used 1990 census data to explore income differences between gay men and heterosexual men. They found that being a gay man resulted in a 15.6 percent decrease in wages compared to being a married heterosexual man, but only a 2.4 percent decrease in wages compared to being a heterosexual unmarried cohabiter. When controls for human capital, race/ethnicity, and location were added, they found that gay men earned less than heterosexual married men in the same occupations.

Clain and Leppell (2001) also used 1990 census data[7] to examine the effect of sexual orientation on income. They included interactions of a sexual orientation dummy variable with many independent variables, arguing that the effects of sexual orientation on earnings could be more complex than originally reported by Badgett. They showed that men living with partners of the same sex earned about 22 percent less than men not living with any partner at all; in other words, a man living with another man experienced about a 22 percent wage penalty compared to a man living without a partner. Further, they found that men living with male partners earned 1 percent less than comparable men living with female partners, if they were college-educated, working in blue-collar jobs, and living in the Midwest. They found, on the other hand, that women living with partners of the same sex earned significantly more than women not living with partners. This is particularly true if they were living in the Midwest or if they had minor children. Thus, by incorporating interaction terms, Clain and Leppell showed a slightly different picture of income differences between same-sex and different-sex couples than those revealed in other studies using 1990 Census data.

Just as with studies using GSS data, therefore, studies using 1990 Census data have produced varying results with respect to the existence and the extent of wage differences between homosexual and heterosexual individuals. Although all find a wage penalty for gay men, the extent of this penalty varies, particularly depending on whether the comparison is made with partnered heterosexual men as a whole, married men, or heterosexual cohabiting men. For lesbians, the picture continues to be a confusing one, with some findings indicating that there is no statistically significant difference in earnings between lesbians and heterosexual women when controls are included for the presence of children and part-time work. The differences in outcomes among studies using both GSS data and 1990 census data can be attributed in large part to conflicting perspectives on the best manner in which to construct a model of income differences. How should sexual orientation be measured? Which control variables should be included? What statistical method should be employed to measure these income differences?

In this chapter, we use data from the 2000 Census and attempt to unite the methodologies and findings from past studies, and to tease out and perhaps resolve some of the conflicts in the literature about the effect of sexual orientation on income.

Method

This is an analysis of differences in income derived from wages. Our data from the 2000 5 percent Census Bureau Public Use Microdata Sample file thus exclude individuals who did not report being in the labor force. Further, we exclude all individuals whose reported earnings were less than $1000, and we include a control for the number of weeks worked in the previous year. In addition, we only compare partnered individuals due to the absence of information in the census data on unpartnered gay men or lesbians. Consequently, our sample includes only individuals who indicated that they are part of an unmarried partnership (both same-sex and different-sex) or who are married.

The dependent variable is the natural log of income derived from wages; we hence interpret our results in terms of percent differences in income.[8] The independent variables measure human capital characteristics that have been shown to affect individual earnings, as well as demographic and social characteristics which also might have an impact. We are primarily concerned with examining the effect of sexual orientation on income. This variable is measured as a dummy variable, coded 1 if an individual self-identifies as being in a same-sex unmarried partner relationship, and 0 if in a different-sex partnership (either an unmarried partnership or marriage). Based on the results from prior research, we predict that being a partnered gay male will result in a wage penalty, whereas being a partnered lesbian is likely to result in no statistically significant advantage once we introduce individual-level controls.

We also include several variables measuring human capital characteristics. Studies examining the factors that attribute to income differences often include such human capital characteristics as level of education, occupation, and experience (Badgett 2001; Allegretto and Arthur 2001; Clain and Leppell 2001; Klawitter and Flatt 1998). These variables provide important information about potential productivity, skills, or experience, which are likely to be economically rewarded by employers (Badgett 2001); consequently, controlling for these characteristics accounts for differences in income which can be easily explained by legitimate competing economic resources. In these analyses, we have included a measure of the level of education, coded 1 if the individual has earned a college degree or higher.[9] We have measured potential experience by the respondent's age in years.[10] Finally, we included a variable measuring the occupational income score of the respondent's occupation. Some earlier studies have included a categorical measure of occupation, such as whether the respondent worked in professional, clerical, or labor occupations (Berg and Lien

2002; Allegretto and Arthur 2001; Clain and Leppell 2001; Badgett 1995). We opted to provide more occupational detail by including an occupational income score as a measure of occupational differences. This variable assigns to persons in each occupation a score based on median earnings within that occupation and thus represents the material rewards accruing to persons in different occupations. By including this variable, we are able to control for occupational differences which are likely to result in earnings differences; as an individual's occupational income score increases, his or her income should also increase due to income expectations associated with that occupation.

In addition to individual-level variables capturing human capital characteristics, we have also included measures of several important social and demographic variables known to affect earnings. First, we included a dummy variable indicating whether the individual is of a race other than white, as nonwhite individuals are likely to experience a wage penalty (Durden and Gaynor 1998; Siegel 1965). In addition, we included a dummy variable indicating whether an individual is Hispanic, due to the wage penalty commonly associated with Hispanic ethnicity (Durden and Gaynor 1998; Poston et al. 1976). This penalty is often thought to accrue from language barriers; hence we also included a variable measuring ability to speak fluent English.

Other studies examining the earnings of women in particular have found that they are adversely affected by both the presence of children in the household, as well as by engaging in part-time work (Badgett 2001; Durden and Gaynor 1998; Klawitter 1998). Consequently, we included a dummy variable indicating whether children were present in the household, as well as a variable measuring the number of hours worked in a given week. Finally, we included a variable measuring whether the individual resides in a metropolitan or nonmetropolitan area because residing in a nonmetropolitan area usually results in lower wages.

We then used Ordinary Least Squares (OLS) regression to estimate the effects of these variables on earnings. We conducted four separate analyses: in the first two we compared the earnings of partnered gay men with married men, and the earnings of partnered gay men with cohabiting heterosexual men; in the next two we compared the earnings of partnered lesbians with married women, and then with female heterosexual cohabiters.

Results

Table 8.2 shows the results of the four OLS regressions. In all the equations, we controlled for the 11 independent variables just described. We only present in the table the results indicating the effect of sexual orientation on earnings, since this is the variable with which we are most concerned; the other independent variables serve as controls.

TABLE 8.2. Results from Four OLS Regression Analyses: Percent Difference in Earnings Between Same-Sex Partners and Heterosexual Partners*

Comparison Group	Percent Difference in Earnings
Partnered Gay Men vs. Heterosexual Married Men	−9.0%[†]
Partnered Gay Men vs. Heterosexual Unmarried Partners	+2.6%[†]
Partnered Lesbians vs. Married Women	+6.0%[†]
Partnered Lesbians vs. Heterosexual Unmarried Partners	+12%[†]

*Although unreported, all four analyses include the 11 independent variables indicated in the text.
[†]Coefficients are statistically significant when p ≤ .05.

In our first analysis, we compare the earnings of partnered gay men to married men. We find that, all else being equal, gay men earn approximately nine percent less than married men. This finding of a wage penalty of gay men compared to married men is consistent with findings from earlier studies, although the penalty is notably smaller than in any of the studies using 1990 Census data, where the wage gap was approximately 15 percent or greater (see Table 8.1).

When comparing gay men with cohabiting heterosexual men, however, a new finding emerges. All else being equal, gay men are shown to earn approximately 2.6 percent more than cohabiting heterosexual men. This is the first time that a *wage advantage* has been shown for gay men, indicating a departure from earlier findings. Thus, it appears that partnered gay men earn less than married heterosexual men, but slightly more than cohabiting heterosexual men.

Turning to the results for women, one sees quite a different picture of the relationship between sexual orientation and income. Compared to married women, lesbians earn approximately 6 percent more, all else being equal. Similarly, lesbians earn approximately 12 percent more than cohabiting heterosexual women. Partnered lesbians, therefore, appear to have a sizable wage advantage over partnered heterosexual women, especially over cohabiting women. The finding of a wage advantage for lesbians is consistent with earlier GSS-based research (see Table 8.1), but inconsistent with earlier census-based research. Our findings, therefore, stand in contrast to earlier research using 1990 census data to examine income differences.

Discussion and Implications

Perhaps due to our use of 2000 U.S. Census data, we have shown two substantive findings that stand in contrast to earlier research. First, our findings indicate that a wage penalty exists for gay men when compared to married men, but a *wage advantage* when gay men are compared to cohabiting heterosexual men. This is the first time that a wage advantage has been shown for gay men over any heterosexual group. Although prior studies have found a much greater wage gap between married men and gay men than between gay men and heterosexual cohabiting men, all have revealed a wage penalty for gay men in relation to all heterosexual males. Our finding of a wage advantage of 2.6 percent thus indicates an important shift since 1990 in the relationship between income and homosexuality.

This difference could be attributed to a number of factors. Changing attitudes toward homosexuality during the 1990s could have resulted in a decrease in discrimination based on sexual orientation. Although research using both 1990 and 2000 census data has not found the presence of a state-level antidiscrimination law to result in a statistically significant effect on income (Klawitter and Flatt 1998), it is nonetheless important to note that the majority of these laws were passed during the 1990s. The mere passing of these laws could be viewed as some evidence of changing attitudes toward homosexuality in employment situations, perhaps accounting in part for some of the shift from a wage penalty to a wage advantage.

Regardless of the explanation, this finding is significant in that it highlights the fact that the wage penalty experienced by gay men seems to be more attributable to their status as unmarried individuals than to their sexual orientation. It is only when compared to married men that gay men experience a wage penalty, raising questions concerning the appropriate method to address wage differentials. Perhaps the failure of antidiscrimination laws to have a statistically significant effect on income (Klawitter and Flatt 1998) can be attributed to the fact that these laws, while providing a remedy for individuals who experience direct discrimination,[11] do not address the heart of the cause of wage inequality between heterosexuals and homosexuals: the ability to marry. Although cohabiting heterosexuals are also faced with the marriage penalty that results from their unmarried status, they ultimately have the option of entering into a legal union and gaining the benefits associated therewith. If same-sex couples would incur these same benefits from a legal union, then perhaps it is through the recognition of such unions, rather than through antidiscrimination laws, that income differences can be reduced.

In addition to the new picture painted of wage differences for gay men, our analysis also reveals a large and statistically significant wage advantage for lesbians that persists even when controls were added for part-time work and the presence of children in the household. This stands in contrast with earlier findings using 1990 census data, which showed that lesbians' wage advantages compared to heterosexual women disappeared when controls were added for full-time work and the presence of children (Klawitter 1998; Klawitter et al. 1998). Our findings are more consistent with studies using GSS data that found fairly large wage advantages even when controls were introduced for the presence of children (Black et al. 2003). The disparity between our results and those of Klawitter and colleagues (1998) could be attributable to differences in the 2000 data classification system compared to 1990; the 2000 data are likely more accurate.

Once again, therefore, it appears that lesbians have an income advantage over heterosexual women that persists even after controlling for individual characteristics. As previously noted, Badgett (2001, 1995) and Berg and Lien (2002) have offered a number of suggestions for lesbians' wage advantage. Perhaps the most likely prospect is that homosexuality, for women, may have beneficial connotations in the realm of employment. As we have controlled for any wage effects due to the presence of children or to part-time work, lesbians' wage advantage cannot be attributable to these factors. It is possible, however, that employers may *perceive* that lesbians have greater labor force attachment than heterosexual women and reward them accordingly. Further, lesbians may be more readily accepted into male-dominated professions as "one of the guys," permitting them to excel in areas in which heterosexual women are barred. Indeed, studies have shown that heterosexual men are often more hostile toward gay men than toward lesbians, indicating perhaps more of an acceptance of female than male homosexuality (Kite and Whitley 1996; Herek 1991).

An additional explanation for the contrasting findings of gay men and lesbians could be connected with the limitations of using a cross-sectional data set. Lesbians might earn more than heterosexual women because they are less likely to enter and exit the labor force for child-care purposes. Although we have controlled for the presence of children in the household, the data do not permit us to assess whether the woman leaves the workforce to care for the child. In female same-sex partnerships, economic constraints might not permit one of the partners to remain at home to care for a child; heterosexual females, on the other hand, are usually better able to stay at home with a child due to the support they receive from the (often) higher earnings of the male partner. If this is the case, heterosexual women might experience an earnings loss over time due to repeated entry and exit from the labor force, which could account for the lesbian "wage advantage." Collecting new data on child-care patterns of same-sex couples would help shed light on the plausibility of this explanation for the lesbian wage advantage.

Conclusion

From the findings presented in this chapter, it would appear that a major shift occurred during the 1990s, one that has resulted in wage gains for both gay men and lesbians over heterosexuals. It is important to bear in mind, however, that statistical techniques such as regression analysis are limited in what they are able to reveal about the presence of discrimination. Regression analysis rests on an assumption that the unexplained difference in earnings between homosexual and heterosexual individuals is perhaps the result of discrimination, in favor of one group or the other. The difference can, however, also be due to other factors that have been omitted from the model as control variables, but which nonetheless exert an influence on determining one's income. In the model used in this chapter, we incorporated eleven individual characteristics that have been shown through prior research to play an important role in predicting income; we also estimated models with additional independent variables to ensure that we selected the best model. We feel confident both that our model presents a sound estimate of income differences based on sexual orientation, and that the model documents a real shift in income differences compared to studies using 1990 data.

This study, as well as most of the earlier studies, does not incorporate independent variables controlling for the influence of contextual characteristics on an individual's income, however. For example, residence in a state with a higher gross state product might result in a higher income. If gay men and lesbians disproportionately reside in states with higher incomes, then failure to control for this factor may well tend to skew the regression results. In separate work not reported here, we conducted a multilevel analysis that included controls for both the individual independent variables discussed in this chapter, as well as controls for state-level characteristics.[12] We find that when these state-level characteristics are included along with the individual-level characteristics, the wage advantage for gay men over cohabiting heterosexual men *disappears*.

When contextual characteristics are taken into account, gay men experience a wage penalty, rather than a wage advantage, compared to cohabiting heterosexual men. This finding emphasizes the importance of considering contextual characteristics when studying income differences. Relying solely on the OLS results, one can certainly argue that income differences between homosexual and heterosexual individuals appear to have decreased since 1990. One would not want to argue, however, that gay men now have a wage advantage over cohabiting heterosexual men because the inclusion of contextual characteristics demonstrates otherwise.

Finally, the results discussed in this chapter have important implications concerning the role of marriage on the earnings patterns of same-sex partners. Gay men have a wage penalty compared to married men, but a wage advantage compared to cohabiting heterosexual men. Conversely, lesbians have a greater wage advantage when compared to cohabiting heterosexual women than to married women. Past research has demonstrated that marriage results in a wage benefit for men, but not for women (Waite and Gallagher 2000). Thus, at first it is not surprising that being unmarried results in a greater wage penalty for gay men, but not for lesbians. Some studies, however, have suggested that some of the income benefits derived from marriage for men can be attributable to men changing workplace behaviors in response to assumed marital responsibilities, as well as to receiving a benefit from a woman's care of the home and children (Waite and Gallagher 200). Thus, traditional gender roles support some of men's marital income benefits. Whether these benefits would play out in the same manner for same-sex couples is uncertain.

Other studies have suggested that employers tend to discriminate in favor of married men, believing married men to be more dedicated workers and more deserving of pay raises (Waite and Gallagher 2000). If employer discrimination plays a role in the marriage premium, then gay men will experience a wage penalty regardless of whether their own marital relationships adhere to traditional gender roles. Given the fact that we have shown that married men have an almost 9 percent income advantage over gay men, the denial of legally recognized marriage to same-sex partners takes on important economic consequences. Understanding the causes and implications of this marriage premium could perhaps shed light on the intersections of economics, gender, and the importance of legally recognized unions. In the previous section of this book, we examined more closely some of the issues surrounding marriage and family, including the manner in which family size, economic investments, and union status vary based on sexual orientation.

CHAPTER 9

≈

Sexual Orientation and Occupational Segregation

In 1964, the U.S. government enacted Title VII of the Civil Rights Act, prohibiting employment discrimination on the basis of race, color, religion, sex, or national origin. Subsequently, women and racial/ethnic minorities have drawn on this legislation in making inroads toward reducing employment discrimination. Although many of the elite professions remain dominated by white males, Title VII has permitted women and minorities to gain some access to these professions and to other professional occupations. The relative success of Title VII has led some lawmakers to seek similar protection for other disadvantaged groups. Indeed, some of the presidential candidates in the 2004 campaign argued that a federal law should be enacted to prohibit employment discrimination based on sexual orientation.

When such legislation is posed, policy makers might consider turning to social scientists for evidence that gay men and lesbians need employment protection. In particular, they might wish to know whether gay men and lesbians earn less than similarly situated heterosexuals (an issue explored in Chapter 8), and whether they are segregated, perhaps unwillingly, into different occupations than heterosexuals. This chapter takes a first step toward addressing this second question by examining the distribution of homosexual and heterosexual individuals in the professional occupations.

Prior studies have examined income differentials based on sexual orientation, but none to our knowledge have explored their differential distribution in particular occupations. Analyses based on income differences can show whether gay men and lesbians are paid an equivalent salary to heterosexuals within the same occupation, but they do not reveal whether they are segregated from heterosexuals in particular occupations. In this chapter, we focus on professional occupations because these are generally the most coveted, characterized by status, honor, autonomy, high education, and specialized training (Sokoloff 1992). The exclusion or inclusion of gay men and lesbians in professional occupations could demonstrate that they are underrepresented in the professions, suggesting the need for discussion about whether a federal antidiscrimination law based on sexual orientation is needed.[1]

The Effect of Sexual Orientation on Employment

Sexual Orientation, Income, and Occupation

Until recently, studies exploring the influence of sexual orientation on work suffered from the lack of representative data. As a result, there have been few quantitative studies examining the impact of sexual orientation on income or occupational segregation that were generalizable. As noted in Chapter 8, the few representative studies that have been conducted have relied on data from the General Social Survey, the National Health and Social Life Survey, and the unmarried partner questions in the 1990 and 2000 census questionnaires. These studies have focused on the relationship between sexual orientation and income and have demonstrated a wage penalty for gay men and an income advantage for lesbians (Badgett 1995; Black et al. 2003; Klawitter and Flatt 1998; Klawitter 1998; Allegretto and Arthur 2001; Clain and Leppell 2001; Berg and Lien 2002). Income differences between homosexual and heterosexual individuals could be due to discrimination (both against gay men, and perhaps in favor of lesbians), but could also be due at least in part to differences in occupation. If gay men, for instance, tend to work in occupations that pay less than those of heterosexual men, their income disparities could be based on these occupation differences.

Homosexual and heterosexual individuals could be segregated into different occupations for several reasons. Human capital theory suggests that entry into a particular occupation requires certain levels of education and skills (Reskin and Padavic 1994). Gay men and lesbians might, then, be segregated into particular occupations if they possess, or lack, these skills. Socialization theory, in contrast, contends that socialization creates a preference for different kinds of work and only teaches different groups the skills needed for those supposedly "typical" jobs (Reskin and Padavic 1994). Gay men and lesbians could be socialized to believe certain careers are more appropriate for their sexual orientation and might, consequently, develop only the skills to pursue those occupations. The end result would be that homosexual individuals are concentrated in different occupations than heterosexual ones.

Fear of discrimination could also lead gay men and lesbians to work in particular occupations. Escoffier (1975) suggests that homosexual individuals might be more willing to choose an occupation with lower pay if it permitted the person to disclose his or her sexual orientation with few repercussions. Similarly, gay men and lesbians might be more likely to be hired into the more tolerant and, often, lower-paying occupations (Badgett 1995). In this way, discrimination in some occupations would act to limit available choices (Elliot 1993). For instance, studies have shown that many are unaccepting of gay men and lesbians working as teachers, especially in elementary schools (Elliot 1993; Fassinger 1993; Klawitter and Flatt 1998). The bias against hiring homosexual individuals to teach children is so strong that the states of Minnesota and Connecticut prohibit employment discrimination based on sexual orientation in all areas *other than those that involve work with minor children* (Klawitter and Flatt 1998). In contrast, college and university environments seem to be more accepting of homosexuality (Fassinger 1993). These different levels of tolerance could well encourage gay men and lesbians to teach at universities, rather than in primary or secondary schools.

Similarly, gay men and lesbians have been limited in their ability to pursue occupations in various branches of government. Legal decisions in the 1960s, 1970s, and 1980s excluded gay men and lesbians from government positions requiring a high security clearance, citing as a justification the alleged fact that they are susceptible to blackmail with the threat of revealing their sexual orientation (*McKeand v. Laird* 1973; *Adams v. Laird* 1969; *Padula v. Webster* 1987). The ban on homosexual individuals in the military also serves as a deterrent to many gay men and lesbians when selecting an occupation. Some occupations, therefore, are more accepting of homosexuality than others. Opportunities and choices hence play a significant role in the segregation of the workforce. Gay men and lesbians may not freely choose stereotypical or lower-paying occupations, but might settle for positions where they believe they will be accepted.

Due to the impacts of these forces on occupational choice, some research has sought to assess the effects of occupational differences on income disparities. Using GSS data, Badgett (1995) controlled for the managerial, professional/ technical, clerical/sales, and craft/operative occupations and found that occupational differences accounted for some of the income difference between lesbians and heterosexual women. She found that lesbians are less likely to work in managerial or clerical/sales positions, more likely to work in craft/operative and service positions, and about equally as likely as heterosexual women to work in professional/technical occupations (Badgett 1995; Badgett and King 1997). Significantly, half of the lesbians and bisexual women in her sample fell into the craft/ operative and service occupations, which are the lowest-paying occupations. Klawitter (1998), however, used 1990 census data and found that gay men and lesbians were more likely to be in the highest-paid occupations, such as managerial and professional positions, and less likely to be in technical/sales or operator/ fabricator positions.

Research has found that occupational differences based on sexual orientation tend to vary by sex. Badgett (1995) noted that including a control for occupation increased the negative effect of homosexuality on income by as much as 37 percent for men. In addition, gay male respondents were less likely to be in managerial or blue-collar occupations, and more likely to be in professional/technical and service occupations. She concluded that her "results suggest that gay/bisexual men are in higher-paying occupations but earn less than heterosexual men within these categories," but indicated that "occupational sorting might be observed at a finer level of detail" (1995: 736). Black and his colleagues (1997), in contrast, concluded that much of the observable pay difference between gay men and heterosexual men is attributable to the occupational choices of the gay men.

These studies indicate that occupational segregation is an important factor in determining the income and status of gay men and lesbians in the workforce. This chapter extends the above research and analyzes occupational segregation at a "finer level," by examining the role that sexual orientation plays in distributing individuals in the professions.

Sexual Orientation Discrimination in Employment

During the days leading up to the 2004 presidential election, candidates John Kerry and Howard Dean promoted federal legislation prohibiting employment discrimination based on sexual orientation. Their discussions were bolstered by judicial decisions seen as victories for gay men and lesbians, including the Supreme Court's decision striking down Texas's law against same-sex sodomy, and the Massachusetts Supreme Court's ruling giving same-sex couples marriage rights equal to those of opposite-sex couples (*Lawrence et al. v. Texas* 2003; *Goodridge et al. v. Department of Public Health* 2003). These legal victories suggested that perhaps the time is nearing for the enactment of a federal law prohibiting discrimination based on sexual orientation.

This chapter describes the extent to which occupational segregation of homosexual from heterosexual individuals exists in the professions. It does not focus specifically on the causes. It is well known that occupational segregation occurs either by choice or exclusion. Thus the demonstration that segregation exists is not direct evidence of employment discrimination. Nonetheless, findings of occupational segregation are a first step toward understanding whether there is discrimination based on sexual orientation and, if so, whether legislation might be needed to address existing discrimination.

Examining Occupational Segregation

Selecting the Sample

This chapter uses data from the 2000 Census 5 percent Public Use Microdata Sample file, specifically the data described and used in some of the previous chapters on same-sex partners and heterosexual partners. As discussed in Chapter 1, one of the possible problems with these data is that individuals identifying as unmarried partners on the census could possess different characteristics from those who do not so identify. This could be problematic in the analyses we undertake in this chapter if individuals in certain occupations are more likely to identify as unmarried partners than those in other occupations. Our results could thus be biased to reflect an overrepresentation of gay men and lesbians in some occupations, and an underrepresentation in others. We noted in Chapter 1, however, the strong evidence that the individual characteristics of same-sex unmarried partners are similar to those captured by other data sources, suggesting little bias in the use of census data.

Due to the focus here on the workforce, we restrict the sample to individuals between the ages of 18 and 65 who reported that they were in the labor force. We compare the occupations of "homosexual individuals," that is, those who identified as same-sex unmarried partners, to "heterosexual individuals," that is, those who identified either as married or as heterosexual cohabiters. We selected only those individuals who were employed in one of the 33 largest professions (see Table 9.1) so as to keep the study to a manageable size and to avoid problems that might result were we to select smaller professions (a possible problem owing to our use of a 5 percent sample of the census records).

TABLE 9.1. The 33 Largest Professional Occupations and Their Corresponding Nam-Powers Occupational Scores, U.S., 2000

Profession	Nam-Powers Scores
Male Professions	
Elite	
Physicians & Surgeons	100
Lawyers	99
Nonelite	
Computer Software Engineers	94
Civil Engineers	94
Electrical & Electronics Engineers	94
Chief Executives	93
Mechanical Engineers	93
Personal Financial Advisers	92
Architects	92
Misc. Engineers, Including Agricultural & Biomedical	91
Computer Programmers	90
Industrial Engineers	90
Computer Scientists & Systems Analysts	89
Network Systems & Data Communication Analysts	84
Clergy	75
Musicians & Singers	51

(*continued*)

TABLE 9.1. (*continued*)

Profession	Nam-Powers Scores
Gender-Neutral Professions	
Pharmacists	97
Psychologists	93
Secondary School Teachers	86
Postsecondary Teachers	86
Accountants & Auditors	85
Editors	79
Human Resources Specialists	77
Writers & Authors	76
Counselors	75
Designers	67
Artists	56
Female Professions	
Registered Nurses	83
Elementary & Middle School Teachers	83
Librarians	82
Special Education Teachers	80
Social Workers	77
Preschool & Kindergarten Teachers	45

Construction of the Indexes

Two indexes[2] were constructed to compare the occupations of homosexual and heterosexual individuals. The first is an index of representation[3] and measures the proportion of same-sex partners in the profession relative to the proportion of same-sex partners in the labor force overall; an analogous index was constructed for heterosexuals. It was also calculated for each profession by sex. We thus have six indices for each profession (same-sex partners as a whole; gay men; lesbians; heterosexuals as a whole; male heterosexuals; and female heterosexuals). Results are presented in terms of the actual percentage that homosexual/heterosexual individuals are over- or underrepresented in the profession compared to the expected percentage based on their population in the labor force.

The second is an index of relative advantage and compares how over- or underrepresented same-sex partners are *in relation to partnered heterosexuals*, controlling for the differences of each group in the labor force overall.[4] The index was also calculated by sex, resulting in three indexes for each profession:

same-sex partners/partnered heterosexuals; gay men/heterosexual males; and lesbians/heterosexual females. We present our results in percentages; they reflect the degree to which same-sex partners are over- or underrepresented in a profession compared to partnered heterosexuals.

We also categorize each profession according to its gender composition and prestige[5] as follows: elite male professions, nonelite male professions, gender-neutral professions, and female professions (Sokoloff 1992, see Table 9.1). The two indexes were then calculated for each of the four occupational categories. These data allow us to determine whether same-sex partners are concentrated in the more prestigious, powerful, and highly paid male professions, or in the lower-status, less prestigious, lower-paying female professions.

Findings

Same-Sex Partners in the Professions: An Overview

Some have argued that gay men and lesbians are primarily found in the more privileged occupations (Badgett 2001; Black et al. 2000), although quantitative data have not previously been used to support such an assertion. Our examination of the presence of same-sex partners in the 33 largest professions appears to support this argument: they are represented to their advantage in the more desirable professions.

Table 9.2 shows that same-sex partners are slightly overrepresented in the 33 largest professions; there are 9 percent more same-sex partners in the professions than one would expect based on their proportion in the labor force. Both partnered gay men and lesbians are overrepresented, with 14 percent more lesbians and 4 percent more gay men in the professions than one would expect. This overrepresentation of homosexual individuals in the largest professions is not surprising, however, given the results of prior studies indicating that homosexual individuals tend to have relatively high levels of education (Blumstein and Schwartz 1983; Laumann et al. 1994; Klawitter and Flatt 1997).

Partnered heterosexuals, in contrast, are as represented in the professions as their proportion in the labor force, that is, they are neither over- nor underrepresented (see Table 9.2). When they are examined by gender, however, we see that heterosexual women are actually overrepresented by 21 percent, an amount close to, although exceeding, the overrepresentation of lesbians. On the other hand, *heterosexual men* are underrepresented; there are 17 percent fewer heterosexual men in the professions than one would expect based on their proportion in the labor force. This underrepresentation of heterosexual males and overrepresentation of heterosexual females, however, could be attributed to the professions selected (the largest professions are female-dominated, including elementary and middle school teachers and registered nurses).

TABLE 9.2. Indexes of Representation for Homosexual and Heterosexual Individuals and Indexes of Relative Advantage for Homosexual Individuals Compared to Heterosexuals in the 33 Largest Professions Considered as an Aggregate, U.S. 2000

Index of Representation for Same-Sex Partners	Index of Representation for Gay Men	Index of Representation for Lesbians	Index of Representation for All Heterosexuals	Index of Representation for Male Heterosexuals	Index of Index of Representation for Female Heterosexuals	Index of Relative Advantage for Same-Sex Partners	Relative Advantage for Gay Men	Index of Relative Advantage for Lesbians
+9%	+4%	+14%	±0%	−17%	+21%	+10%	+26%	−6%

Given these results, it is no surprise that when gay men and lesbians are compared with heterosexuals, gay men are overrepresented and lesbians are underrepresented (Table 9.2). Same-sex partners are 10 percent more likely to be in the professions compared to heterosexuals. The difference is small for women, with lesbians having a disadvantage of only 6 percent compared to heterosexual females. For men, however, the difference is substantial; gay men are 26 percent more likely to be in the largest professions than are heterosexual men.

These findings suggest a strong advantage for gay men in the largest professions. The data in Tables 9.3 and 9.4, however, show that while same-ex partners are overrepresented in the professions overall, they are not distributed in them in the same way as heterosexuals. As shown in Table 9.3, same-sex partners as a whole are only overrepresented in elite male and gender neutral professions, and are underrepresented in the nonelite male and female professional categories.

The differences are more striking when examined by sex. Gay men are overrepresented in both types of male professions; they are overrepresented by 42 percent in the elite male professions, and there are 14 percent more gay men in the nonelite male professions than one would expect. On the other hand, in the gender-neutral professions gay men are overrepresented by 29 percent and are underrepresented by 35 percent in the female professions. Overall, then, gay men are most overrepresented in the elite male professions, and most underrepresented in the female professions.

Lesbians, like gay men, are overrepresented in three of the professional categories. Notably, lesbians are overrepresented in the elite male professions by 15 percent, but are underrepresented in the nonelite male professions by 27 percent. Gender-neutral professions also contain an overrepresentation of lesbians; 42 percent more lesbians are in these professions than expected based on their proportion in the labor force. In the female professions, lesbians are also overrepresented by 22 percent. Lesbians, therefore, are most overrepresented in gender-neutral professions, and most underrepresented in the nonelite male professions.

In contrast, Table 9.3 shows that partnered heterosexuals fall into the occupational categories more as expected. Heterosexual males are overrepresented in the elite male and nonelite male occupations, by 35 percent and 45 percent, respectively. They are underrepresented in both the gender-neutral and the female occupations by 22 percent and 75 percent, respectively. Heterosexual men are most overrepresented, then, in the nonelite male occupations, and most underrepresented in the female occupations.

Heterosexual females, on the other hand, are overrepresented in the gender-neutral and female professions, and underrepresented in both male professions. They are most overrepresented in the female professions, where there are 93 percent more heterosexual women than one would expect. In the gender-neutral professions, they are overrepresented by 27 percent. In contrast, in the elite male and nonelite male professions, heterosexual women are underrepresented by

TABLE 9.3. Indexes of Representation for Homosexual and Heterosexual Individuals in Occupational Groups Categorized by Status and Sex, U.S., 2000

Occupational Category	Index for All Same-Sex Partners	Index for Gay Men	Index for Lesbians	Index for All Heterosexuals	Index for Male Heterosexuals	Index for Female Heterosexuals
Elite Male	+28%	+42%	+15%	±0%	+35%	−45%
Nonelite Male	−7%	+14%	−27%	±0%	+45%	−56%
Gender-Neutral	+36%	+29%	+42%	±0%	−22%	+27%
Female	−6%	−35%	+22%	±0%	−75%	+93%

TABLE 9.4. Indexes of Relative Advantage for Homosexual Individuals Compared to Heterosexuals in Occupational Groups Categorized by Status and Sex, U.S., 2000

Occupational Category	Index for All Same-Sex Partners	Index for Gay Men	Index for Lesbians
Elite Male	+29%	+5%	+109%
Nonelite Male	−7%	−21%	+67%
Gender-Neutral	+36%	+67%	+12%
Female	−6%	+158%	−37%

45 percent and 56 percent, respectively. Heterosexual women are thus most overrepresented in female professions, and most underrepresented in nonelite male professions.

Although the gender differences between same-sex partners and heterosexual partners are striking, the index of relative advantage provides even greater insight about how sexual orientation affects occupational segregation by gender. Table 9.4 shows that gay males, compared to heterosexual males, are overrepresented in all the occupational groups other than the nonelite male category, most notably in the female professions where they are 158 percent more likely to be found than heterosexual males. Similarly, lesbians are overrepresented in elite and nonelite male professions and gender-neutral professions compared to heterosexual females; in particular, they are 109 percent more likely to be in the elite male professions than heterosexual females. Notably, lesbians are *underrepresented* in female professions compared to heterosexual females; they are 37 percent less likely to work in the female professions than heterosexual females. Thus, homosexual individuals appear to be more likely to cross gender lines in the professions than heterosexual individuals: gay males work in female professions at a far greater rate than heterosexual males, and lesbians in male professions more so than heterosexual females.

Same-Sex Partners in Specific Professions

Our results so far show that same-sex partners are more likely than partnered heterosexuals to cross gender lines in the professions. Of the 33 largest professions, however, which are most likely to attract same-sex partners? Compared to heterosexuals, in which of the professions are gay men and lesbians most over- and underrepresented?[6]

The data in Table 9.5 show the professions in which same-sex partners are over- and underrepresented. Overall, they are underrepresented in 14 of the professions and overrepresented in 19. Generally, they are overrepresented in those professions concerned with physical and psychological difference and disability (e.g., psychologists, counselors, physicians, or special education teachers), those connected with the computer industry (e.g., computer programmers, network architects), those that could be seen as focusing on effecting change (e.g., lawyers and social workers), and those connected with creative expression (e.g., designers, artists, or architects). Same-sex partners are generally underrepresented in the engineering professions and teaching professions, excluding postsecondary teachers. At first glance, these data suggest that the underrepresentation of same-sex partners as teachers of young children may be a result of the societal disapproval shown in public opinion polls about homosexual individuals working with young children. We discuss this possibility in greater detail below in the conclusion.

Once again, exploring the role that gender plays in the occupations of same-sex partners is instructive. Gay men are underrepresented in 15 of the professions and overrepresented in 18. They are most overrepresented as architects, designers, musicians, writers and authors, artists, editors, and in occupations in the computer industry. Generally, these fall primarily into the artistic and design categories. In contrast, gay men are most underrepresented in the engineering professions and in the teaching professions (other than postsecondary teaching), as well as among clergy and registered nurses. Like same-sex partners as a whole, both the teaching and engineering occupations have a significant shortage of gay men. Further, although we noted earlier that gay men are more likely than heterosexual men to work in the female professions, our data dealing with individual occupations demonstrate once more that they are still significantly underrepresented in these professions.

Partnered lesbians are underrepresented in 14 professions, overrepresented in 17, and at parity in 2 (physicians and personal financial advisers). They are most overrepresented as psychologists, counselors, social workers, writers, editors, and secondary education teachers. They are also overrepresented in the four female professions of librarians, special education teachers, social workers, and registered nurses. Although these occupations differ thematically from those of gay men, concentrating more on the counseling than on the artistic, those in which they are underrepresented are more similar. They are most underrepresented in the engineering professions and as preschool and elementary school teachers. Unlike gay men, however, they are also significantly underrepresented in computer-related occupations. Further, lesbians are notably underrepresented as chief executives, that is, as owners or primary operators of businesses.

TABLE 9.5. Indexes of Representation for Homosexual Individuals in the 33 Largest Professional Occupations, U.S., 2000

Occupation	Index for All Same-Sex Partners	Index for Gay Men	Index for Lesbians
Chief Executives	−25%	−8%	−41%
Human Resources Specialists	+29%	+26%	+32%
Accountants & Auditors	−12%	−10%	−14%
Personal Financial Advisers	−8%	−16%	−1%
Computer Scientists & Systems Analyst	+34%	+51%	+18%
Computer Programmers	+18%	+48%	−11%
Computer Software Engineers	+12%	+40%	−15%
Network Systems & Data Communication Analysts	+66%	+91%	+42%
Architects	+88%	+196%	−15%
Civil Engineers	−34%	−27%	−41%
Electrical & Electronics Engineers	−52%	−42%	−62%
Industrial Engineers	−28%	−23%	−33%
Mechanical Engineers	−58%	−48%	−67%
Misc. Engineers, Including Agricultural & Biomedical	−45%	−37%	−52%
Psychologists	+226%	+81%	+364%
Counselors	+66%	+9%	+121%
Social Workers	+107%	+27%	+182%
Clergy	−48%	−37%	−58%
Lawyers	+31%	+31%	+30%
Postsecondary Teachers	+54%	+22%	+85%
Preschool & Kindergarten Teachers	−40%	−63%	−18%
Elementary & Middle School Teachers	−25%	−44%	−7%
Secondary School Teachers	−15%	−35%	+5%
Special Education Teachers	+13%	−30%	+54%
Librarians	+48%	+29%	+67%
Artists	+85%	+110%	+61%
Designers	+94%	+168%	+23%
Musicians & Singers	+81%	+161%	+4%
Editors	+97%	+92%	+102%
Writers & Authors	+126%	+120%	+131%
Pharmacists	−28%	−9%	−47%
Physicians & Surgeons	+26%	+54%	−1%
Registered Nurses	−4%	−36%	+27%

Same-Sex Partners and Partnered Heterosexuals in the Professions:
A Comparison

The basic patterns of over- and underrepresentation of gay men and lesbians in
the professional occupations are the following: gay men are most overrepresented in creative and artistic professions; lesbians are most overrepresented in
counseling and psychological professions. How do these patterns compare with
those of heterosexual males and females? Table 9.6 shows that the specific professions in which same-sex partners are concentrated tend to differ from those
of heterosexuals, providing further evidence that sexual orientation plays a role
in occupational segregation.

Compared to partnered heterosexuals, same-sex partners are underrepresented in 14 of the 33 professional occupations being analyzed and overrepresented in 19. The primary occupations in which they are overrepresented require
skills involving creativity, psychology/counseling, and/or are careers involving social change. Same-sex partners are overrepresented as postsecondary teachers relative to heterosexuals, supporting prior research that homosexual individuals may
be more likely to pursue careers, or to be hired, in higher education because university environments tend to be more tolerant of alternative lifestyles.

The ten professions in which same-sex partners are underrepresented are
mainly engineering, which are where heterosexuals, particularly males, are much
more likely to be employed. Same-sex partners are less likely than heterosexuals to
work as preschool and kindergarten teachers, elementary and middle school teachers, or secondary teachers. This difference could well be due to public prejudice regarding homosexual individuals working with children; it could also result from
the fact that fewer lesbians choose to work in these female-dominated careers.

There are also gender differences in the indexes of relative advantage (see
Table 9.6). Gay men compared to heterosexual men are underrepresented in 10 of
the professions, overrepresented in 22, and at parity in one (lawyers). The 12 in
which gay men are very strongly overrepresented are mainly in the so-called female professions. For example, gay men are a full 1,600 percent more likely to
work as preschool or elementary school teachers than are heterosexual men. High
levels of overrepresentation, although not at such an extreme level, are also seen for
gay men in many of the other female professions, including librarians, registered
nurses, social workers, and special education teachers. In addition, gay men are
much more likely than heterosexual men to work in creative professions, such as
designers, editors, artists, writers and authors, and architects. Finally, gay men are
highly concentrated in professions involving psychology/counseling. In contrast,
relative to heterosexual males, gay males are underrepresented in the engineering
professions and in the clergy.

Compared to heterosexual females, partnered lesbians are underrepresented
in 10 of the professions and overrepresented in 23. Notably, although lesbians are
underrepresented in the engineering professions relative to their proportion in the
labor force, they are overrepresented relative to heterosexual women. In fact,

TABLE 9.6. Indexes of Relative Advantage for Homosexual Individuals Compared to Heterosexual Individuals in the 33 Largest Professions, U.S., 2000

Occupation	Index for All Same-Sex Partners	Index for Gay Men	Index for Lesbians
Chief Executives	−25%	−39%	+59%
Human Resources Specialists	+30%	+89%	−6%
Accountants & Auditors	−12%	+20%	−34%
Personal Financial Advisers	−9%	−34%	+48%
Computer Scientists & Systems Analysts	+34%	+25%	+60%
Computer Programmers	+18%	+18%	+30%
Computer Software Engineers	+12%	+4%	+50%
Network Systems & Data Communication Analysts	+67%	+44%	+148%
Architects	+90%	+105%	+100%
Civil Engineers	−34%	−56%	+216%
Electrical & Electronics Engineers	−52%	−65%	+127
Industrial Engineers	−28%	−51%	+115%
Mechanical Engineers	−58%	−70%	+183%
Misc. Engineers, Including Agricultural & Biomedical	−45%	−62%	+144%
Psychologists	+235	+158	+253%
Counselors	+67%	+79%	+50%
Social Workers	+109%	+227%	+63%
Clergy	−48%	−60%	+63%
Lawyers	+31%	−2%	+127%
Postsecondary Teachers	+55%	+21%	+89%
Preschool & Kindergarten Teachers	−41%	+1600%	−63%
Elementary & Middle School Teachers	−25%	+56%	−48%
Secondary School Teachers	−15%	−15%	−20%
Special Education Teachers	+13%	+220%	−22%
Librarians	+49%	+512%	−16%
Artists	+87%	+60%	+32%
Designers	+96%	+299%	−11%
Musicians & Singers	+83%	+153%	+11%
Editors	+99%	+150%	+159%
Writers & Authors	+129%	+180%	+87%
Pharmacists	−29%	−13%	−44%
Physicians & Surgeons	+26%	+12%	+88%
Registered Nurses	−4%	+446%	−40%

lesbians are overrepresented in almost all of the other nonelite male professions relative to heterosexual women, as well as the elite male professions of physicians and lawyers. Generally, then, lesbians tend to be overrepresented in male professions relative to heterosexual women and underrepresented in every female profession except social workers. This comparison paints a picture of sexual orientation creating two very different career tracks for women.

Conclusion

In this chapter we examined a hitherto unexplored area, the extent to which homosexual individuals are segregated in the professions. The data show that same-sex partners are overrepresented in the professions as a whole, and are concentrated in fields that focus on creativity, psychology/counseling, and law/social work. They are most underrepresented in the engineering and teaching professions.

Had we restricted our analysis to the assessment of the over- and underrepresentation of same-sex partners in particular occupations, we would have overlooked important patterns in the data. This would have been due to the fact that the distribution of same-sex partners in the professions is dramatically affected by sex. Gay males are significantly more likely to work in female professions than heterosexual males, although they are underrepresented in female professions as a whole. Similarly, lesbians are more likely than heterosexual females to work in both the elite and nonelite male professions, but are not as likely to work in the so-called female professions. Thus, although lesbians are actually overrepresented in the female professions relative to their numbers in the labor force, they are less likely to work in these professions than their heterosexual counterparts.

These findings suggest that gay men and lesbians are more likely to cross gender boundaries in the professions than are heterosexual men and women. At the same time, if one examines the representation of gay men and lesbians in the professions (Table 9.3) rather than their representation relative to heterosexuals (Table 9.4), one sees that gay men are overrepresented in the male occupations and lesbians are overrepresented in the female professions. Thus, even though gay men and lesbians are more likely than heterosexuals to cross gender boundaries in the professions, it is important to recognize that they still remain fairly segregated in sex-typed occupations. They are simply *less* sex-segregated than heterosexuals. Also, our data indicate that gay males and lesbians are more overrepresented in gender-neutral professions than are heterosexuals (Table 9.3), providing still further support that homosexual individuals may be less wedded to occupations with strong sex segregation.

Finally, these initial analyses enable us to distinguish between segregation resulting from sexual orientation, as opposed to that resulting from sex. For example, consider the representation of gay men and lesbians in the teaching professions. We found that gay men are underrepresented in all of the teaching professions, other than postsecondary teaching. These findings may result from the fact that gay men are often excluded from the teaching of young children because the public perceives them to be a danger to children. But when we compare the representation of gay men to heterosexual men in these professions, we find that gay men are much more likely to be teachers than heterosexual men; our data show that gay men are 16 times more likely to work as a preschool or kindergarten teacher than heterosexual men. This finding supports the notion that the underrepresentation of gay men in this profession is a consequence more of their sex than their sexual orientation. Their sexual orientation actually makes them *less* underrepresented as teachers than their heterosexual counterparts.

Lesbians, however, are underrepresented in the teaching professions when their sex would suggest that they should be overrepresented. Relative to heterosexual women, lesbians are far less likely to work as teachers. Thus, for women, sexual orientation rather than sex is the better explanation of the representation of lesbians in these particular professions. Our analyses, although exploratory, nevertheless reveal some of the ways in which the interrelations of sex and sexual orientation result in segregation.

It is important to note, however, that all of the comparisons we report in this chapter are limited to data involving only partnered heterosexual and homosexual individuals. We would hypothesize that unpartnered women (particularly unpartnered heterosexual women) are more likely to work in the professions than are partnered, and might even have higher representation in occupations outside of the female-dominated professions. Unpartnered women might be more likely to pursue demanding professional occupations prior to marriage and/or children. We would anticipate that unpartnered men, on the other hand, might be less likely to work in professional occupations because partnership might propel them into higher-paying professional occupations. Thus, an analysis of unpartnered individuals might demonstrate an even larger male/female disparity within the professions than was observed herein. An examination of occupational segregation that is inclusive of unpartnered individuals is, therefore, suggested for future research in this area.

Although we have been able to shed some light on the manner in which sexual orientation leads to occupational segregation, our results reported in this chapter are largely descriptive. We have not presented any direct quantitative evidence regarding the correlates and causes of segregation in the professions by sexual orientation. Gay men and lesbians may choose certain professions out of personal interest, may select the professions they are socialized to believe are appropriate for persons of their sexual orientation, or may choose professions in which they believe their sexual preference will be tolerated. They may not "choose" particular professions at all; they could well be limited in their choices due to discriminatory hiring practices. Additional research on this underexplored topic is needed to gain an understanding of the causes behind the segregation of homosexual individuals in the professions, as well as in the other occupations.

CONCLUSION

❧

Implications for Law, Policy, and Future Research on Sexual Orientation

In the chapters of this book, we have examined the manner in which sexual orientation affects an assortment of demographic outcomes. We used data from the 2000 U.S. Census to both ask and to explore a series of social demographic issues that have heretofore been unexamined, or underexplored, due to the lack of large nationally representative data sets. Our findings demonstrate that, in every instance, sexual orientation has differential demographic consequences for homosexual and heterosexual individuals. These results indicate that the incorporation of sexual orientation into demographic analyses is warranted. This personal characteristic of sexual orientation, much like sex, age, or race, has been shown here to have an important effect on population outcomes.

Many of our findings also have legal and policy implications concerning the role of sexual orientation in the family, the workplace, and in the community. In this concluding chapter, we bring together some of these results in a discussion of the ways in which the demography of sexual orientation can shape and inform law and policy.

In addition to showing the implications of our findings for sexual orientation policy, we consider some of the future research needs in the demography of sexual orientation. Specifically, we discuss data and theoretical developments suggested by our current findings. As noted in our Introduction, we believe that the analyses in this book provide a foundation for future research on the demography of sexual orientation.

Legal and Policy Implications

In 2003, the United States Supreme Court heard arguments in an appeal by two men from Texas who were convicted of engaging in "deviate sexual intercourse" between individuals of the same-sex, a violation of Texas law (*Lawrence v. Texas* 2003). The state of Texas argued that the promotion of morality was a legitimate state interest justifying the maintenance of a law that prohibited same-sex sodomy. The Court, however, reversed the conviction, ruling that the statute violated the men's liberty and privacy interests. Specifically, the Court's majority opinion stated:

> The petitioners are entitled to respect for their private lives. The State cannot demean their existence or control their destiny by making their private sexual conduct a crime. . . . The Texas statute furthers no legitimate state interest which can justify its intrusion into the personal and private life of the individual. . . . [T]hose who drew and ratified the Due Process Clauses of the Fifth Amendment or the Fourteenth Amendment . . . knew times can blind us to certain truths and later generations can see that laws once thought necessary and proper in fact serve only to oppress. As the Constitution endures, persons in every generation can invoke its principles in their own search for greater freedom. (*Lawrence* 2003: 578–579)

Both the holding in this case, as well as much of the legal reasoning provided therein, have been viewed as strong precedent for future legal challenges to legislation that distinguishes between individuals in homosexual and heterosexual relationships. The Court cautioned "against attempts by the State, or a court, to define the meaning of the [homosexual] relationship or to set its boundaries absent injury to a person or abuse of an institution the law protects" (*Lawrence* 2003: 567). Thus, in dicta, the Court has set forth the ground rules for any future litigation: the state should establish "injury to a person or abuse of an institution" in order to warrant an intrusion on the constitutional rights of gay men and lesbians.

Since *Lawrence*, judicial decisions have already begun to delineate whether and when legal distinctions can be made based on sexual orientation. For example, the Kansas Supreme Court considered a case in which different penalties were applied in cases of underage sex when they involved homosexual conduct (*Kansas v. Limon* 2005). A lower court held that the state had legitimate interests in harsher punishments for homosexual conduct in order to protect children's traditional development, fight disease, and protect traditional values. The Kansas Supreme Court rejected these arguments, relying on *Lawrence* in ruling that "moral disapproval of a group cannot be a legitimate governmental interest." This holding is particularly notable in that the court specifically rejected the state's arguments about moral values, as well as other state interests such as protecting a child's physical or psychological well-being.

For an equal protection case not involving a category requiring elevated scrutiny (such as race or sex), the state is usually given a great deal of leeway in establishing that the law has a "rational basis." Consequently, the court's rejection of the state's arguments is significant, and signals that lower courts view the Supreme Court's decision in *Lawrence* as one that either demands, or at least permits, a movement toward a more critical analysis of laws making distinctions based on sexual orientation.

With this legal movement as a backdrop, we have presented in this book a series of demographic analyses of the structure and dynamics of same-sex partnering. We have suggested that many of our analyses have legal and policy implications that we believe are particularly relevant at this time of legal transition. In this concluding chapter, we now highlight some of the developing legal and policy concerns in the areas touched on in our book, and summarize some of the findings that bear on these issues.

Legal Findings Related to Spatial Distribution and Mobility

Policy makers, as well as marketers, have become increasingly interested in determining where gay men and lesbians live and, in conjunction, with the factors that draw them to particular residential areas. In some areas, such as Oakland, California, and Spokane, Washington, there have been movements initiated by local governments and activists to identify and create gay enclaves (Zamora 2004; Geranios 2005). Other policy makers and economists contend that the presence of gay men and lesbians in communities provides tangible economic benefits. The economist Richard Florida (2002), for example, argues that the future economic success of communities depends on attracting individuals employed in creative industries. He contends that this so-called creative class is particularly attracted to areas with high levels of recreational and cultural amenities, as well as a diversity of lifestyles, including gay and lesbian lifestyles. Owing to these kinds of arguments, locating concentrations of same-sex partners and developing methods to attract them via friendly policies have become matters of attention for some policy makers.

In both Chapters 3 and 5, we demonstrate that sexual orientation affects residential choice. We show in Chapter 5 that sexual orientation has a statistically significant effect on the initial decision to migrate. Further, once individuals have migrated, we provide data in Chapter 3 that support the notion that sexual orientation results in residential segregation. For policy makers seeking to either attract a greater number of same-sex partners to an area, or to address enclave issues within a city (such as in Oakland and Spokane), these findings indicate that the residential patterns of gay men and lesbians are not random. Rather their decisions to move and their location decisions in cities are linked to their orientation.

The spatial distribution of same-sex partners in both metropolitan and non-metropolitan areas of the United States is analyzed in Chapter 2. These findings are relevant for policymakers who wish to determine the locations of high concentrations of same-sex partners. They also illustrate that gay men and lesbians reside in large numbers in nonmetropolitan, as well as in metropolitan areas. We further examine whether the presence of sodomy laws or state antidiscrimination laws increase the concentration of same-sex partners. Our results indicate that such legislation, whether negative or friendly, does not appear to be strongly and significantly associated with prevalence levels of gay men and lesbians.

This finding is supported by our respondents in the qualitative interview data analyzed in Chapter 4. Although all of our respondents noted that the presence of a liberal political climate was important in selecting a residence, only 40 percent indicated that specific legislation was also important. Further, some distinguished between legislation that signaled opposition to homosexual individuals, and that which provided specific benefits; friendly legislation seemed less important in determining residential choices than the presence of laws or policies that denied rights.

Our findings in these chapters thus indicate that same-sex partners are distributed throughout the United States, regardless of legislation. Policy makers seeking to capitalize on any existing financial or social benefits derived from the presence of a gay male and lesbian population would be best served by avoiding legislation that curtails the rights of these individuals. Although we did not find that friendly legislation affected the residential choices of same-sex partners, incorporating such considerations in future statistical models examining migration and settlement decisions would surely provide additional insight.

Legal Findings and the Family

Disputes related to the family and sexual orientation have been at the forefront of legal debates during the past decade. Disagreements over the legalization of same-sex marriage have resulted in both federal and state legislation and litigation. Congress passed the Defense of Marriage Act in 1996, which defines marriage as existing solely between a man and a woman, thus denying federal marriage benefits to same-sex couples (Gerstmann 2004). In 2004, then President George W. Bush called for a federal constitutional amendment that would define marriage as existing between a man and a woman. Although this amendment did not garner sufficient support in Congress, similar amendments have passed in growing numbers at the state level. At the time of this writing (May 2008), 26 states have enacted constitutional amendments banning same-sex marriage;[1] in contrast, only the state of Massachusetts has legalized same-sex marriage. Many of the debates over same-sex marriage are based on concerns about the lack of stability of such unions, the dissimilarity between same-sex couples and heterosexual couples, and the meaning of these differences for children living in same-sex families (Tepperman and Blain 2006).

The analyses we report in Chapter 7 go to the heart of this debate; we examine many indicators of attachment in relationships to determine whether same-sex couples are dissimilar from heterosexual couples. Our findings demonstrate that same-sex couples tend to fall in between married heterosexual couples and cohabiting heterosexual couples on measures of attachment, such as household assets and wealth, the presence of children in the household, and employment. Since the census data do not permit same-sex couples to distinguish between long-term marriage-like relationships, and cohabiting relationships, it is not surprising that same-sex couples fall between the two heterosexual couple types on these indicators. This finding supports the notion that same-sex partners do not drastically differ from heterosexual couples on measures of attachment, suggesting that same-sex relationships are not as different from heterosexual ones as opponents of same-sex marriage have argued.

We also sought in Chapter 7 to examine the effects of state-level laws on attachment indicators. We theorized that if states had enacted local Defense of Marriage Acts, for instance, then attachment levels of same-sex partners would be affected negatively by this state expression of opposition to their unions. We find, however, no statistical relationship between the presence of such laws and the attachment measures examined. This suggests that laws forbidding same-sex marriage do not negatively affect the attachment levels of gay and lesbian couples; these couples will retain comparable levels of attachment irrespective of whether same-sex marriage is sanctioned by the state. Conversely, it is possible that a formal Defense of Marriage Act does not have a statistical effect on attachment because, even in the absence of such a law, same-sex marriage has not been legally *sanctioned*, and couples in all states are equally affected by the denial of this right.

Various conservative groups announced an initiative for the 2006 national elections to pass laws prohibiting the adoption of children by gay male and lesbian couples (Stone 2006). In support of such legislation, they contend that children need both a male and female role model in order to develop properly. Consequently, it is claimed that being raised in same-sex families is not in a child's "best interest." As of May 2008, 4 states have laws that restrict adoption by same-sex couples and/or single individuals, and in 15 states same-sex adoption is permitted only in certain jurisdictions.[2] In addition to adoption rights, there have also arisen disputes over the rights of both single individuals and gay men and lesbians to have children via reproductive technologies. For example, in Indiana in 2005, Senator Patricia Miller proposed a bill that would have required any individual seeking to have a child through medically assisted methods to be married (Associated Press 2005). Parents would have been required to obtain a certificate from a licensed child placement agency verifying their marital status and providing other background information. Although this particular bill was withdrawn before it reached a vote, there are similar laws in other states limiting the ability of same-sex couples to have children through alternative reproductive means, such as surrogacy.[3]

We report findings in Chapter 6 that support the notion that such existing and proposed legislation has little effect on same-sex individuals who are currently partnered. In states where gay men and lesbians already experience limited or nonexistent adoption rights, the presence of these limitations does not have a significant effect on the odds of their having a child residing with them in the household. These laws, therefore, do not seem to discourage gay men and lesbians from establishing families of their own. This is perhaps best explained by our finding that the odds of having a child in the household dramatically increase if an individual reports having been in a prior heterosexual relationship. In other words, individuals who identify their marital status as divorced, separated, or widowed have much higher odds of having children in the household. The children of same-sex partners, therefore, might often predate the same-sex partnership, that is, these are children who were born into a heterosexual union.

Limiting adoption or reproductive rights will, undoubtedly, affect the ability of many gay men and lesbians to have children. Our findings suggest, however, that fewer homosexual families will be affected than one might anticipate if the children are largely coming from heterosexual relationships. This phenomenon, however, might change over time. As gay men and lesbians continue to come out at increasingly earlier ages, they may be less likely to enter into heterosexual marriages that produce children. Over the long term, laws that limit adoption and the use of alternative reproductive technologies by same-sex couples are more likely to have a negative impact on the odds of having children.

Legal Findings Related to Employment

As of May 2008, 20 states in the United States had adopted laws prohibiting discrimination in private employment on the basis of sexual orientation. Half of all the states in the United States had similar laws for public employees. The majority of these laws were adopted during and following the 1990s. We noted in Chapter 8, however, that few quantitative analyses have been undertaken that examine the effects of these antidiscrimination laws on the labor market outcomes of gay men and lesbians. Klawitter and Flatt (1998), drawing on 1990 Census data, found no statistically significant relationship between the presence of these laws and average earnings. The absence of an effect of antidiscrimination laws on earnings could, perhaps, be attributable to the relatively low numbers of complaints filed under these laws, signaling a lack of efficacy, a lack of knowledge, or both related to this legislation.

In Chapter 8, however, we present findings that support the notion that income differentials based on sexual orientation have diminished since the 1990s. Notably, after controlling for a host of individual characteristics, we report that gay men experience a wage advantage when compared to cohabiting heterosexual men. This is the first time that such a wage advantage has been found for gay men. The fact that there appears to have been a decline in the wage differential based on sexual orientation during the 1990s could well be indicative of changing attitudes toward homosexuality during this decade.

Although the presence of a state-level antidiscrimination law has not been found to have a statistically significant effect on income (Klawitter and Flatt 1998), it is nonetheless notable that the majority of these laws were passed during the same period in which there occurred an equalizing of earnings. Local government officials have attested that these laws have not only increased the awareness of sexual orientation discrimination, but have also reduced the occurrence of such discrimination (Button et al. 1995). Despite the fact that this sentiment has not been borne out statistically, the increased awareness of sexual orientation discrimination that both fostered the passing of these laws and that spread throughout the country as a result of their passing, could have contributed in part to the earnings changes over the past decade.

Our findings in Chapter 8 also suggest another possible explanation for the failure of state antidiscrimination laws to alter wage differentials based on sexual orientation. As previously noted, gay men experience a wage advantage when compared to cohabiting heterosexual men; it is only when compared to married men that gay men experience a wage penalty. We believe that these findings indicate that it is largely the unmarried status of gay men, rather than their orientation, that results in their wage disadvantage compared to heterosexual men.[4] Consequently, the failure of antidiscrimination laws to have a statistically significant effect on income differences could be the result of a disconnect between these laws and the heart of the cause of wage inequality between homosexual and heterosexual men: the ability to marry. Unmarried heterosexual men also experience the same wage penalty as gay men; nonetheless, they are legally permitted to enter into unions and gain the economic benefits associated with formally recognized marital status. Given this relationship between marital status and income, it is possible that laws permitting same-sex marriage, rather than antidiscrimination laws, are those that can more directly address current income inequality between gay and heterosexual men.

There are also legal implications in the findings we report in Chapter 9 regarding occupational segregation in the professions based on sexual orientation. Some of the lack of support thus far for a federal antidiscrimination law in employment has been attributed to poor evidence of either income inequality or occupational segregation based on sexual orientation. Chapter 8 demonstrates the existence of income inequality between men and women based on sexual orientation. Chapter 9, in turn, demonstrates the presence of occupational segregation. Gay men, for example, have much higher odds of working in the so-called female professions than do heterosexual males; similarly, lesbians are more likely than heterosexual females to work in both the elite and nonelite male professions. These findings suggest that gay men and lesbians cross gender boundaries in the professions more often than heterosexual men and women. Further, there are specific occupations in which gay men and lesbians are more likely to be concentrated, including those focused on creativity, psychology/counseling, and law/social work. Alternately, we show that they are underrepresented in engineering and teaching professions.

Sexual orientation, therefore, appears to play an important role in segregating individuals into particular occupations. Our analyses do not, however, reveal whether this segregation can be attributable to choice, socialization, fear of discrimination, or actual discrimination. If segregation is due to discrimination, antidiscrimination laws will offer an important remedy for individuals seeking entry into occupations to which they feel excluded. Our analyses provide initial support for such laws. Further research, however, is needed to tease out the causes of the occupational segregation demonstrated in Chapter 9.

The Demography of Sexual Orientation: Implications for Future Research

Males do not represent two discrete populations, heterosexual and homosexual. The world is not to be divided into sheep and goats. It is a fundamental of taxonomy that nature rarely deals with discrete categories. . . . The living world is a continuum in each and every one of its aspects. (Kinsey et al. 1948: 639)

As Kinsey and colleagues (1948) observed, many hold that sexual orientation is not a binary characteristic; rather, individuals can be said to fall along a continuum ranging from entirely heterosexual to entirely homosexual identities. The manner in which persons classify their sexual desires, behaviors, and identities determines their placement along this continuum (Kinsey et al. 1948; Laumann et al. 1994; see also our discussion in Chapter 1 of essentialism and social constructionism).

If sexuality exists along a continuum, then it becomes challenging for social scientists to frame the correct questions dealing with sexual orientation in order to measure its effects. Should the researcher focus on desire, behavior, identity, or a combination thereof? How should questions addressing these varying dimensions of sexuality be framed? And, should the social scientist's "definition" of sexual orientation (i.e., desire, behavior, identity, or a combination) vary depending on the question posed? Researchers are now attempting to get at the heart of many of these questions (Gates and Sell 2006; Black et al. 2000; Laumann et al. 1994). Our findings provide some guidance about how to address these questions, as well as some important methodological and theoretical implications.

We noted in Chapter 1 that two questions on the U.S. Census instrument permit individuals to indirectly label their sexual orientation through a combination of responses to questions dealing with their sex and with their relationship to the head of householder. If an individual identifies as an "unmarried partner" to the head of the household, that is, person #1, and the two individuals are of the same sex, then they are considered to be same-sex partners. This question, therefore, measures sexual orientation in a binary fashion, focused on sexual identity: individuals either identify as same-sex or different-sex partners. Our analyses suggest that defining sexual orientation in this fashion could well lead to different types of outcomes than if the question was asked in a more varied format.

For example, in Chapter 7 we compare the indicators of relationship attachment for individuals in same-sex relationships to those in different-sex relationships. Our results indicate that same-sex couples often fall between married and cohabiting heterosexual couples on these measures. If the census questionnaire permitted same-sex couples to distinguish between marital and cohabiting relationships, it is quite possible that we would find little or no difference in these attachment factors based on sexual orientation. Rather, all individuals in cohabiting relationships might be relatively similar, and all of those in married relationships might be similar. On the other hand, we might determine that sexual orientation remains an important distinguishing characteristic on this issue. Married heterosexual men and married gay men, in particular, might report significantly different levels of attachment, as measured in terms of the presence of children in the household or household income and assets. With the question presented on the census instrument, however, we are unable to capture such distinctions. Instead, our results suggest that same-sex couples have attachment levels that fall between those of married and cohabiting heterosexuals, when this finding could be partly attributable to the manner in which sexual orientation is measured by the census question.

Similarly, in Chapter 8 we examine income differences based on sexual orientation and find that male same-sex partners earn less than married heterosexual men, but slightly more than cohabiting heterosexual men. If being in a marital relationship, even one not formally recognized by law, provides an income benefit to gay men as it does to heterosexual men, then one would expect the income difference between cohabiting gay men and married heterosexual men to increase if we were able to remove married gay men from the analysis. Further, cohabiting gay men might actually earn less than cohabiting heterosexual men if we were able to remove married gay men from the analysis. In addition, we would be further able to tease out the effects of the wage disparity that can be attributable to marital status, as opposed to sexual orientation, if we could distinguish between these two types of relationships for gay men.

In our analyses, we attempt to adjust for this data limitation by comparing same-sex partners with both married and cohabiting heterosexuals. Nonetheless, the results we report in these chapters suggest the need for a comprehensive, nationally representative data-set that would permit such fine measurement distinctions. We do not anticipate changes to the question format contained in the census or in the American Community Survey in the near future. In future U.S. censuses, however, there will necessarily be some gay men and lesbians with legally recognized marriages that were granted by the state of Massachusetts.

If other states follow Massachusetts, then the U.S. Census Bureau will need to decide how to classify these legally sanctioned marriages. Will they lead to the development of a different category than unmarried partner? Will individuals who participate in civil unions or who are married in commitment ceremonies that are not legally recognized by a state continue to be lumped into the unmarried partner category? Such questions regarding relationship status will likely create greater classification challenges for the Census Bureau in coming years.

Indeed, in some other nations, changes are being made to their census questions in recognition of the changing legal status of the relationships of gay men and lesbians. The Canadian census questionnaire includes a category for same-sex couples who have entered into common-law marital relationships to identify such relationships on the census form. And in the United Kingdom, the marital status question on the 2011 census will be expanded in order to incorporate changes in the legal recognition of same-sex relationships (Townley 2006). While we recognize the energy and expense that would go into amending the categories associated with same-sex partners in the United States, such an approach could be the most optimal manner of improving the data and knowledge on same-sex partners.

Another insight that can be gleaned from the census design of the United Kingdom concerns the manner in which they phrase questions about the relationship among household members. As of 2001, the U.K. census asks how each individual is related to *all other members of the household*, rather than asking only how each individual is related to the head of household. A household relationship question in this format would make it possible to see how every member of the family is related to one another. More specifically for our research concerns, one could determine to which partner family members were related, for example, how children (or other family members) in the household are related to the unmarried partner who is not the head of household. This format could provide more accurate insight into the demographics of same-sex families.

In addition to the questions about relationship status, a question that directly asks individuals about sexual orientation would, of course, solve many of the questions of data validity associated with using the census data. Perhaps most dramatically, it would allow for all gay male and lesbian individuals who self-identify to be enumerated, whether single, partnered, married in heterosexual unions, and so forth. This would be significant in that it is perhaps likely that many of the demographic issues explored in this work would differ for single gay men and lesbians. For example, single individuals might be more likely to have migrated within the past five years than would partnered ones; this could be attributable, in part, to a desire to seek residential locations with a larger same-sex dating pool and/or anonymity, which would aid in forming relationships. Further, marriage has been found to provide a powerful boost to income for men (Waite and Gallagher 2000). The manner in which this effect would play out for gay men and lesbians is unclear. It is possible that partnered gay men experience an earnings boost as a result of their partnered (and, in some cases, married) status; on the other hand, partnered gay men might be less willing or able to hide their sexual orientation, which could result in an earnings penalty. Consequently, the census data could reflect a skewed picture of income differences based on sexual orientation in that these results are perhaps not entirely transferable to the gay and lesbian population as a whole. This could also be the case for other demographic issues examined in this book. A question directly addressing sexual orientation, then, could aid in exploring the manner in which outcomes differ for single and partnered gay men and lesbians.

Although the U.S. Census Bureau is unlikely to add such a question out of privacy concerns, the census questionnaire has for decades included questions about other personal, private demographic characteristics such as race, ethnicity, ancestry, and age. We have shown in this book that sexual orientation is a characteristic with almost as much influence as, if not more than, race, ethnicity, ancestry, and age in the prediction of demographic outcomes. This suggests to us that it would perhaps make sense to collect such data. Further, some have advocated for the inclusion of such a question on censuses in other countries in order to both collect demographic data and to "monitor equality legislation and improve the service provision to lesbian, gay and bisexual people" (Townley 2006; see also McManus 2003).

One might wonder, however, whether individuals would respond to a question about sexual orientation on the census, or whether gay men and lesbians would feel targeted by these questions. In the in-depth interviews we conducted in Chapter 4, we asked respondents whether they would answer a census question that asked, point-blank, about sexual orientation. Only one respondent answered in the negative, citing the Holocaust as an example of what could go wrong with such information. However, all other respondents indicated a general willingness to provide such information and to "be counted." These results, though, could be attributable in part to the fact that all of our respondents reside in the San Francisco Bay Area and perhaps feel more secure in their sexuality because of the locations of their residence. If gay men and lesbians residing in more rural and/or conservative areas were asked a similar question, the outcome might well be different.

Although it is unlikely that we will see a question dealing directly with sexual orientation on the census questionnaire, it is important to keep in mind that the current census question is one which, similarly, addresses orientation through an individual's *identification*. This approach to sexual orientation is particularly useful in analyses where the possible effects of discrimination are being measured (McManus 2003). For instance, in a labor market analysis, it might be more important to look at whether individuals identified as gay men or lesbians in order to determine whether they are likely to have disclosed their identity in the workplace and, thus, made themselves vulnerable to discrimination (Baumle and Poston 2005; Badgett 2001).

In analyses attempting to assess the way in which sexual orientation affects individual decisions such as migration, however, a broader measure of sexual orientation would be more useful. As we discussed in Chapter 5, a gay man or lesbian might choose to migrate to an area in order to escape a restrictive environment, experience more sexual freedom, or both. If this is the case, then the individual might or might not choose a gay male or lesbian identity; rather, some who choose to migrate due to orientation might experience same-sex sexual desire, but not yet openly identify. In such a case, a combination of sexual desire, behavior, and identity could better capture the range of individuals to be included in such analyses. At this time, however, the census provides the only data-set for analyzing the effect of sexual orientation on migration. Consequently, the need for a consideration of new data-sets that consider multiple dimensions of sexuality is important for future studies.

We noted in Chapter 1 that the U.S. Census is not the only available data-set for examining issues of sexual orientation. There are, however, no perfect data-sets for examining the gay male and lesbian population at present. There are just as many limitations associated with the other data-sets, such as size, question format, and the absence of questions on demographic issues. The 2000 U.S. Census, however, is the largest nationally representative data-set with which we can study issues of social demography related to sexual orientation. In spite of its limitations, it allows for the enumeration of a significant part of the gay male and lesbian population and, then, the examination of the characteristics and demographic outcomes of same-sex households and relationships. Further, given the large sample size of gay men and lesbians provided by the census, one has access to a data set that is the most diverse with regard to race, ethnicity, and class. Consequently, the census continues to be a valuable tool for social scientists studying the social demography of sexual orientation. Future research would benefit from both the adaptation of the current questions on the census, as well as the development of additional or supplemental data sets to examine these issues. With such tools, additional momentum can be made in both substantive and theoretical developments in the demography of sexual orientation.

APPENDIX

APPENDIX TABLE 3.1. Same-Sex Unmarried Partner Sample Size and City Populations

City	% of Gays in City*	Number of Gays in City	% of Lesbians in City*	Number of Lesbians in City	Total City Population	% of Same-Sex in Nation†
New York	17.29%	30,028	17.53%	21,776	8,008,278	4.36%
Los Angeles	8.89%	15,444	7.69%	9,552	3,694,820	2.10%
Chicago	6.53%	11,340	6.16%	7,650	2,896,016	1.60%
Wash DC	3.09%	5,362	1.54%	1,918	572,059	0.61%
San Francisco	7.54%	13,098	3.79%	4,706	776,733	1.50%
Atlanta	2.56%	4,440	1.53%	1,906	416,474	0.53%
Philadelphia	2.63%	4,568	3.26%	4,046	1,517,550	0.72%
Boston	2.25%	3,902	1.91%	2,378	589,141	0.53%
Houston	4.74%	8,230	5.47%	6,798	1,953,631	1.26%
Dallas	4.14%	7,184	3.34%	4,152	1,188,580	0.95%
Seattle	3.16%	5,495	3.61%	4,480	563,374	0.84%
Oakland	1.32%	2,294	2.46%	3,060	399,484	0.45%
Phoenix	2.95%	5,118	3.16%	3,928	1,321,045	0.76%
San Diego	3.49%	6,060	3.09%	3,838	1,223,400	0.83%
Riverside	0.34%	590	0.50%	616	255,166	0.10%
Minneapolis	1.65%	2,868	1.91%	2,376	382,618	0.44%
Detroit	0.94%	1,632	1.51%	1,872	951,270	0.29%
Tampa	0.99%	1,724	0.97%	1,204	303,447	0.25%
Denver	1.96%	3,396	1.96%	2,436	554,636	0.49%
Ft. Lauderdale	1.67%	2,896	0.66%	822	152,397	0.31%
Miami	0.94%	1,640	0.80%	994	362,470	0.22%
Portland	1.70%	2,956	2.94%	3,648	529,121	0.56%
Baltimore	1.22%	2,114	1.71%	2,122	651,154	0.36%
Orange	0.23%	404	0.34%	422	128,821	0.07%

(continued)

APPENDIX TABLE 3.1. (*continued*)

City	% of Gays in City*	Number of Gays in City	% of Lesbians in City*	Number of Lesbians in City	Total City Population	% of Same-Sex in Nation[†]
Orlando	1.11%	1,928	0.90%	1,120	185,951	0.26%
Sacramento	1.07%	1,854	1.57%	1,952	407,018	0.32%
St. Louis	0.86%	1,496	0.88%	1,098	348,189	0.22%
Newark	0.35%	616	0.56%	694	273,546	0.11%
Las Vegas	0.85%	1,478	0.91%	1,130	478,434	0.22%
Columbus	1.88%	3,262	2.31%	2,872	711,470	0.52%
San Jose	1.48%	2,578	1.89%	2,352	894,943	0.41%
Austin	1.74%	3,018	2.42%	3,010	656,562	0.51%
San Antonio	1.37%	2,380	2.24%	2,776	1,144,646	0.43%
Cleveland	0.68%	1,188	0.87%	1,082	478,403	0.19%
Pittsburgh	0.55%	948	0.72%	890	334,563	0.15%
New Orleans	1.23%	2,138	1.13%	1,398	484,674	0.30%
Indianapolis	1.44%	2,504	1.80%	2,238	791,926	0.40%
Kansas City	1.20%	2,084	1.41%	1,756	441,545	0.32%
Fort Worth	0.94%	1,626	1.34%	1,666	534,694	0.28%
Charlotte	1.04%	1,800	1.17%	1,454	540,828	0.27%
TOTALS	100.00%	173,681	100.00%	124,188		25.06%

*Percentage is the number gay or lesbian unmarried partner households in the city divided by the total same-sex population in all 40 cities.

[†]Percentage is the number of same-sex unmarried partner households in city divided by the total population of same-sex unmarried partners in the nation.

APPENDIX TABLE 3.2. Eight Exposure Indexes of Homosexuals to Heterosexuals, 40 U.S. Cities, 2000

City	Gays to All Heterosexuals	Lesbians to All Heterosexuals	Gays to Married Heterosexuals	Gays to Unmarried Heterosexuals	Gays to Lesbians	Lesbians to Married Heterosexuals	Lesbians to Unmarried Heterosexuals	Lesbians to Gays
Atlanta	0.880	0.910	0.716	0.164	0.026	0.739	0.171	0.060
Austin	0.972	0.974	0.835	0.137	0.012	0.842	0.132	0.012
Baltimore	0.959	0.968	0.757	0.202	0.015	0.768	0.200	0.014
Boston	0.903	0.937	0.743	0.159	0.020	0.788	0.149	0.033
Charlotte	0.979	0.982	0.859	0.120	0.008	0.866	0.116	0.010
Chicago	0.954	0.968	0.809	0.145	0.012	0.827	0.141	0.018
Cleveland	0.960	0.978	0.762	0.198	0.009	0.789	0.189	0.010
Columbus	0.946	0.968	0.775	0.171	0.016	0.818	0.150	0.018
Dallas	0.941	0.968	0.840	0.101	0.012	0.866	0.103	0.021
Wash DC	0.883	0.932	0.714	0.169	0.018	0.759	0.172	0.049
Denver	0.938	0.955	0.755	0.183	0.019	0.800	0.154	0.027
Detroit	0.979	0.980	0.772	0.206	0.009	0.769	0.211	0.008
Fort Worth	0.984	0.986	0.892	0.093	0.007	0.900	0.087	0.006
Ft. Lauderdale	0.924	0.940	0.766	0.157	0.013	0.777	0.163	0.047
Houston	0.960	0.975	0.858	0.101	0.012	0.882	0.093	0.014
Indianapolis	0.971	0.980	0.814	0.157	0.009	0.831	0.148	0.010
Kansas City	0.958	0.968	0.809	0.150	0.014	0.835	0.133	0.017
Las Vegas	0.984	0.984	0.859	0.125	0.006	0.858	0.127	0.008
Los Angeles	0.956	0.973	0.826	0.130	0.010	0.849	0.124	0.017
Miami	0.960	0.973	0.820	0.140	0.010	0.829	0.144	0.016
Minneapolis	0.943	0.945	0.754	0.189	0.022	0.774	0.171	0.027

(continued)

APPENDIX TABLE 3.2. (*continued*)

City	Gays to All Heterosexuals	Lesbians to All Heterosexuals	Gays to Married Heterosexuals	Gays to Unmarried Heterosexuals	Gays to Lesbians	Lesbians to Married Heterosexuals	Lesbians to Unmarried Heterosexuals	Lesbians to Gays
New Orleans	0.913	0.956	0.732	0.182	0.017	0.787	0.168	0.026
New York	0.869	0.877	0.747	0.122	0.009	0.766	0.111	0.111
Newark	0.978	0.976	0.786	0.191	0.010	0.775	0.201	0.009
Oakland	0.947	0.944	0.798	0.150	0.029	0.790	0.153	0.021
Orange	0.989	0.989	0.918	0.071	0.005	0.920	0.069	0.005
Orlando	0.964	0.968	0.804	0.160	0.012	0.807	0.161	0.020
Phoenix	0.975	0.979	0.842	0.132	0.009	0.847	0.132	0.012
Philadelphia	0.953	0.969	0.783	0.170	0.013	0.810	0.159	0.015
Pittsburgh	0.968	0.976	0.814	0.154	0.011	0.833	0.142	0.012
Portland	0.960	0.960	0.789	0.171	0.020	0.800	0.160	0.016
Riverside	0.986	0.986	0.870	0.117	0.006	0.871	0.115	0.006
Sacramento	0.960	0.965	0.787	0.173	0.017	0.809	0.156	0.017
San Antonio	0.986	0.987	0.890	0.096	0.006	0.893	0.094	0.005
San Diego	0.924	0.947	0.768	0.156	0.022	0.812	0.135	0.034
San Francisco	0.821	0.867	0.667	0.154	0.035	0.722	0.145	0.097
San Jose	0.981	0.983	0.884	0.097	0.008	0.890	0.093	0.009
Seattle	0.917	0.937	0.727	0.191	0.029	0.774	0.163	0.035
St. Louis	0.959	0.965	0.768	0.191	0.014	0.774	0.191	0.019
Tampa	0.967	0.974	0.816	0.151	0.010	0.818	0.156	0.015

NOTES

An Introduction to the
Demography of Sexual Orientation

1. States with laws prohibiting discrimination on the basis of sexual orientation include California, Connecticut, Hawaii, Illinois, Maine, Maryland, Massachusetts, Minnesota, Nevada, New Hampshire, New Jersey, New Mexico, New York, Rhode Island, Vermont, and Wisconsin. A sexual orientation antidiscrimination law was enacted in the District of Columbia in 1973.

2. The population studies journals in the JSTOR database include the following: *Demography, Family Planning Perspectives, International Family Planning Perspectives, International Migration Review, Population: English Edition, Population: French Edition, Perspectives on Sexual and Reproductive Health, Population and Development Review, Population Index, Population Studies,* and *Studies in Family Planning.*

3. Riley (2005) notes that demographic research on gender has increased dramatically since 1990. For example, 20 years ago there were virtually no sessions in the Population Association of America's annual meetings that were directly tied to gender issues; now there are usually a number of such sessions.

4. Saenz and Morales (2005) observe that Hauser and Duncan's (1959) *The Study of Population*, considered the classic work on population research, only allotted four pages to the discussion of issues concerning race and ethnicity. It has been primarily during the last two decades that an increase in the demographic interest in issues of race and ethnicity has occurred (Saenz and Morales 2005).

5. Riley (1999) makes a similar observation regarding the surprising exclusion of feminist perspectives from demographic study, given the strong focus on reproductive behavior in the field of demography.

6. See Poston et al. (2005) or Riley (1999) for similar arguments regarding "bringing men in" or "bringing women in" to demographic studies.

7. In support of rejecting the use of "homosexual" as a noun, Boswell (1980: 45) states that "there can be no more justification for retaining a designation out of favor with gay people than for continuing to use 'Negro' when it has ceased to be acceptable to blacks." This is a view different from that of Sullivan (1996: ix–x) who uses the term

189

"homosexual" to refer to "someone who is constitutively, emotionally, and sexually attracted to the same sex." He holds that the word "homosexual" is the "most neutral term available."

8. Queer theory was originally associated with a more radical form of gay, lesbian, bisexual, and transgendered politics which embraced "queer" as a label to denote culturally marginal sexual self-identifications. It has, however, more currently been employed as a theory which challenges the essentialist notion of both homosexuality and heterosexuality (Jagose 1996).

9. During some field work we conducted in the San Francisco Bay Area, for instance, we found that different race and ethnic groups voiced a preference for varying identifying labels.

Chapter 2: Patterns of Same-Sex Partnering in Metropolitan and Nonmetropolitan America

1. The statistical tolerances of the 12 independent variables are all acceptable, ranging from a low of .40 (Baptists per 1,000 population) to a high of .76 (infant mortality rate, and the log of population size). The mean tolerance of the 12 variables is .52.

2. The statistical tolerances of these eight independent variables are all above .91. There is no problem regarding the collinearity of these independent variables.

Chapter 3: The Residential Segregation of Gay Males and Lesbians from Heterosexuals

1. Analyses of residential segregation in countries outside of the United States have also focused largely on dimensions of race and ethnicity; this research has included countries such as England (Collison and Mogey 1959), India (Mehta 1968), Puerto Rico (Schwirian and Rico-Velasco 1971), Egypt (Latif 1974), the Philippines (Costello and Palabrica-Costello 1984), and China (Poston et al. 1998).

2. We opted to use the gay prevalence rate as the indicator of homosexual size owing to the enhanced visibility of gays as compared to lesbians, as stated earlier in this chapter. This hypothesis is drawn from the racial and ethnic studies literature.

3. The independent variables for the OLS equations were chosen based on the results of their zero-order correlations previously mentioned and their statistical tolerances. Due to multicollinearity, we could not use all of the independent variables shown in Table 2.

4. The statistical tolerances of the five independent variables are all acceptable, ranging from .65 (city crime rate) to .84 (for the sodomy law variable). The mean tolerance of the five variables is .75.

Chapter 4: Gay Male and Lesbian Enclaves in the San Francisco Bay Area

1. We acknowledge that these areas are extremely divergent in terms of geographic area covered. In other work (Baumle and Compton 2007), we examine the significance of geographic diversity in gay and lesbian enclaves in more detail. Overall, we maintain

that these areas possess common characteristics, despite the dissimilarity of their geographic boundaries.

2. Although some of our Oakland respondents appreciated the city's attempt to create a gay space, others expressed concern that the district would result in the unfair displacement of low income, minority individuals from the proposed district.

3. Additionally, Guerneville has the second highest prevalence rate of gay male and lesbian couples of all towns with at least 50 couples and third for all "zip code areas" in the nation with at least 50 couples (Gates and Ost 2004). On further examination of the census data in Sonoma County, we found the census tract with the highest lesbian prevalence rate was in the Santa Rosa–Cotati area, and the second and third tracts with the highest lesbian prevalence rate were in the Guerneville area (see Figure 4).

4. To highlight our approach, in each city we visited known gay male and lesbian bars, restaurants, and coffeehouses. While at these venues, we observed the interactions and modes of dress of patrons, as well as their numbers. Further, we paid particular attention to outward displays of GLBT (gay, lesbian, bisexual, and transgender) affiliation, as suggested both by the institutions and the patrons; such displays might include stickers, buttons, or ribbons indicating a particular identity, modes of dress, selection of a décor that was suggestive of the gay male and lesbian culture, and/or a venue name which indicated a particular clientele. We took detailed field notes, recording our observations, as well as recording many of the institutions and related observations through photographic evidence. Further, we collected newspapers, flyers, advertisements, and other items indicative of a gay and/or lesbian presence in each enclave.

5. In separate work, additional interviews were conducted for 40 subjects, ten from each enclave (Baumle and Compton 2007). The overall patterns reported in this chapter are consistent with the findings from the larger study.

6. Interviews were primarily conducted in person, and ranged in length from a little over an hour to two and a half hours, with the average interview being about an hour and a half long. We also conducted some interviews via telephone and email exchanges, when interview subjects were unavailable during our visit but still wanted to participate in the study. Additional information regarding interviewing methods is available, on request, from the authors.

7. There is, however, a lesbian-owned bar in Petaluma that hosts gay and lesbian events, but the subjects were either unaware of the presence of this bar, or felt that it was only a "lesbian bar" one night a week; none had visited the bar. Field research supported the notion that this bar was patronized by heterosexual locals, as well as by lesbians from throughout the county. Events on some nights resulted in a stronger draw for the lesbian community, whereas on other nights the bar took on the appearance of a men's biker bar.

Chapter 5: Factors Affecting the Migration Decision of Gay Men and Lesbians

1. We introduce these interaction terms in a separate model, as the inclusion of the interactions do not permit the straightforward interpretation of the direct effect of the same-sex partner variable on interstate migration. This is attributable to the fact that the same-sex partner variable is incorporated into the interaction term. Consequently, we have created a separate model to analyze the effects of the interaction terms.

2. We report in Table 2 the odds ratios for all variables included in Model 1. We only discuss the results for the sexual orientation variable, however, since this is the variable with which we are concerned for the purposes of this analysis. The remaining control variables behaved in the expected manner.

3. Our findings in Chapter 9 indicate that gay men and lesbians are more likely to cross gender boundaries in professional occupations than are heterosexuals; nonetheless, they work predominantly in sex-segregated occupations, just as heterosexual men and women do.

Chapter 6: Characteristics of Same-Sex Families

1. Families of choice are defined more by emotional ties rather than by legal terms and can embrace friends, lovers, coparents, children and/or relatives from prior relationships who serve as caregivers to one another, providing emotional and/or material support (Weston 1991; Cahill et al. 2002).

2. GLBT families are generally thought of as consisting of either a single gay male, lesbian, bisexual, or transgendered parent with one or more children, or a gay or lesbian couple with or without children (Cahill et al. 2002).

3. However, the heterosexual assumptions associated with most family theories and studies and/or the relative lack of popularity of GLBT studies could also contribute to the dearth of research in this field.

4. Smith and Gates (2001) assert that at the very least there are just over 600,000 same-sex unmarried partner households in the United States recorded by the 2000 Census, an enumeration confirmed by our work (see Chapter 1).

5. These organizations include the American Academy of Pediatrics, the American Psychological Association (APA), the National Association of Social Workers in conjunction with the APA, the American Psychoanalytic Association, and the American Academy of Family Physicians.

6. See the Introduction to our book for a discussion about the lack of demographic studies on sexual orientation.

7. We examined the statistical tolerances for the independent variables and found that all were above .78, indicating that all these independent variables may be included in a single regression equation.

8. While we recognize the assumptions associated with deeming "separated," "divorced," and "widowed" as categories that solely describe heterosexual relationships, in the eyes of the law and the Census Bureau (the Census Bureau derives these categories from federal law), same-sex marriage is not recognized; thus, these categories associated with marriage would not be considered applicable to same-sex relationships.

9. When state-level characteristics are disaggregated to the individual level, a number of statistical assumptions are violated; multilevel modeling permits regressions at both the individual and state level, thereby avoiding the concerns associated with disaggregation.

10. We first partitioned the variance in the dependent variable, the presence of children, at the level of the individual and the state; we found a statistically significant amount of variance at the state level, thus justifying a multilevel analysis. Also, our multilevel model employed the same independent variables as the first model except that we dropped the household income variable (due to its skewed nature and minimal effect in the previous model).

Chapter 7: The Effects of Sexual Orientation on Dimensions of Family Attachment

1. Most of these findings are based on data from the Study of Income Dynamics, the National Health and Social Life Survey, the Health and Retirement Survey, and the National Longitudinal Survey on Youth.

2. Note that, as reflected in Chapter 8, gay men earn less than married men in analyses conducted at the individual, rather than the household, level and that include controls for other individual characteristics.

3. For more discussion of gender effects on income among same-sex couples, see Chapter 8.

4. See Chapter 6 for a discussion of multilevel modeling.

Chapter 8: The Economic Cost of Homosexuality

1. In addition to studies relying on the GSS and U.S. Census data, Carpenter (2004) reported results from a creative use of the Center for Disease Control's Behavioral Risk Factor Surveillance System, a large telephone-based nationally representative survey that includes questions on income and whether the respondent is in a same-sex or different-sex relationship. Although the details of his analysis are not reported here, Carpenter found that a wage penalty exists for both male and female same-sex households, with the penalty for same-sex female households being greater than that for the male households.

2. Badgett (2001) presents an instructive discussion about the implications of disclosure for discrimination in the workplace, noting that discrimination can certainly occur even in cases of nondisclosure if coworkers suspect that a particular employee is a gay man or lesbian. Consequently, individuals who engage in homosexual behavior, but do not identify as gay men or lesbians, could still experience workplace discrimination despite their failure to disclose their identity. Nonetheless, individuals who openly identify as gay men or lesbians and do disclose are certainly more likely to be directly vulnerable to workplace discrimination.

3. Notably, however, the relationship is in the negative direction, although insignificant, indicating that being a lesbian leads to a wage penalty, rather than an advantage.

4. Badgett found that as the definition for what constitutes homosexuality becomes more stringent (i.e., the number of same-sex sexual partners increases), the negative effect on income increases.

5. Klawitter and Flatt (1998) also found that male same-sex couples had about 11 percent lower household income than married couples; this finding was unexpected, as one would anticipate that two males would earn more money than a couple comprised of a male and a female, due to the gender gap in earnings.

6. Klawitter (1998) did observe, however, that the payoffs for human capital were lower for women in same-sex couples; despite the fact that they possessed greater human capital, they were being rewarded to a lesser degree for these attributes than were women who were not in same-sex couples.

7. Clain and Leppell used the one percent Public Use Microdata Sample, and not the five percent sample used in the other studies cited above.

8. This percentage is calculated by transforming the coefficient for the direct effect of orientation on earnings (b) as follows: $(e^b - 1) \times 100$.

9. Although we wished to provide finer detail concerning educational attainment by including years of education, we were unable to do so because the 2000 Census question on education does not ask the respondent to report individual years of school completed; rather, educational attainment is reported in categories of uneven size.

10. As noted by Badgett (2001), economists measure experience by subtracting years of education from the respondent's age (minus 5 years for years spent at the pre-kindergarten stage). As Badgett encountered when working with the NHSLS data, however, we were unable to do so due to the absence of data on the number of years of educational attainment (see previous note). Consequently, we used age as a measure of experience (Badgett 2001), and included education as another independent variable in the equation.

11. Klawitter and Flatt (1998) also argue that these laws are not widely implemented at either the state or local level, which could attribute to the absence of a statistically significant effect of the laws on income.

12. The state-level characteristics included in the analysis were presence in the state of a sodomy law, presence in the state of a homosexual sodomy law, percent in the state voting Republican, gross state product per capita, percent of the GSP attributable to manufacturing, presence in the state of an antidiscrimination law, a measure of gay/lesbian concentration, and percent in the state of Southern Baptists.

Chapter 9: Sexual Orientation and Occupational Segregation

1. Of course, occupational segregation can be due to either choice or exclusion; thus the existence of segregation is not evidence of discrimination. Nonetheless, knowledge about the specific professions that gay men and lesbians choose or to which they have access can shine light on the manner in which sexual orientation influences one's choice of profession, the stereotypes leading to their exclusion from particular occupations, or both.

2. The two indexes used in this study mirror those employed by Sokoloff (1992) in an examination of women and race in the professions.

3. The index of representation for homosexual, as well as that for heterosexual, individuals was calculated as follows:

$$\frac{(\text{\# of homosexual (or heterosexual) individuals in the profession} \ / \ \text{\# of persons in the profession})}{(\text{\# of homosexual (or heterosexual) individuals in the labor force} \ / \ \text{\# of persons in the labor force})}$$

4. The index of relative advantage is calculated by dividing the index of representation of the disadvantaged group by that of the advantaged group; in this case, the index of representation for a profession for homosexual individuals was divided by that for heterosexuals.

5. A profession was labeled "male" if it had 30 percent or fewer females, "gender-neutral" if it was 30.1 to 70 percent female, and "female" if it was 70.1 to 100 percent female. Occupational prestige was measured using the 2000 Nam-Powers occupational status scores, which are calculated based on the relative education required and income level of each profession, with scores ranging from a low of 1 to a high of 100.

6. Although the index of representation was calculated for heterosexual individuals for each profession, as well as for homosexual individuals, we will not present these results here; instead they will be reflected in our empirical results using the index of relative advantage.

Conclusion: Implications for Law, Policy, and Future Research on Sexual Orientation

1. These states include Alaska, Arkansas, Georgia, Kansas, Kentucky, Louisiana, Michigan, Mississippi, Missouri, Montana, Nebraska, Nevada, North Dakota, Ohio, Oklahoma, Oregon, Texas, and Utah. In 2005, Nebraska's amendment was struck down by a federal court; this decision has been appealed.

2. As of 2006, Colorado, Nebraska, Ohio, and Wisconsin do not permit same-sex couples to adopt; Alabama, Alaska, Delaware, Hawaii, Indiana, Iowa, Louisiana, Maryland, Minnesota, Nevada, New Mexico, Oregon, Rhode Island, Texas, and Washington allow same-sex couples to adopt in some jurisdictions.

3. The following states prohibit surrogacy agreements for all unmarried couples in some or all circumstances: Florida, Indiana, Louisiana, Michigan, Nebraska, Nevada, New York, North Dakota, Texas, Utah, and Virginia; in addition, such surrogacy agreements are prohibited in the District of Colombia.

4. It is important to reiterate that when we (Baumle and Poston 2005) estimated models incorporating both individual and state-level controls, gay men were shown to experience a small wage disadvantage compared to heterosexual cohabiting men. Even here the difference between gay men and married men is greater than that between gay men and cohabiting heterosexual men.

BIBLIOGRAPHY

Abrahamson, Mark. 2002. *Urban Enclaves: Identity and Place in America*. New York: St. Martin's Press.

Adams v. Laird, 420 F.2d 230 (D.C. Cir. 1969).

Alba, Richard D. and Victor Nee. 2003. *Remaking the American Mainstream: Assimilation and Contemporary Immigration*. Cambridge, MA: Harvard University Press.

Alba, Richard D., John R. Logan, and Kyle Crowder. 1997. "White Ethnic Neighborhoods and Assimilation: The Greater New York Region, 1980–1990." *Social Forces* 75:883–909.

Alba, Richard D., John R. Logan, Wenquan Zhang, and Brian Stults. 1999. "Strangers Next Door: Immigrant Groups and Suburbs in Los Angeles and New York." In *A Nation Divided: Diversity, Inequality and Community in American Society*, edited by Phyllis Moen, Henry Walker, and Donna Dempster-McClain. Ithaca, NY: Cornell University Press.

Allegretto, Sylvia A. and Michelle M. Arthur. 2001. "An Empirical Analysis of Homosexual/Heterosexual Male Earnings Differentials: Unmarried and Unequal?" *Industrial and Labor Relations Review* 54:631–46.

Allen, Katherine R. and David H. Demo. 1995. "The Families of Lesbians and Gay Men: A New Frontier in Family Research." *Journal of Marriage and Family* 57:111–27.

Associated Press. 2005. "Bill Would Limit Reproduction Procedures for Gays, Singles." October 4, 2005. Retrieved October 20, 2005 (http://wthr.com/Global/story.asp?S=3936139).

Babbie, Earl. 2006. *The Practice of Social Research*, 11th ed. Belmont, CA: Wadsworth Publishing.

Baca Zinn, Maxine and D. Stanley Eitzen. 1999. *Diversity in Families*. 5th ed. New York: Longman.

Badgett, M. V. Lee. 1995. "The Wage Effects of Sexual Orientation Discrimination." *Industrial and Labor Relations Review* 48: 726–39.

———. 2001. *Money, Myths, and Change: The Economic Lives of Lesbians and Gay Men*. Chicago, IL: The University of Chicago Press.

Badgett, M. V. Lee, Colleen Donnelly, and Jennifer Kibbe. 1992. *Persuasive Patterns of Discrimination against Lesbians and Gay Men: Evidence from Surveys across the United States*. Washington, DC: National Gay and Lesbian Task Force Policy Institute.

Badgett, M. V. Lee and Mary C. King. 1997. "Lesbian and Gay Occupational Strategies." Pp. 73–85 in *HomoEconomics: Capitalism, Community, and Lesbian and Gay Life*, edited by Amy Gluckman and Betsy Reed. New York: Routledge.

Badgett, M. V. Lee and Marc A. Rogers. 2003. *Left Out of the Count: Missing Same-sex Couples in the 2000 Census*. Amherst, MA: Institute for Gay and Lesbian Strategic Studies.

Barrett, Richard E. 1994. *Using the 1990 U.S. Census for Research*. Thousand Oaks, CA: Sage Publications.

Baumle, Amanda K. and Dudley L. Poston, Jr. 2005. "The Cost of Being Homosexual: Multilevel Analyses." Paper presented at the annual meeting of the Southern Demographic Association, Oxford, Mississippi, November 4.

Becker, Gary. 1957. *The Economics of Discrimination*. Chicago, IL: University of Chicago Press.

Bellafante, Ginia. 2004. "Two Fathers, With One Happy to Stay at Home." *New York Times* (January 12): A1, A17.

Berg, Nathan and Donald Lien. 2002. "Measuring the Effect of Sexual Orientation on Income: Evidence of Discrimination." *Contemporary Economic Policy* 20:394–414.

Bianchi, Susan and Daphne Spain. 1996. "Women, Work and Family in America." *Population Bulletin* 51:1–46.

Black, Dan A., Gary A. Gates, Seth G. Sanders, and Lowell J. Taylor. 1997. "The Effects of Sexual Orientation on the Wages of Men." Working paper, Heinz School of Public Policy and Management, Carnegie Mellon University.

Black, Dan A., Gary Gates, Seth G. Sanders, and Lowell J. Taylor. 2000. "Demographics of the Gay and Lesbian Population in the United States: Evidence from Available Systematic Data Sources." *Demography* 37:139–54.

Black, Dan A., Gary A. Gates, Seth G. Sanders, and Lowell J. Taylor. 2002. "Same-Sex Unmarried Partner Couples in Census 2000: How Many Are Gay and Lesbian?" Working Paper.

Black, Dan A., Gary Gates, Seth G. Sanders, and Lowell J. Taylor. 2003. "Why Do Gay Men Live in San Francisco?" *Journal of Urban Economics* 51:54–76.

Black, Dan A., Hoda R. Makar, Seth G. Sanders, and Lowell Taylor. 1998. "The Effects of Sexual Orientation on Earnings." Working paper, Heinz School of Public Policy and Management, Carnegie Mellon University.

Black, Dan A., Hoda R. Makar, Seth G. Sanders, and Lowell J. Taylor. 2003. "The Earnings Effects of Sexual Orientation." *Industrial and Labor Relations Review* 56:449–69.

Blumstein, P. and Pepper Schwartz. 1983. *American Couples*. New York: William Morrow and Company.

Boswell, John. 1980. *Christianity, Social Tolerance, and Homosexuality*. Chicago, IL: The University of Chicago Press.

Boyd, Robert L. 1998. "The Storefront Church Ministry in African American Communities of the Urban North during the Great Migration: The Making of an Ethnic Niche." *The Social Sciences Journal* 35:319–32.

Bradford, Judith, Kirsten Barrett and Julie A. Honnold. 2002. *The 2000 Census and Same-Sex Household: A User's Guide*. New York: The National Gay and Lesbian Task Force Policy Institute.

Brines, Julie and Kara Joyner. 1999. "The Tie that Binds: Principles of Cohesion in Cohabitation and Marriage." *American Sociological Review* 64:333–55.

Buckland, Fiona. 2002. *Impossible Dance: Club Culture and Queer World Making*. Middleton, CT: Wesleyan University Press.

Bumpass, Larry L. and James A. Sweet. 1989. "National Estimates of Cohabitation." *Demography* 26:615–25.

Bunting, Eve. 1987. *Will You Be My POSSLQ?* San Diego, CA: Harcourt Brace Jovanovich.

Burr, Jeffrey A., Lloyd B. Potter, Omer R. Galle, and Mark A. Fossett. 1992. "Migration and Metropolitan Opportunity Structures: A Demographic Response to Racial Inequality." *Social Science Research* 21: 380–405.

Burstein, Paul. 1985. *Discrimination, Jobs, and Politics: The Struggle for Equal Opportunity in the United States Since the New Deal*. Chicago, IL: The University of Chicago Press.

Butler, Judith. 1990. *Gender Trouble*. New York: Routledge.

Button, James W., Barbara A. Rienzo, and Kenneth D. Wald. 1995. "Where Local Laws Prohibit Discrimination Based on Sexual Orientation." *Public Management* 77:9–14.

Cahill, Sean, Mitra Ellen, and Sarah Tobias. 2002. *Family Policy: Issues Affecting Gay, Lesbian, Bisexual, and Transgendered Families*. New York: The National Gay and Lesbian Task Force Policy Institute. www.ngtlf.org.

Califia, Pat. 1997. "San Francisco: Revisiting 'The City of Desire.'" Pp. 177–196 in *Queers in Space*, edited by Gordan Brent Ingram, Anne-Marie Bouthillette, and Yolanda Retter. Seattle, WA: Bay Press.

Carpenter, Christopher. 2004. "New Evidence on Gay and Lesbian Household Incomes." *Contemporary Economic Policy* 22:78–94.

Carrington, Christopher. 2000. *No Place Like Home: Relationships and Family Life Among Lesbians and Gay Men*. Chicago, IL: University of Chicago Press.

Casper, Lynne M. and Philip N. Cohen. 2000. "How Does POSSLQ Measure Up? Historical Estimates of Cohabitation." *Demography* 37:237–45.

Castells, Manuel and Karen Murphy. 1982. "Cultural Identity and Urban Structure: The Spatial Organization of San Francisco's Gay Community." Pp. 237–59 in *Urban Policy Under Capitalism*, edited by Norman I. Fainstein and Susan S. Fainstein. London: Sage.

Center for Disease Control and Prevention (CDC). 2004. "CDC HIV/AIDS Surveillance Report: HIV Infection and AIDS in the United States, 2004." Atlanta, GA: Center for Disease Control. Retrieved on January 7, 2006 (www.cdc.gov/hiv/stats.htm).

Cianciotto, Jason and Sean Cahill. 2003. *Education Policy: Issues Affecting Lesbian, Gay, Bisexual and Transgendered Youth.* New York: The National Gay and Lesbian Task Force Policy Institute.

Clain, Suzanne Heller and Karen Leppell. 2001. "An Investigation into Sexual Orientation Discrimination as an Explanation for Wage Differences." *Applied Economics* 33:37–47.

Collins, Alan. 2004. "Sexual Dissidence, Enterprise and Assimilation: Bedfellows in Urban Regeneration." *Urban Studies* 41:1789–1806.

Collison, Peter, and John Mogey. 1959. "Residence and Social Class in Oxford." *American Journal of Sociology* 64:599–605.

Compton, D'Lane R. and Dudley L. Poston, Jr. 2005. "An Appraisal of the 2000 U.S. Census Data on Same-sex Unmarried Partners." Paper presented at annual meeting of American Sociological Association. Philadelphia, PA. August 2005.

Cooke, Thomas and Adrian Bailey. 1996. "Family Migration and the Employment of Married Women and Men." *Economic Geography* 72:38–48.

Costa, Dora L. and Matthew E. Kahn. 2000. "Power Couples: Changes in the Locational Choice of the College Educated, 1940–1990." *Quarterly Journal of Economics* 115:1287–1315.

Costello, Michael A. and MariLou Palabrica-Costello. 1982. "Changing Patterns of Residential Segregation, by Occupational Status, in a Philippine City." *Philippine Studies* 32:290–304.

D'Emilio, John and Estelle B. Freedman. 1988. *Intimate Matters: A History of Sexuality in America.* New York: Harper & Row, Publishers.

de Leeuw, Jan. 2002. "Introduction." Pp. xix–xxii in Stephen W. Raudenbush and Anthony S. Bryk, *Hierarchical Linear Models: Applications and Data Analysis Methods.* 2nd ed. Thousand Oaks, CA: Sage Publications.

Demo, David H. and Katherine R. Allen. 1996. "Diversity within Lesbian and Gay Families: Challenges and Implications for Family Theory and Research." *Journal of Social and Personal Relationships* Aug.: 415–34.

Demo, David H., Katherine R. Allen, Mark A. Fine. 2000. "An Overview of Family Diversity: Controversies, Questions, and Values." *Handbook of Family Diversity.* New York: Oxford University Press.

Department of Justice. 2004. *Hate Crimes Statistics, 2004.* Washington, DC: Department of Justice.

Donohue, John. J. III and James Heckman. 1991. "Continuous Versus Episodic Change: The Impact of Civil Rights Policy on the Economic Status of Blacks." *Journal of Economic Literature* 29:1603–43.

Duncan, Otis Dudley and Beverly Duncan. 1955. "Residential Distribution and Occupational Stratification." *American Journal of Sociology* 60:493–503.

Durden, Garey and Patricia Gaynor. 1998. "More on the Cost of Being Other than White and Male: Measurement of Race, Ethnic, and Gender Effects on Yearly Earnings." *The American Journal of Economics and Sociology* 57:95–103.

Elliot, John E. 1993. "Lesbian and Gay Concerns in Career Development." Pp. 25–44 in *Homosexual Issues in the Workplace*, edited by Louis Diamant. Washington, DC: Taylor & Francis.

Ericksen, Karen Paige and Karen F. Trocki. 1994. "Sex, Alcohol and Sexually Transmitted Diseases: A National Survey." *Family Planning Perspectives* 26: 257–63.

ERS/USDA. 1995. "1989 ERS County Typology Codes." Washington, DC: Economic Research Service, U.S. Department of Agriculture.

Escoffier, Jeffrey. 1975. "Stigmas, Work Environment, and Economic Discrimination Against Homosexuals." *Homosexual Counseling Journal* 2:8–17.

Farley, Reynolds. 1977. "Residential Segregation in Urbanized Areas of the United States in 1970: An Analysis of Social Class and Racial Differences." *Demography* 14:497–518.

Farley, Reynolds, and William Frey. 1994. "Changes in the Segregation of Whites from Blacks during the 1980s: Small Steps towards a More Integrated Society." *American Sociological Review* 59:23–45.

Fassinger, Ruth E. 1993. "And Gladly Teach: Lesbian and Gay Issues in Education." Pp. 119–42 in *Homosexual Issues in the Workplace*, edited by Louis Diamant. Washington, DC: Taylor & Francis.

Fields, Jason and Charles L. Clark. 1999. "Unbinding the Ties: Edit Effects of Marital Status on Same Gender Couples." Population Division Working Paper No. 34, Fertility and Family Statistics Branch. Washington, DC: U.S. Census Bureau.

Fong, Eric and Kumiko Shibuya. 2000. "The Spatial Separation of the Poor in Canadian Cities." *Demography* 37:449–59.

Fossett, Mark A. and Cynthia M. Cready. 1998. "Ecological Approaches in the Study of Racial and Ethnic Differentiation and Inequality." Pp. 157–94 in *Continuities in Sociological Human Ecology*, edited by Michael Micklin and Dudley L. Poston, Jr. New York: Plenum Press.

Foucault, Michel. 1978. *The History of Sexuality: An Introduction, Vol. 1.* New York: Vintage Books.

Frisbie, W. Parker, and John D. Kasarda. 1988. "Spatial Processes." Pp. 629–66 in *Handbook of Sociology*, edited by Neil J. Smelser. Newbury Park, CA: Sage.

Frisbie, W. Parker, and Dudley L. Poston, Jr. 1978. "Sustenance Differentiation and Population Redistribution." *Social Forces* 57:42–56.

Gamson, Joshua. 1996. "Must Identity Movements Self-Destruct?: A Queer Dilemma." Pp. 395–420 in *Queer Theory/Sociology*, edited by Steven Seidman. Cambridge, MA: Blackwell Publishers.

Gates, Gary J. and Jason Ost. 2004. *The Gay and Lesbian Atlas.* Washington, DC: The Urban Institute Press.

Gates, Gary and Randall L. Sell. 2006. "Measuring Gay and Lesbian Couples," in *The Handbook of Measurement Issues in Family Research*, eds. Sandra Hofferth and Lynne Casper. Mahwah, NJ: Lawrence Erlbaum Associates.

Geranios, Nicholas K. 2005. "Spokane's Gays Seek Own District." *The Seattle Times.* January 16, 2005. Retrieved on May 4, 2006 (http://seattletimes.nwsource.com/html/localnews/2002152263_gayspokane16.html).

Gerstmann, Evan. 2004. *Same-Sex Marriage and the Constitution.* New York: Cambridge University Press.

Glick, Paul C. 1984. "American Household Structure in Transition." *Family Planning Perspectives* 16:205–11.

Glick, Paul C. and A. J. Norton. 1977. "Marrying, Divorcing, and Living Together in the U.S. Today." *Population Bulletin* 32:4–34.

Glick, Paul C. and Graham B. Spanier. 1980. "Married and Unmarried Cohabitation in the United States." *Journal of Marriage and the Family* 42:19–30.

Goodridge et al. v. Department of Public Health, 798 N.E.2d 941 (Mass. 2003).

Gottman, John M., James Murray, Catherine C. Swanson, Rebecca Tyson, and Kristin R. Swanson. 2002. *The Mathematics of Marriage: Dynamic Nonlinear Models.* Cambridge, MA: MIT Press.

Graves, Philip E. 1980. "Migration and Climate." *Journal of Regional Science* 20:227–37.

Green, John C., James L. Guth, Layman A. Kellstedt, and Corwin E. Smidt. 1995. "Evangelical Realignment: The Political Power of the Christian Right Wins One." *The Christian Century* (July 5–12):676–77.

Greenwood, Michael J. 1997. "Internal Migration in Developed Countries." Pp. 647–720 in *Handbook of Population and Family Economics*, edited by Mark R. Rosenzweig and Orden Stark. Amsterdam: Elsevier.

Guest, Avery and James Weed. 1976. "Ethnic Residential Segregation: Patterns of Change." *American Journal of Sociology* 81:1088–1111.

Gunderson, Morley. 1989. "Male-Female Wage Differentials and Policy Responses." *Journal of Economic Literature* 27:46–72.

Guth, John L. 1995. "South Carolina: The Christian Right Wins One." *PS: Political Science and Politics* 28:8–11.

Hamby, Chris. 2005. "Utah's Mormon Influence Creates First Amendment Challenges." First Amendment Center, July 21, 2005. Retrieved on May 9, 2006 (http://www.firstamendmentcenter.org/news.aspx?id=15569).

Hauser, Philip M. and Otis D. Duncan, eds. 1959. *The Study of Population: An Inventory and Appraisal.* Chicago, IL: University of Chicago Press.

Hawley, Amos H. 1950. *Human Ecology: A Theory of Community Structure.* New York: Ronald Press.

Hawley, Amos H. 1968. "Human Ecology." Pp. 323–32 in *International Encyclopedia of the Social Sciences*, edited by David L. Sills. New York: Crowell, Collier, and Macmillan.

Hawley, Amos H. 1981. *Urban Society.* Rev. ed. New York: Ronald Press.

Herek, Gregory M. 1991. "Stigma, Prejudice and Violence against Lesbians and Gay Men." In *Homosexuality: Research Implications for Public Policy*, edited by John C. Gonsiorek and James Weinrich. Newbury Park, CA: Sage Publications.

Hernandez, Donald J. 2006. Personal e-mail communication with Dudley Poston. January 28.

Hinde, Andrew. 1998. *Demographic Methods.* New York: Edward Arnold.

Howard Dean for America. 2003. "Ensuring Civil Rights and Justice for All." Howard Dean for America. Retrieved November 11, 2003 (http://www.deanfor america.com/site/PageServer?Pagename=policy_statement_civilrights).

Ingram, Gordan Brent, Anne-Marie Bouthillette, and Yolanda Retter. 1997. "Queer Zones and Enclaves: Political Economies of Community Formation." Pp. 171–75 in *Queers in Space*, edited by Gordan Brent Ingram, Anne-Marie Bouthillette, and Yolanda Retter. Seattle, WA: Bay Press.

Jacobsen, Joyce and Laurence M. Levin. 1997. "Marriage and Migration: Comparing Gains and Losses from Migration for Couples and Singles." *Social Science Quarterly* 78:688–709.

Jagose, Annamarie. 1996. *Queer Theory: An Introduction*. New York: New York University Press.

Kaiser Family Foundation. 2004. "Reported AIDS Cases among Adults and Adolescents by Transmission Category, Cumulative through December 2004." Washington, DC: Kaiser Family Foundation.

Kalton, Graham. 1983. *Introduction to Survey Sampling*. Newbury Park, CA: Sage Publications.

Kansas v. Limon, 122 P.3d 22 (Kan. 2006).

Karp, Herbert H. and K. Dennis Kelly. 1971. *Toward an Ecological Analysis of Intermetropolitan Migration*. Chicago, IL: Markham Publishing Company.

Katz, Jonathan. 1995. *The Invention of Heterosexuality*. New York: Penguin Books.

Kinsey, Alfred C., Wardell B. Pomeroy, and Clyde E. Martin. 1948. *Sexual Behavior in the Human Male*. Philadelphia, PA: W. B. Saunders and Company.

Kite, Mary E. and Bernard E. Whitley, Jr. 1996. "Sex Differences in Attitudes toward Homosexual Persons, Behaviors, and Civil Rights: A Meta-Analysis." *Personality and Social Psychology Bulletin* 22:336–53.

Klawitter, Marieka M. 1998. "The Determinants of Earnings for Women in Same-Sex and Different-Sex Couples." Paper prepared for presentation at Allied Social Science Associations meetings, Chicago, January 1998.

Klawitter, Marieka and Victor Flatt. 1998. "The Effects of State and Local Antidiscrimination Policies on Earnings for Gays and Lesbians." *Journal of Policy Analysis and Management* 17:658–86.

Knopp, Lawrence. 1990. "Social Consequences of Homosexuality." *Geographical Magazine* (May): 20–25.

Krysan, Maria. 2002. "Whites Who Say They'd Flee: Who are They, and Why Would They Leave?" *Demography* 39:675–96.

Kurdek, Lawrence. 1987. "Perceived Emotional Support from Family and Friends in Members of Homosexual, Married, and Heterosexual Cohabiting Couples." *Journal of Homosexuality* Winter: 57–68.

Kurdek, Lawrence. 1992. "Relationship Stability and Relationship Satisfaction in Cohabitating Gay and Lesbian Couples: A Prospective Longitudinal Test of the Contextual and Interdependence Models." *Journal of Social and Personal Relationships* 9:125–42.

Lambda Legal. 2006. "Overview of State Adoption Laws." New York: Lambda Legal. Retrieved May 19, 2006 (www.lambdalegal.org/cgi-bin/iowa/documents/record2.html?record=1923).

Latif, Abdel H. 1974. "Residential Segregation and Location of Status and Religious Groups in Alexandria, Egypt." Pp. 423–32 in *Comparative Urban Structure: Studies in the Ecology of Cities*, edited by Kent P. Schwirian. Lexington, MA: D. C. Heath.

Laumann, Edward O., John H. Gagnon, Richard T. Michael, and Stuart Michaels. 1994. *The Social Organization of Sexuality: Sexual Practices in the United States*. Chicago, IL: University of Chicago Press.

Lauria, Mickey and Lawrence Knopp. 1985. "Toward an Analysis of the Role of Gay Communities in the Urban Renaissance." *Urban Geography* 6:152–69.

Lawrence et al. v. Texas, 123 S. Ct. 2472 (2003).

Lee, Everett S. 1966. "A Theory of Migration." *Demography* 3:47–57.

LeVay, Simon and Elisabeth Nonas. 1995. *City of Friends: A Portrait of the Gay and Lesbian Community in America*. Cambridge, MA: The MIT Press.

Lieberson, Stanley. 1963. *Ethnic Patterns in American Cities*. New York: Free Press.

Lillard, Lee A. and Linda J. Waite. 1995. "'Til Death Do Us Part: Marital Disruption and Mortality." *The American Journal of Sociology* 100:1131–56.

Lithwick, Dahlia. 2006. "Why Courts Are Adopting Gay Parenting." *Washington Post*, March 12. Retrieved May 19, 2006 (washingtonpost.com/wp-dyn/content/article/2006/03/10/AR200603102031).

Lofland, John and Lyn H. Lofland. 1995. *Analyzing Social Settings: A Guide to Qualitative Observation and Analysis*. Belmont, CA: Wadsworth Publishing.

Logan, John, Richard D. Alba, and Wenquan Zhang. 2002. "Immigrant Enclaves and Ethnic Communities in New York and Los Angeles." *American Sociological Review* 67:299–322.

London, Bruce. 1986. "Ecological and Political-economic Analyses of Migration to a Primate City: Bangkok, Thailand, ca. 1970." *Urban Affairs Quarterly* 21:501–26.

Long, John S. 1997. *Regression Models for Categorical and Limited Dependent Variables*. Thousand Oaks, CA: Sage Publications.

Massey, Douglas S. 1979. "Effects of Socioeconomic Factors on the Residential Segregation of Blacks and Spanish Americans in U.S. Urbanized Areas." *American Sociological Review* 44:1015–22.

Massey, Douglas S. 1985. "Ethnic Residential Segregation: A Theoretical Synthesis and Empirical Review." *Sociology and Social Research* 69:315–50.

Massey, Douglas S. and Nancy A. Denton. 1987. "Trends in the Residential Segregation of Blacks, Hispanics and Asians: 1970–1980." *American Sociological Review* 52:802–25.

Massey, Douglas S. and Nancy A. Denton. 1988. "The Dimensions of Residential Segregation." *Social Forces* 67:281–315.

Massey, Douglas S. and Nancy A. Denton. 1989. "Hypersegregation in U.S. Metropolitan Areas: Black and Hispanic Segregation Along Five Dimensions." *Demography* 26:373–91.

Massey, Douglas S. and Nancy A. Denton. 1993. *American Apartheid: Segregation and the Making of the Underclass*. Cambridge, MA: Harvard University Press.

Massey, Douglas S. and Brendan P. Mullan. 1984. "Processes of Hispanic and Black Spatial Assimilation." *American Journal of Sociology* 89:836–73.

McKeand v. Laird, 490 F.2d 1262 (9th Cir 1973).

McManus, Sally. 2003. *Sexual Orientation Research Phase 1: A Review of Methodological Approaches*. Edinburgh: Scottish Executive Social Research. Retrieved on May 5, 2006 (http://www.scotland.gov.uk/Publications/2003/03/16650/19351).

Mehta, Surinder K. 1968. "Patterns of Residence in Poona (India) by Income, Education and Occupation (1937–65)." *American Journal of Sociology* 73:496–508.

Mincer, Jacob. 1978. "Family Migration Decisions." *Journal of Political Economy* 86:749–73.

Mohr, Richard. 1998. *Gays/Justice*. New York: Columbia University Press.

Mondimore, Francis Mark. 1996. *A Natural History of Homosexuality*. Baltimore, MD: The Johns Hopkins University Press.

Murray, Stephen O. 1992. "Components of Gay Community in San Francisco." Pp. 107–46 in *Gay Culture in America: Essays from the Field*, edited by Gilbert Herdt. Boston, MA: Beacon Press.

Murray, Stephen O. 1996. *American Gay*. Chicago, IL: Chicago University Press.

Nam, Charles B. and Monica Boyd. 2004. "Occupational Status in 2000: Over a Century of Status-Based Measurement." *Population Research and Policy Review* 23:327–58.

National Center for Health Statistics. 2004. *National Survey of Family Growth, Cycle 6, 2002*. CD-ROM Series 23, Number 4A. Hyattsville, Maryland: National Center for Health Statistics.

National Gay and Lesbian Task Force Organization. 2006. "Adoption Laws in the U.S." New York: National Gay and Lesbian Task Force. Retrieved May 25, 2006 (http://www.thetaskforce.org/downloads/AdoptionLaws.pdf).

National Gay and Lesbian Task Force Organization. 2006. "Foster Care Regulations in the U.S." New York: National Gay and Lesbian Task Force. Retrieved May 25, 2006 (http://www.thetaskforce.org/downloads/FosteringMap.pdf).

Newport, Frank. 2001. "American Attitudes Toward Homosexuality Continue to Become More Tolerant," The Gallup Organization. Retrieved May 25, 2006 (http://www.gallup.com/subscription/?m=f&c_id=10680).

O'Connell, Martin and Gretchen Gooding. 2006. "The Use of First Names to Evaluate Reports of Gender and Its Effect on the Distribution of Married and Unmarried Couple Households." Paper presented at the Annual Meetings of the Population Association of America, Los Angeles, CA, March 30–April 1.

O'Connell, Martin and Gretchen Gooding. 2007. "Editing Unmarried Couples in Census Bureau Data." Housing and Household Economic Statistics Division Working Paper. Washington, DC: U.S. Census Bureau.

O'Reilly, Kathleen and Gerald R. Webster. 1998. "A Sociodemographic and Partisan Analysis of Voting in Three Anti-gay Rights Referenda in Oregon." *Professional Geographer* 50:498–515.

Osgood, C. 1981. *There's Nothing That I Wouldn't Do If You Would Be My POSSLQ*. New York: Holt, Rinehart, and Winston.

Padula v. Webster, 822 F.2d 97, 104 (D.C. Cir. 1987).

Park, Robert E. 1925. "The Concept of Position in Sociology." *Publications of the American Sociological Society* 20:1–14.

Park, Robert E. 1926. "The Urban Community as a Spatial Pattern and a Moral Order." Pp. 3–20 in *The Urban Community*, edited by E. W. Burgess. Chicago, IL: University of Chicago Press.

Patterson, Charlotte J. 2000. "Family Relationships of Lesbian and Gay Men." *Journal of Marriage and Family* 62:1052–69.

Poston, Dudley L., Jr. 2003. "An Appraisal of the Data." Working paper, Texas A&M University.

Poston, Dudley L., Jr. 2005. "Age and Sex." Pp. 19–58 in *Handbook of Population*, edited by Dudley L. Poston, Jr. and Michael Micklin. New York: Kluwer Academic/Plenum Publisher.

Poston, Jr., Dudley, David Alvirez, and Marta Tienda. 1976. "Earnings Differences Between Anglo and Mexican American Male Workers in 1960 and 1970: Changes in the 'Cost' of Being Mexican American." *Social Science Quarterly* 57:618–31.

Poston, Dudley L., Jr., Amanda K. Baumle, and Michael Micklin. 2005. "Epilogue: Needed Research in Demography." Pp. 853–81 in *Handbook of Population*, edited by Dudley L. Poston, Jr. and Michael Micklin. New York: Springer.

Poston, Dudley L., Jr. and W. Parker Frisbie. 1998. "Human Ecology, Sociology, and Demography." Chapter 2 in *Continuities in Sociological Human Ecology*, edited by Michael Micklin and Dudley L. Poston, Jr. New York: Plenum Press.

Poston, Dudley L., Jr., Yuan Gu, and Carol S. Walther. 2003. "The Ecology of Homosexuality: Gay and Lesbian Partnering in the Metropolitan Areas of the United States in 2000." Paper presented at the annual meeting of the Southern Demographic Association, Washington, DC, October 23–25.

Poston, Dudley L., Jr., and W. Parker Frisbie. 2005. "Ecological Demography." In *Handbook of Population*, edited by Dudley L. Poston, Jr. and Michael Micklin. New York: Springer Publishing Company.

Poston, Dudley L., Jr., and M. X. Mao. 1996. "An Ecological Investigation of Interstate Migration in the United States, 1985–1990. *Advances in Human Ecology* 5:303–42.

Poston, Dudley L., Jr., and M. X. Mao. 1998. "Interprovincial Migration in China, 1985–1990." *Research in Rural Sociology and Development* 7: 227–50.

Poston, Dudley L., Jr. and Michael Micklin, eds. 2005. *Handbook of Population*. New York: Kluwer Academic/Plenum Publisher.

Poston, Dudley L., Jr., Michael Micklin, and Jing Shu. 1998. "Spatial Segregation and Social Differentiation in China." Pp. 283–98 in *Continuities in Sociological Human Ecology*, edited by Michael Micklin and Dudley L. Poston, Jr. New York: Plenum Press.

Price-Spratlen, Townsand. 1999. "Livin' for the City: African American Ethnogenesis and Depression Era Migration." *Demography* 36:553–68.

Ramirez, Horacio N. Roque. 2003. "'That's My Place!': Negotiating Racial, Sexual, and Gender Politics in San Francisco's Gay Latino Alliance, 1975–1983." *Journal of the History of Sexuality* 12:224–58.

Reskin, Barbara and Irene Padavic. 1994. *Women and Men at Work*. Thousand Oaks, CA: Pine Forge Press.

Riley, Nancy E. 1999. "Challenging Demography: Contributions from Feminist Theory." *Sociological Forum* 14:369–97.

Riley, Nancy E. 2005. "Demography of Gender." Pp. 109–42 in *Handbook of Population*, edited by Dudley L. Poston, Jr. and Michael Micklin. New York: Kluwer Academic/Plenum Publisher.

Risman, Barbara and Pepper Schwartz. 1988. "Sociological Research on Male and Female Homosexuality." *Annual Review of Sociology* 14:125–47.

Saenz, Rogelio. 1991. "Interregional Migration Patterns of Chicanos: The Core, Periphery, and Frontier." *Social Science Quarterly* 72:135–48.

Saenz, Rogelio and Edli Colberg. 1988. "Sustenance Organization and Net Migration in Small Texas Nonmetropolitan Communities, 1960–1980." *Rural Sociology* 53:334–45.

Saenz, Rogelio and Alberto Davila. 1992. "Chicano Return Migration to the Southwest: An Integrated Human Capital Approach." *International Migration Review* 26:1248–66.

Saenz, Rogelio and M. Christina Morales. 2005. "Demography of Race and Ethnicity." Pp. 169–208 in *Handbook of Population*, edited by Dudley L. Poston, Jr. and Michael Micklin. New York: Kluwer Academic/Plenum Publisher.

Saewyc, Elizabeth M., Greta R. Bauer, Carol L. Skay, Michael D. Resnick, Elizabeth Reis, and Aileen Murphy. 2004. "Measuring Sexual Orientation in Adolescent Health Surveys: Evaluation of Eight School-based Surveys." *Journal of Adolescent Health* 35:345.e1–e.15.

Saewyc, Elizabeth M., Linda H. Bearinger, Robert Wm. Blum, and Michael D. Resnick. 1999. "Sexual Intercourse, Abuse and Pregnancy Among Adolescent Women: Does Sexual Orientation Make a Difference?" *Family Planning Perspectives* 31:127–31.

Sandefur, Gary D. and Jiwon Jeon. 1991. "Migration, Race and Ethnicity, 1960–1980." *International Migration Review* 25:392–407.

Sarantakos, Sotirios. 1996. "Same-Sex Couples: Problems and Prospects."

Schiltz, Marie Ange. 1998. "Young Homosexual Itineraries in the Context of HIV: Establishing Lifestyles." *Population: An English Selection* 10:417–45.

Schwirian, Kent P., and Jesus Rico-Velasco. 1971. "The Residential Distribution of Status Groups in Puerto Rico's Metropolitan Areas." *Demography* 8:81–90.

Seidman, Steven. 1993. "Families We Choose: Lesbians, Gays, Kinship." *Contemporary Sociology* 22:230–31.

Seidman, Steven. 1994. "Queer-ing Sociology, Sociologizing Queer Theory: An Introduction." *Sociological Theory* 12:166–77.

Seidman, Steven. 1996. "Introduction." Pp. 1–29 in *Queer Theory/Sociology*, edited by Steven Seidman. Cambridge: Blackwell Publishers.

Shryock, Henry S., Jacob S. Siegel, and Associates. 1976. *The Methods and Materials of Demography*. Condensed Edition by Edward G. Stockwell. New York: Academic Press.

Sibalis, Michael. 2004. "Urban Space and Homosexuality: The Example of the Marais, Paris' 'Gay Ghetto.'" *Urban Studies* 41:1739–58.

Siegel, Paul. 1965. "On the Cost of Being a Negro." *Sociological Inquiry* 35:41–57.

Simmons, Tavia and Martin O'Connell. 2003. *Married-couple and Unmarried-partner Households: 2000*. Washington, DC: United States Census Bureau. Retrieved May 25, 2006 (www.census.gov/prod/2003pubs/censr-5.pdf).

Sly, David F. 1972. "Migration and the Ecological Complex." *American Sociological Review* 37:615–28.

Smith, Amy. 2005. "KKK Takes Spotlight Away From Other Prop. 2 Backers." *The Austin Chronicle*, November 4. Retrieved on February 21, 2006 (http://www.austinchronicle.com/issues/dispatch/2005-11-04/pols_naked3.html).

Smith, David M., and Gary J. Gates. 2001. Gay and Lesbian Families in the United States: Same-Sex Unmarried Partner Households. *A Human Rights Campaign Report*, August 22.

Smith, Tom W. 1991. "Adult Sexual Behavior in 1989: Number of Partners, Frequency of Intercourse and Risk of AIDS." *Family Planning Perspectives* 23:102–07.

Sokoloff, Natalie J. 1992. *Black Women and White Women in the Professions: Occupational Segregation by Race and Gender, 1960–1980.* New York: Routledge.

Sorrells, Jim. 1999. *Welcome to the Lower Russian River: A Brief History and Guide.* Sebastopol, CA: G-Wiz Graphics and Printing.

Soulforce. 2006. "Discrimination in Adoption and Foster Care of Children" Lynchburg, VA: Soulforce. Retrieved May 19, 2006 (www.soulforce.org/article/647).

Stacey, Judith and Timothy J. Biblarz. (2001). "(How) Does the Sexual Orientation of Parents Matter?" *American Sociological Review* 66:159–83.

Starbuck, Gene H. 2002. *Families in Context.* Belton, CA: Wadsworth

StataCorp. 2005. *Stata, Statistics and Data Analysis, Version 9.1.* College Station, TX: StataCorp.

Steinfels, Peter. 1988. "Southern Baptists Condemn Homosexuality as 'Depraved.'" *New York Times* (June 17): Section B, Page 6, Column 2.

Stokes, Joseph, David McKirnan, and Rebecca Burzette. 1992. "Behavioral versus Self-labeling Definitions of Bisexuality: Implications for AIDS Risk: *International Conference on AIDS* 8 (no. 2), abstract no. PoDD 5199.

Stone, Andrea. 2006. "Drives to Ban Gay Adoption Heat Up in 16 States." *USA Today*, February 20, 2006. Retrieved on April 28, 2006 (http://www.usatoday.com/news/nation/2006-02-20-gay-adoption_x.htm).

Sullivan, Andrew. 1996. *Virtually Normal: An Argument About Homosexuality.* New York: Vintage Books.

Tepperman, Lorne and Jenny Blain. 2006. *Think Twice! Sociology Looks at Current Social Issues,* 2nd ed. Upper Saddle River, NJ: Pearson Education.

Tienda, Marta and Franklin D. Wilson. 1992. "Migration and the Earnings of Hispanic Men." *American Sociological Review* 57:661–78.

Townley, Ben. 2006. "Sexuality Question Out in Census." March 9, 2006. Retrieved on May 5, 2006 (http://uk.gay.com/headlines/9709).

U.S. Bureau of the Census. 1998. *State and Metropolitan Area Data Book 1997–1998.* Washington, DC: U.S. Government Printing Office.

U.S. Bureau of the Census. 2001. "Technical Note on Same-Sex Unmarried Partner Data From the 1990 and 2000 Censuses." Washington, DC: U.S. Census Bureau, Population Division, Fertility & Family Statistics Branch. Retrieved on July 22, 2005 (http://www.census.gov/population/www/cen2000/samesex.html).

U.S. Bureau of the Census. 2003. Washington, DC: U.S. Bureau of the Census. Retrieved on October 1, 2003 (http://www.census.gov/press-release/www/2001/sumfile2.html).

U.S. Bureau of the Census. 2004. "American Community Survey, 2004 Subject Definitions (Revised January 2006)." Washington, DC: U.S. Bureau of the Census. Retrieved on February 3, 2006 (http://www.census.gov/acs/www/Downloads/2004/usedata/Subject_Definitions.pdf).

Valentine, Gill. 1993. "(Hetero)sexing Space: Lesbian Perceptions and Experiences of Everyday Spaces." *Environment and Planning D: Society and Space* 11:395–413.

Vobejda, Barbara. 1998. "Unwed Pairs Make Up 4 Million Households: Number Has Grown Eightfold Since 1970." *Washington Post,* July 27: A10.

Waite, Linda J. 1995. "Does Marriage Matter?" *Demography* 32:483–507.

Waite, Linda J. 2005. "Marriage and Family." Pp. 87–108 in *Handbook of Population*, edited by Dudley L. Poston, Jr. and Michael Micklin. New York: Kluwer Academic/Plenum Press.

Waite, Linda and Maggie Gallagher. 2000. *The Case for Marriage: Why Married People Are Happier, Healthier, and Better off Financially*. New York: Broadway Books.

Walther, Carol S. and Dudley L. Poston, Jr. 2004. "Patterns of Gay and Lesbian Partnering in the Larger Metropolitan Areas of the United States." *Journal of Sex Research* 41:201–14.

Weightman, Barbara A. 1981. "Commentary: Towards a Geography of the Gay Community." *Journal of Cultural Geography* 1:106–12.

Weston, Kath. 1991. *Families We Choose: Lesbians, Gays, Kinship*. New York: Columbia University Press.

White, Michael J. and David P. Lindstrom. 2005. "Internal Migration." Pp. 311–46 in *Handbook of Population*, edited by Dudley L. Poston, Jr. and Michael Micklin. New York: Kluwer Academic/Plenum Publisher.

Wikipedia. 2006a. "Dubuque, Iowa." *Wikipedia, The Free Encyclopedia*. Retrieved on May 9, 2006 (http://en.wikipedia.org/wiki/Dubuque%2C_Iowa#History).

Wikipedia. 2006b. "Key West, Florida." *Wikipedia, The Free Encyclopedia*. Retrieved on March 1, 2006 (http://en.wikipedia.org/wiki/Key_West_Florida).

Woolwine, David. 2000. "Community in Gay Male Experience and Moral Discourse." Pp. 5–37 in *Gay Community Survival in the New Millennium*, edited by Michael R. Botnick. New York: The Haworth Press.

Zamora, Jim Herron. 2004. "Gays in the Mainstream." *San Francisco Chronicle*. June 25, 2004: B1, B7.

Zita, Jacquelyn N. 1992. "Male Lesbians and the Postmodernist Body." *Hypatia* 7:106–27.

Authors

Amanda K. Baumle is Assistant Professor of Sociology at the University of Houston. She specializes in demography, social inequality, and the sociology of law. Prior to obtaining her PhD in sociology at Texas A&M University, she earned a JD from the University of Texas and practiced labor and employment law. Her current research explores issues involving the demography of sexual orientation, labor demography, and gender inequality in the legal practice.

D'Lane Compton is Assistant Professor of Sociology at the University of New Orleans. Her areas of emphasis are social psychology and gender and sexuality. Her current research investigates the demography of sexual orientation and theoretical properties of stigma development and dissolution.

Dudley L. Poston Jr. is Professor of Sociology, the George T. and Gladys H. Abell Endowed Professor of Liberal Arts, and Director of the Asian Studies Program, at Texas A&M University. He previously served on the faculties of Cornell University and the University of Texas. His current research focuses on the demography of China and South Korea, and the demography of sexual orientation. At Texas A&M University, he teaches undergraduate and graduate classes in demography, demographic methods, and statistics.

INDEX

213